ASIAN AMERICANS AND CHRISTIAN MINISTRY

Edited by
Inn Sook Lee
Timothy D. Son

WIPF & STOCK · Eugene, Oregon

Wipf and Stock Publishers
199 W 8th Ave, Suite 3
Eugene, OR 97401

Asian Americans and Christian Ministry
By Lee, Inn Sook and Son, Timothy D.
Copyright©1999 Lee, Inn Sook
ISBN 13: 978-1-60608-546-2
Publication date 2/11/2009
Previously published by Voice Publishing House, 1999

In memory of

The Reverend Woon Hyung Lee and
Kwonsa Grace Ungcho Chun Lee

and to

The Reverend and Mrs. Yong Taek Son

Contents

Preface

"As long as one stays in the state of the wounded, one can not fully participate in the redemptive work of God"

This is a statement written by one of the leading social psychologists. Asian American leaders, I believe, are particularly interested in looking at this statement and wish to explore our unique experiences in the larger American society from the Christian perspective, longing for healing and achieving a sense of wholeness. We believe that this volume is precisely an effort to explore our predicaments in the wilderness of cultural marginality with the spirit of yearning for a full participation in the redemptive work of God.

Historically Chinese, Japanese, Koreans and Asian Indians first immigrated to this country around the turn of this century, and Filipinos, Vietnamese, and Taiwanese started to come in large groups in the early part of the 1970's. The Asian American Christian communities have gathered their efforts in support of the new immigrants. The churches have been serving them not only as their "spiritual home," providing nurture, comfort and uplifting of spirituality during their times of adjustment, but also as a generative womb leading the alienated life of immigrants toward meaningful integration.

The articles included in the present volume are geared around those that provide the theoretical and theological foundations that help us understand Asian American predicaments and those that explore psychosocial experiences individually and collectively. Also included are articles which incorporate theological and biblical insights to the unique experiences encountered in the Asian American faith communitics with the hope to reconstruct a better future.

We are happy to say that the most of the articles were written by Dr. Inn Sook Lee's former students at Princeton Theological Seminary. It gives us a deep sense of gratitude to see them grow as visionary teachers and prophets who can not only provide intellectual and spiritual guidance in their ministerial contexts, but also stir the purposeful direction of the future Asian American churches in the midst of ambiguity and uncertainty. We would like to express our sincere appreciation to the writers for their unique contributions to this volume. We particularly express our thanks to them for their willingness to walk with us through the tedious process of editing the articles.

We would like to express our sincere appreciation to the faculty of Princeton Theological Seminary for their hearty support and encouragement expressed toward Dr. Inn Sook Lee during past ten years as she has been teaching number of courses as a visiting lecturer and as the first Asian American woman professor. Without their approval and confidence shown toward her as an educator, it would not have been possible for her to continue to teach here at Princeton.

We are also thankful to Mr. Jung Phil Kim, Mr. Cy S. Lee, and Rev. Chester Kim for their expertise in the computer technology which had provided valuable assistance in putting the volume together. A sincere thanks are expressed to Mrs. Eun Hee Lee, Dr. and Mrs. Jamo Kang, Ms. Jean Shim, Mrs. Chung Hee Kim and Mr. Isaac De Son for their generous support with their important resources. We are also grateful to Ms. Eunny Lee, Mr. Richard Kong, Ms. Ginny Landgraf, and Ms. Hyun Kyung Choi for their invaluable assistance in preparation of this volume for publication. Last but not least, we wish to express our heartfelt appreciation to Dr. Sang Hyun Lee of Princeton Theological Seminary and Professor Angella M. Pak for their selfless support and encouragement rendered for this publication.

May God's abundant blessings be with all those who are faithful to the calling of Jesus Christ by dedicating their lives by the way of nurturing and ministering those who are suffering, and yet determined to continue the pilgrimage of establishing God's realm on earth with a full sense of peace and justice.

Inn Sook Lee and
Timothy D. Son
November, 1999
Princeton, New Jersey

Chapter One

The Taste of a Nickel Coke:
Stories of the Japanese American Women of the Internment

Haruko Nawata Ward

Introduction

Among the diverse members of the Asian American population, Japanese Americans experienced a unique form of racial discrimination in the years of 1942 to 1947. After the attack on Pearl Harbor by the Japanese navy on December 7, 1942, the American public and government reacted in what in retrospect seems to have been the making of the Japanese Americans on the West Coast a scapegoat at the end of a long history of American Euro-centric racism against Orientals. The evacuation and relocation (or internment) of the entire population of Japanese American ancestry was the culmination of political, judicial and total systematic racism.

Not much study has been done on how the experience of this systematic racism affected the identity formation of Japanese American women due to a lack of research during the evacuation. It has been pointed out that the effect was so deep that these Japanese Americans were incapable of speaking about their feelings for a long time. Others suggest the notion of *haji*, the shame of which any talk is a social taboo. Some see that their negative experience of being singled out as a target ethnic minority resulted in the rapid assimilation of the second and third generations of Japanese immigrants after the war. Others understand that they became successfully assimilated to the larger American society despite the internment experience because of their long installed sense of civil obedience due to Confucian teaching. The internment is a very important subject to be studied by the Christian church, which takes inclusiveness and the value of personhood seriously.

1. Meeting with the Japanese American Woman

In 1990-91 I had an opportunity to work with a Japanese American woman in a church setting. I soon discovered that this woman had experienced internment and that she normally avoided mentioning that part of her life in conversations. She was totally Americanized linguistically and culturally. But I also noticed that she valued her identity as a Japanese American, and that she was eager to learn about Japanese culture to be empowered as a Japanese.

In order to encourage Asa to share her experience, I asked her to give a five minute talk on her life as an older Asian American woman so that the younger women might gain wisdom. This was planned in the context of a "Heritage Day" in the Asian/Asian American Women's Cultural Exchange program at the church. I did not specify to Asa if her talk should include her experience of internment. At first she was very hesitant to speak in public. She said that two minutes would suffice for her to cover 70 years of life. A week later she called me to say that after starting to read and write about her family, her friends and her own story of internment, she felt that she could talk for ten minutes.

On the day of the presentation, once she started to tell these stories, the time froze. The stories were so compelling that nobody noticed that half an hour had past before Asa stopped to take a breath. She said that this was her first time ever to tell her story of internment to anybody. For 48 years she had kept silent. Until that day she had not discovered the voice that could articulate her story, and the ears that were willing to listen to that voice. By telling her story Asa relived the emotions she had during the internment; saw her relationship with her father, mother and siblings in a new perspective; realized that her Christian faith supported her all through the years, and came to accept her "negative" heritage as worth talking about provided a safe and empathetic environment.

2. Storytelling as a Possible Method for Healing

Recent feminist therapists and counselors have discovered the therapeutic power of stories for their clients. In the analysis of the function of stories and myths in human psychological formation, Joan Laird laid out 6 dimensions of stories. I will summarize these in the following[1]:

1. Storytelling is a central device in the construction of human self and meaning. "Like the ritual, [it helps] us to bear witness, to see ourselves mirrored in a collective identity."
2. Stories "help us to order the world, to sort out, explain, and integrate events in a striving for continuity and coherence; they are social touchstones, mediating a complex, cybernetic feedback process between the personal and the social, meshing one's inner and outer history."
3. Stories "also order and preserve the past, creating and transmitting tradition, providing continuity of experience and meaning."
4. "Stories play a crucial role in socializing family members. They are models for action, telling family members how to master challenges as well as what should be feared or avoided."
5. Stories "also serve to explain the unexplainable and rationalize the irrational, mediating family paradoxes by both displaying and screening them at the same time."

Thus stories give structural frameworks to the history of one's past, perspectives to order the present situation, and models for present and future action. In the experiences of trauma, crisis and important transitions, families often formulate stories as a means of providing continuity between past, present and future.

When the social oppression is overwhelming, the family's and individual's ability to formulate stories is diminished. As examples of social oppression Laird gives such historical incidents as "Nazi Holocaust, the Vietnam War, the Argentinean 'Dirty War'," and such personal and family events as incest, abortion, and murder, as well as migration, geographic and emotional cutoffs, poverty, despair, conflict, and communicative disease.[2] These painful and shameful experiences mute the individual's and family's voice. There is only "unstory."[3] I would add the Japanese Americans' "unstory" until recent years to this category. This shameful and painful internment included all the familial and personal crises stated above within the larger social context of structural racism.

Asa, my friend, was able to regain the voice when she and other former internees of the Heart Mountain Relocation Center decided to write and publish a private collection of their stories in 1989 to commemorate President Reagan's signing the Act of Redress. She also regained another voice in telling her story in the church to an audience who did not share her experience. These were occasions for her own therapeutic moments of healing. In telling her story to the group of Asian American women (Chinese, Korean, Malaysian, Indonesian, Filipino and Japanese), Asa caused a deep echoing in the audience's voice to respond by telling their own stories. Laird points out characteristics of women's story telling:

> Women not only begin to connect themselves with other women and to discover new possibilities for their lives, but also have new opportunities to tell the stories of their oppression and of their poverty.[4]

Indeed many women in the group were able to courageously share stories of their experiences of racism and sexism in their heritage after hearing Asa.

Morishima laments on the "sadly" lacking scientific information and reading sources such as individual diaries.[5] He is also skeptical of the objective value of the "recollections" of internees "which were distorted by ten to fifteen intervening years". To supplement the lack of "scientific data" which has been gathered on the effects of the Japanese American internment experience, another approach to the study of this particular experience may be taken. Stories can give light to one's present understanding of the past event rather than scientifically accurate documentation of the past. For a therapeutic purpose the stories are practical.

Fortunately, *And Justice for All*, a volume of the stories of Japanese American internees, was published in 1984.[6] By analyzing the stories we may be able to see how these women recovered their identities as Americans and Japanese, how they recollected the experiences to reconstruct their present lives, how they viewed the cultural and social structure of their traumatic experiences, what issues of family relationships developed after experiencing the internment, and what issues of faith emerged. In the following (section 5) I would like to reconstruct a general overview of women in families in internment camps. In a later section (section 6) I would like to introduce specific cases of two Japanese American women.

3. An Attempt to Reconstruct a General Overview of Women in Families in Internment Camps

Most studies have shown that in Asian cultures women's identity is very much intertwined with family identity, and for a therapist to differentiate the concept of family between American (Western or Euro centric) and Asian cultures is important. Most studies on Asian American women have been interpreted within the context of traditional Buddhist-Confucian influence. Their ethical teachings have perpetuated a hierarchical social structure and particular roles. Among first generation (*issei*) Japanese American women at the time of internment these structures and roles were predominant. In the traditional East Asian framework, "personal actions reflect not only on the individual and the nuclear and extended families, but also on all the preceding generations of the family since the beginning of time."[7]

At the time of internment, when radical discontinuity occurred in all areas of life, family and the sense of history may have been the only continuity and security that these *issei* women had. Arranged marriages for familial survival and sometimes for political ends have been practiced commonly in the East Asian cultures. Many of the *issei* women were "picture brides" because of the racist quota system imposed on the Asian American immigrants by the Oriental Exclusion Act of 1882 and the Gentlemen's Agreement of 1907. In the patrilinear structure of married life, women were trained to serve men.

In her autobiographical essay *Beyond Manzanar* Jeanne Wakatsuki Houston reminiscences about her mother still serving her socially displaced husband in the internment camp who no longer had functional authority as the male head and breadwinner of the household. She assumed and continued the role of wife before, during and after internment. She understood his humiliations out there in the white world, and elevated his position in the house. "After all, was he not doing this for his family, protecting her, acting as the buffer between herself and that alien *hakujin* world?"[8] Even after his social position was made low during internment and his rage was turned against his family, she understood and "she so patiently endured him during those times."[9] In general the role of the wife as a servant to her husband and family was a secured position in the *issei* woman's world.

This does not mean that all *issei* women were not contributing financially to the families. Morishima points out that the stereotypical role of the middle class woman as one who stays home and takes care of the family while the man head earns a living was not necessarily applicable to the Japanese American families in the 1940's. The farmer women shared the same labor with their husbands, but did not earn wages for themselves. In the immigrant-run stores and small businesses on the West Coast, women "undoubtedly made contributions to the family equivalent to those made by their husbands."[10] While mothers and older daughters worked as laborers, younger daughters were given responsibility of looking after the smaller siblings. Both *issei* and *nisei* (second generation) women then had a role of family caretaker and minor wage earner.

The dysfunction within Asian American families caused by the breakdown in communication between the first generation immigrants and their children is another element worth consideration. In the case of Japanese Americans the primal issues that the *issei* women may have faced before the internment were centrally focused around differences between their womanhood in Japanese cultural and familial background and the American society's expectations. The major reason given for the Oriental Exclusion Act was that the Asians were of an inassimilable race. Behind the assimilation theory, there was a definite Anglo-Conformist view, in which "the minorities were expected to adopt the characteristics of the dominant majority as rapidly as possible."[11] Surely with the language barrier and Confucian Japanese attitude of *enryo*,[12] *issei* Japanese women were never very assertive in American society.[13] For those *nisei* women who were under forty years of age at the time of the internment, the social cut off was a traumatic experience. As American citizens of Japanese ancestry, their identity was shaken on both fronts. They were denied their educational and social upbringing as Americans, although their parents had tried to assimilate them totally into the society. They were accused of treason because of their blood. They were also at crucial stages of life when they experience childhood, teenage changes, independence, courtship and marriage. With the internment their vision of becoming free, assertive, and independent American women was shattered. Within the small confines of the relocation camps, they were unable to live as individual American women, and forced to adapt to a group oriented system of Japanese family values. Interestingly after the conflictual discourses and testing of their identities, many *nisei* women chose to become ardent supporters of the Confucian Japanese *koko*[14] values, in which they served their parents and parents-in-law or minors sincerely and devotedly.

In his autobiographical recollection of the internment years, entitled *Issei and Nisei* Daisuke Kitagawa makes a succinct statement that the extended families that were brought together in segregation camps functioned differently from the normal Asian extended families. "Under the false pretense of being one big family, they were compelled to endure an almost absolute absence of privacy."[15] The fact was that the stall-units for each families allotted in the camp were so small, divided only by thin wooden walls through which sounds easily passed, and that they were uncomfortable in both extreme hot and cold weather. Members of the family did not stay together in the rooms except to sleep. Families had to share communal bathrooms, which was a degrading and embarrassing experience.

The family units were without their own cooking facilities. The (stereo)typical women's identity as the managers of the household kitchen was taken away. Kitagawa summarized this minor crisis as follows:

> As wife and mother, a woman prepares every meal for her family, within a budget based on the family income--which normally is what her husband earns taking into consideration the likes and dislikes of all the members of the family; and she does all this without upsetting the nutritional balance required to keep everybody healthy. Under normal circumstances her role is taken for granted. Not even the woman herself is always conscious of it. In the relocation center she was no longer in charge of her family meals. Then, and only then, did it become clear, at least to me, what a work of art it is for her to prepare meals for her family every day of the week. . . . Looking at the same situation from the reverse side, what is set on

> the family table is nothing other than a visible and tangible sign of the invisible and imponderable love and care of her who is at the center of the family.[16]

One would wonder how the *issei* mother and wife such as Houston, who almost ritualized the cooking for serving and feeding the family at the table, felt at the communal mess hall, where children would sit with their peers, and all the "conversation was generally innocuous."[17] The practice of eating at the mess hall symbolized the breakdown of family relationships in the camp. It most affected children. Kitagawa continues:

> The family table and family kitchen are thus sacramental means by which children feed on their parents' love and by which all the members grow together to solidify their mutual relationships.[18]

In the mess hall children received neither parental love nor instruction. Morishima sarcastically states that it was the happiest time for children who "banded together with minimal adult supervision in the relatively safe confines of a barbed wire enclosure."[19] He also points out the parental neglect and psychological punishment imposed on the children.[20] According to Kitagawa the *issei* parents were unable to discipline their children, and *nisei* children's growing lack of respect for their parents were the major reason for the family breakdown.

The constant surveillance by the authorities was another factor which may have affected the children's identity formation. "[T]he center was a place where Caucasian people governed and Japanese people were governed. Everything they saw, day in and day out, indicated that racial difference was identical with a caste distinction."[21] Racism by skin color was ingrained into their psyche deeply. Morishima regrets that there has been no study of the lasting impact of discipline and neglect on the interned children. Apparently no specific studies on the impact on the mother child relationship has been conducted. But Umemoto, who had seen the interned children's drawing which depicted such things as barbed wire, wonders how the early childhood experience in the camp affected their identity formation and later adult lives. Many of the children did not remember the life outside of the camp, and many of them never had experienced the life outside of it. The relationships between young lovers were also strained by the constant surveillance by the military personnel, their parents and the community itself.[22]

The uprooted and confined families were left with much time and ennui. The creative means of passing time such as work corps jobs, furniture making, gardening, flower arrangement classes, as well as drinking and gambling, only gave momentary release of tension. Kitagawa says that to the *issei* women who had worked hard to serve the family, "the life in a relocation center was really and truly a well-earned and highly deserved holiday. It meant liberation from lives of continuous drudgery. For the first time in their lives, they had something akin to free time in a substantial amount, and in many different ways they blossomed out."[23] They found companionship with other women in cultural classes and at the job sites. Kitagawa sees this as positive preparation for the more Americanized and independent life outside of the camp. But it is doubtful that these women truly enjoyed the "vacation" because they did not know when and where they would be going out or if they ever would in future. I rather think that the women used their creativity in the community (the "altered" family) in their best capacity. In actuality many women did continue to spend time in childcare (especially when they were infants and sick), in nursing the sick (because there was no adequate hospital care in the camps), and taking care of the old and invalid parents-in- law. Women's creativity may have cheered up some of the demoralized atmosphere. Kitagawa does describe the low morale throughout the life in the camp in general and in the school set up for children.

What immediate result did the overruling atmosphere of disappointment, alienation, failure of assimilation, tension, stress and low self-esteem bring to the formation of the *nisei* women's psychological world? Based on his survey undertaken in 1966 (20 years after the immediate experience of the internment), Kitano defines the general Japanese American reaction to the internment using the term *shikataganai*. It is a form of passivity "related to a fatalistic orientation whereby an individual resigns himself [sic] to certain external conditions." It is a form of tolerance. "[I]t is indicative of a style of life which counsels patience, tolerance, and repression."[24] Kitano conducted a serious of survey. In responding to the survey statement: "If someone tries to push you around, there is very little that you can do about it," 39% of *issei*, and 29% of *nisei* responded positively compared to 6% of Caucasian. To the statement, "I would not shout or fight in public, even when provoked," 70% of *issei* and 69% of *nisei* responded positively, while 51% of Caucasians answered that they would shout. There is no gender breakdown to this data. But it can be assumed that women in the interment centers showed similar *shikataganai* attitude.[25] Interestingly many of the women in *And Justice for All* stated that at the time of writing their stories (1980's) they did not recall feeling anger at the time of internment (1940's). In fact the anger was internalized. Eventually the "center became a fantastically nice community to live in."[26] In the secluded, isolated, alienated, constantly surveyed camps in desert places, the *issei* became more and more morbid. College age *nisei* started locating the schools and work who would sponsor them to go out of the relocation centers. Those who volunteered to go in the army to fight against the army of "the Japanese emperor" with much agony or with true patriotism, fought in major engagements to prove their American identity ("including a hundred or so members of the Women's Army Corps").[27] Many culturally displaced *kibei* found positions as language teachers/interpreters in military intelligence work with front-line units in the Pacific.[28] The ones who stayed in the centers were the older *issei* and women with small children.

Issei created a fantasy land of false security:

> They appeared to be deliberately trying to forget what had happened to them in the immediate past and to look forward again to their retirement to Japan. The *issei* had transferred themselves to a world of fantasy. Distant past and remote future became more real to them than the immediate past and the immediate future, or even the present. For *issei* American society lost its reality. The fence that enclosed them became an impenetrable wall which set them apart from that society, which to them became virtually a distant land, . . . unknown and unknowable. . . . Such a sociopsychological climate

inclined religious people all the more to religious preoccupations.[29]

The mood among these *issei* Christians became more otherworldly, "in the sense of escaping the harsh reality of the here and now."[30] Also the "symptoms of depressive paranoia and persecution complex" developed. Rumors were fabricated about the loved ones who went out before them. *Issei* parents would indulge in the mysterious fascination of rumor telling and believing rumors about their children.[31] There is no specific mention of the *nisei* women who remained with their *issei* parents-in-law and small children if they were affected by the eschatological religious atmosphere, and fancying over their older sons and husbands outside the camp.

Educated in the American systems although in segregated schools, or in isolation from Japanese schools until the time of the internment, the *nisei* women must have been greatly shocked at their government's treatment of its own citizens. Reeducated in Japanization during the internment, they must have suffered a severe identity crisis. But not many social scientists or clergy cared to record *nisei* women's stories of the time of internment. Nor did they themselves speak out in a loud voice of resistance except some.[32] In the early 1980's "the public hearings of the Commission of the Wartime Relocation and Internment of Civilians enabled hundreds of the survivors of America's concentration camps to come forth and tell their stories publicly."[33] What were the scars and damages that were deeply affecting these women's inner lives to keep them silent for such a long time?

4. Post Traumatic Stress

These *nisei* women may have suffered something akin to what is currently called post traumatic stress syndrome (PTSD). Japanese women have a high propensity to experience a sense of shame, *haji*. The power of shame to silence those suffering from PTSD is universal. "Shame causes the private self to retreat into numbness, to repress feelings and dampen personal engagement with others."[34] Shame is often imposed on the victims of most "sincere" fabrications such as the media's not mentioning the existence of the relocation camps while repeatedly broadcasting about Pearl Harbor.

It is hard to know what went on inside of the Japanese American *nisei* women between the time of internment and the time of storytelling. Studies indicate that not many Asian Americans utilize community mental health facilities probably because of their distrust of the white institutions. Also the sense of shame-stigma of mental illness was still very strong among the Japanese American *issei* and *nisei*.[35]

Kitano criticizes de Vos' theory which attributes major reasons for the survival and strength of the internees to the capacity of the Japanese community and family dynamics itself to "absorb the stress" of racism. Most of the needs and opportunities were taken care of within the Japanese American community with only minimal contact with the larger society. Instead Kitano gives the concept of *gaman* as another major factor. *Gaman* is "the internalization" of problems. Japanese generally "do not bother others . . . He [sic] might 'eat his [sic] own heart out' and yet exhibit few overt signs of disturbance."[36] The availability of two alternate systems such as the *kibei* system (sending the children for schooling in Japan) and more permanent emigration to Japan provided another way of handling problems caused by stress. Counseling and hospitalization happened only as a last resort. According to McGoldrick, at times of severe traumatic experience such as immigration to the USA, most traditional resources of emotional survival may be exhausted. If the family's handling of stress fails, a dysfunction within the family is created.[37]

Did these Japanese American *issei* and *nisei* women suffer such PTSD symptoms as the relentless re-experiencing of the feelings of fear and helplessness "that terrorized them during their ordeal"?[38] Did they suffer from such symptoms as flashbacks and nightmares? These women did experience many layers of trauma, such as sudden loss of social location, of home and belongings, cultural conflict as ethnic persons, sudden move to another location, integration to imposed "Japanese" culture, imprisonment, family disintegration, and severe dehumanization by the structural human evil of racism:

> After a trauma, individuals feel disconnected from the rest of the community, isolated by their intense grief and rage at the unwelcome intrusion in their lives. The sense of fear and helplessness, of their frailty in the face of

> more powerful forces that can swoop down and change their lives, threatens to overwhelm.[39]

In reading the following women's stories, I would like to examine the traces of trauma and how these women have dealt with it in the past, and how these women are communicating it to us readers of today. In so doing, it will become apparent that faith played a crucial part in survival and healing from trauma.

5. From *And Justice for All*: Japanese American *Nisei* Women's Stories

In the above section 4, I tried to give an overview of the "typical" Japanese American woman in the family. Each woman's story, though, is different, as each woman experienced the internment from her particular background. Here I would like to look more closely at two individual experiences.

A. An Orphan Girl's Story

Helen Murano came into the camp under an already traumatic family situation. Her parents and brother died from tuberculosis, a dreaded communicative disease. Her older sister, Mary, also had been hospitalized for TB, and she died a week before the family was interned, leaving Helen at age 15, and her brothers 11 & 13. The history of TB stigmatized her family in the Japanese community. Even for charity the Japanese community was hesitant to help these orphaned children. Helen repeatedly described the alienation she felt toward her Japanese American friends and relatives. Because of her feelings toward the Japanese community, she preferred to stay with Caucasian families. It was a time right after the Depression, and it was hard to find the right foster families. Helen felt more comfortable in the Caucasian world than in the Japanese world.

Experiencing Mary's death was very traumatic. Mary had been the family's spiritual/psychological caretaker as the oldest daughter, and Helen had had a good relationship with her. They were 9 years apart. Helen must have looked to Mary for support and directions. At the time of writing after 48 years, it was still hard to "talk about" the situation around the death of Mary. The evacuation order had been already issued,

Japanese Americans were under curfew, and Helen needed to receive permission to go to see her dying sister in a hospital in the next town. It took her an entire day to receive permission. She felt indignation at the bureaucratic unkindness showed to her. She did not make it in time for Mary's death. Looking at the empty bed, sinking in a deep sense of abandonment she repeated in her heart: "They have done it."[40] Her resentment toward the Japanese American community increased at Mary's funeral at the church. She felt that people were cold and afraid of Helen and her brothers because of possible TB contagion.

Helen could have stayed with her Caucasian foster family, but felt a family responsibility to go to the internment camp with her brothers. Her foster mother and Helen packed camp clothes as if it was for summer camp. The life in the camp was also traumatic, because this was her first time to live among Japanese Americans. The small room and the heat were overwhelming. She felt confused, bitter, and angry toward the American government who had done this and the Japanese who had done this to the child that was her. This experience was more than she could handle.[41] She entertained suicidal thoughts:

> I felt it might be a solution if I just did away with my brothers' and my own life. I thought that. I entertained that as a possibility, as a solution, and then abandoned it. But I thought this because it was so black for me at one point, you know. If your country is doing this to you, and if your people are doing this to you . . . I just couldn't see a way out of a big black hole.[42]

Helen did seek counseling. But in the Assembly Center "there were no persons, no agency, no group there to counsel" not only her but anybody. "No social workers, no social service agency of any kind." When Helen asked for help because of her suicidal thoughts, she was "directed by someone in charge to the infirmary" which treated injuries.[43]

Helen overcame her suicidal thoughts by turning her attention to the care of her younger brothers. At the death of Mary, Helen, who was 15, declared herself as the head of the family. As they drove back from the hospital Helen spoke to her brothers as they played in the back seat of the car: "You know, now I'm the head of the family, and I'm telling you that Mary just died, and out of respect you should not play."[44] From then on, Helen took charge of the family. She managed to obtain full beds for the three of them using her "feminine wiles."[45] She lied to get a typing job even though she did not type. She often skipped school in order to spend many hours washing her brother's clothes. She made the younger siblings study, and they ate together as a family. She insisted on praying before the meals. She made the boys be home by a certain time. The responsibility and her sense of leading the family gave her purpose to go beyond her despair:

> I came around feeling that nobody's going to do this to me. I'm going to prevail, my will is going to prevail, my own life will prevail. I'm not going to kill myself, I'm going to prevail. . . . I made up my mind that my two brothers and I would show everybody. We were orphans, yes; we had come from an unhealthy family, a tubercular family, and we were like pariahs, but I made up my mind, and I told my brothers that we will excel, and we will be better than anybody so that they'll be sorry.[46]

So did all three. The three orphans worked their way through college and medical school and became socially successful after their resettlement. They survived with a strong sense of family and with Helen's strong leadership. She attributed this inner strength to something that her parents instilled in her. Also she saw "unseen hands" beyond her own strength leading the orphans throughout their lives.[47] Helen repeatedly tells of the adults' indifference to the teenage orphans as the most traumatic experience. Helen and her brothers never received any financial support. They also had no emotional support from the community.[48] No adult nurturing of any kind. The people were so wrapped up in their own misery in camp, in their own unhappiness, in their own problems, which is only to be expected, that nobody had anything to give to anybody else. It didn't occur to them that maybe they were needy in other ways. Helen did find some social ties with her teenage peers. It was important for her identity formation as a Japanese American herself to form friendships with, take leadership roles for and to date other Japanese American teenagers.

Confinement was a constant stress for this teenage girl. Helen describes her feelings so eloquently at the time of leaving the internment:

> I felt wonderful the day I left camp. We took a bus to the railroad siding and then stopped someplace to transfer, and I went in and bought a Coke, a nickel Coke. It wasn't the Coke, but what it represented -- that I was free to buy it, that feeling was so intense. You can get maudlin, sentimental about freedom; but if you've been deprived of it, it's very significant. When I ran in there as a teenager to buy that Coke, it was the freedom to buy it, the freedom to run out and do it.[49]

Helen Murano says that at the time of internment these feelings were not articulated. Now by writing she can refocus her life. She concludes her story saying: "But did it have to be that bad for me to have this feeling?"[50] of being a stronger and better person because of the internment experience.

B. A Disintegrated Family

The internment experience definitely affected and altered Violet's life and family. It resulted in a totally disintegrated family over three succeeding generations. Violet says, "whether they call this injustice or inhumanity, I don't know, and history must decide. But for me it was an individual tragedy that should never have happened, and I don't think that it could ever be remedied by anyone or any government."[51] Five traumatic episodes stand out among the many crises: childbirth, the death of her mother-in-law, repatriation to Japan and divorce, the death of her own mother by atomic bomb, and separation with two children.

Violet was married with two children (7 and 5) and was pregnant with the third at the time of evacuation. She had just had a tumor operation. Physically sick and at the last stage of pregnancy, the life in the assembly center was miserable. The smell of the racetrack (which was the center), heat, food poisoning, allergies to the alfalfa which grew in their room, two small children and her sick mother-in-law were traumatic enough. The hospital that she stayed in during her treatment for food poisoning and childbirth had "no roof, no windows, hardly anything."[52]

With the new born baby the family had to move to the internment camp in Jerome, Arkansas. During the 5 days and nights train trip, with the shades drawn "for security reasons"[53] and no air, no formula and no sanitation for the baby, Violet was not allowed to get up or get off the train. She was with the children and parents-in-law, while her husband was taken to build the Fresno Internment Center in Jerome by an earlier train. The baby developed pneumonia and was hospitalized for a long time during her infancy at Jerome. The baby did survive many crises in the hospital. The weather in Jerome was terrible for this California family.

In Jerome, the infamous question 27 & 28 plagued the family.[54] Violet's husband, who was the only son, refused to answer the questionnaire, and decided to repatriate with his *issei* father. Violet also wrote "seek repatriation with the family."[55] Later she tried to reverse the answer and to stay in the U.S.A., but this was not granted. All the persons who did not answer yes to question no. 27 were "segregated" to Tule Lake Internment Camp, Kansas.

On the train to Kansas, Violet was responsible again for her sick child and her sick mother-in-law. (Men were sent first). Her very sick mother-in-law had to be taken off the train and stayed in an unfamiliar hospital in Kansas for two months. No one was allowed to accompany this *issei* woman who "did not speak any English at all."[56] The diagnosis to her condition given was "motion sickness." But in fact she was suffering from cancer. While at Tule Lake she was again taken from her family at Violet's request to be treated in a specialized cancer unit outside of the camp. Violet soon regretted her decision when two MPs "armed with rifles" came to get her. Her mother-in-law cried saying: "They're going to kill me. . . . I've been hospitalized so long since I came into the camp, I'm a nuisance, and they are going to kill me . . . I don't want to go. Don't let them take me." During her stay in the cancer unit, MPs placed her on constant surveillance. "She couldn't understand what the doctor had said to her." After a short stay in the hospital, she came back to the camp and died.[57]

While in Tule Lake, Violet's husband and her brother were arrested as "undesirable enemy aliens" when they protested the shortage of food in the camp. Her brother was taken to the "torture chamber of the Tule Lake stockade."[58] Her husband was sent to the Santa Fe camp in New Mexico, and eventually deported. Because of military censorship, he could not communicate with his family. He went to Nagasaki, Japan, where he started another family. Violet later divorced him.

After the death of his wife, Violet's father-in-law "became a different man."[59] He was very disturbed. He carried his wife's cremated ashes everywhere in a box tied to his body by a white cloth. His US account($27,000 in 1942), a life savings of forty years' labor in the USA, was frozen and was "considered enemy assets."[60] When he repatriated as a mentally disturbed person to Japan, his rented houses, land and other possessions there in Japan also were taken away under MacArthur's Land Reform Act. He stayed with ten other relatives in his tenant farm house and died in utter poverty, and nobody erected a tombstone for him. Violet is very indignant about the tragedy of her father-in-law, who fell in the crack between two nations' laws. She says: "But people shouldn't be too self-centered, too selfish and take advantage of another race or a situation such as ours and make profit out of it."[61]

When in 1946 Violet and her children repatriated to Japan, she looked for her mother in Hiroshima, only to find her in her last days suffering from the burns and radiation illness from the atomic bomb. Her home and all her possessions were destroyed. When they recognized each other, they "did more crying" than they did talking.[62] In Japan Violet and her children were seen as members of an underclass. They were not "real" Japanese. Meanwhile they had lost their American citizenship. The American embassy could not help those who did not have the means to support themselves. In post-war Japan the barter system was the only means of acquiring food for survival. Violet's relatives were very reluctant to accept the new returnees. Violet finally secured a job with British occupation forces as an interpreter trainer. She was paid "the wages of indigenous personnel."[63] During this time the most traumatic experience happened which affected her relationship with her son and daughter till the time of writing. She made a decision to send her 12 year old son and later her daughter (at the same age) to USA. The children were passed from home to home, and Violet received many requests from the foster parents to come and retrieve the children. Because of the restrictions on visas and finances (she had borrowed money from

American forces), it was not possible. The children, after many hardships, were accepted into warm homes, and successfully finished their education. Her son became a college professor, and her daughter a registered nurse.

But the children who had to be independent so early decided that [their mother] let them go because [she] did not want them.[64] The children (including their child) have cut themselves off from their mother, who eventually came back to the USA, remarried, and kept contact with the foster parents. Violet kept her last daughter because she felt that she was more responsible for ("owed to") the daughter's infancy.[65] The impossibility of being with her children when they needed her most in the USA "tormented" her to "the end."[66] But because her children could not have been better off if they had stayed in Japan, she knows "in [her] own mind" that what [she] did for the children, for [herself], for others, was the best course that [she] was able to take. [She has] no regrets whatsoever."[67]

While living through so many family tragedies Violet dealt with many existential and faith questions. The self-recrimination of "What have I done? What have I done to deserve this?" bothered her for a long time.[68] Her children also asked "Why?" in tears.[69] She witnessed her devout Buddhist mother-in-law suffer and confess: "I prayed and I prayed and I prayed. . . . Sometimes the *hotokesama* 'Buddha' did not answer me."[70] Upon her death bed, she did not complain about the unjust treatment she received. Instead she said: "I must have done something in my other life for *hotokesama* to ignore me or not listen to me."[71]

Violet "kept it to [her] self."[72] This internalization of "why? why? why?" kept her feeling ill for a long time. She was angry but at the same time she was numbed to "tell all these things to anybody" by the thought: "But what good does it do. It should only make me sick."[73] The question led her to conversion to Catholicism after the war. In Japan Violet was helped by a Catholic priest constantly. She said that the "last six months since [she] started reliving" her life, "it was very hard." But at the end of her story she says: "I have more peace of mind now."[74]

6. Faith and Christian Response

All the stories that these women tell about their traumatic experiences of internment record the existential question, "Why?" Why did this have to happen to them individually and as an ethnic group? Most of the former internees that contributed stories to *And Justice For All* were Christians. They testified that their faith in the vindicator God did give them some eschatological hope and that faith in the co-sufferer God did give them daily strength for survival. As stated in section 4, the Christians in the internment became somewhat otherworldly. What was crucially missing for them was a *koinonia* of suffering with the rest of the global church. In wrestling with questions of the "neighbors", they had to deal with the fact that their Caucasian friends were no neighbors, nor were the rest of the ethnic groups in the USA.

Here I would simply like to point out the failure and inability of the church to distinguish the Christian understanding of justice from the civil Christianity that was practiced in the earlier half of the twentieth century in America. Reflecting the time of mounting tension toward detention of the Japanese Americans Kitagawa writes:

> The Churches had been curiously silent for all those months, except that at almost every hearing of the Tolan Committee there were church representatives testifying against any mass evacuation. But there had been no organized effort made by the Christian churches to prevent such a measure's being adopted by the government. It was obvious that churchmen were opposed to it as a matter of principle, but nothing was done beyond that.[75]

Even the Presbyterian denomination which had been known for their work for the justice for the immigrants was so "caught up in the anti-Japanese hysteria fanned by the media."[76] The denomination itself was absolutely unable to see what was at stake. Their primary concern at the moment was "the preparation for closing" the Japanese American church and "entrusting it into proper and caring authorities."[77] In the minutes of the session of the Christ United Presbyterian Church "one would not know that a major crisis was affecting the church and the Japanese American community." The minutes of the meetings of the Presbytery did not record any trace of the fate of the Japanese American church. Neither the Japanese American Presbyterians nor the Caucasian

Presbyterians did anything to speak-out against this injustice. Before the war broke out, the conversion of *nisei* to Christianity was only viewed from the perspective of cultural assimilation to mainstream America. As "traitors" to the country, the Japanese American Christians were marginalized in the church as failures of inculturation. "The Japanese Christians in the camps, . . . by and large felt that the denominations abandoned them in their time of need."[78]

Instead of raising the fundamental issues of justice, the denominations started ministry to the evacuees. Yuri Takeishi, on the morning of the evacuation, walked to the place of assembly with a few essential things. She and her sons had slept on the floor the night before. Her husband had been arrested by the FBI. In the place of assembly she saw a church group which "had some hot coffee and doughnuts for us, . . . which helped a lot."[79] Emi Somekawa thought that she had had a good relationship with the Caucasian family "that lived right across the street" with whom her family "went to church together."[80] But through the internment years neither this family nor the church appear among the pictures of her visitors.

Helen Murano had constant contact with a Baptist home missionary woman, and was sponsored by a Presbyterian family to get out of the camp. Quakers are known to have been the only group that did protest directly to the civil authority. (I have not been able to obtain records of documentation of their activities.) By and large the Protestant Federation of Christian Church "ministered" to the internees as outsiders of the Christian fellowship.

Yoshiye Togasaki, a woman doctor, appreciated Quaker, Catholic, Episcopal and Unitarian ministries (of which exact documentation is not available to me at this time of writing.) Just to show the extent of her disappointment with other major Protestant churches, I quote her:

> [T]he president of the Council of Churches of the State of California said to me the filthiest darn things, things like, You're just a traitor, and How do I know how to trust you? I don't know you from anything . . .you're Japanese, so you're not trustworthy. And there were a lot of dirty cusswords in between. Unfortunately, I went to

> him to ask him to speak on behalf of the employees down at City Hall so that they would not be fired. . . . But I got nowhere with him or with the health officer of the city of Los Angeles.[81]

The ministry for the evacuees was conducted by the Japanese American evacuee Christian and Buddhist ministers. Their overall counseling was evaluated as excellent by those who utilized their services. The Christian preaching was not adequate to answer the deep existential questions of the internees. "By and large, the messages were not filled with anger, frustration or denunciations of the impending evacuation. For the most part they spoke of the need of faith to undergird persons in this experience, for holding on to hope despite an uncertain future, and for Christian love in the midst of this crisis."[82] White preachers who were invited to speak from time to time in the camp also spoke of personal piety and not of the deeper questions of faith. Mary Tsukamoto remembers:

> I remember Dr. Allen Hunter, who spoke to us. Some of us asked him to teach us how to pray. I said we feel like hating everybody; we just can't stand so many people all around us. Wherever we go we're with everybody, and there is no privacy. He said, tomorrow morning when you get up, you just know that every single person in that camp, 5,600 people, every one of them has a halo over his head. Each one is trying to grow tall enough to fit under that halo. He said that each one of us is trying his very best to be a good person and I never forgot that.[83]

Preaching Christian love and forgiveness to face the injustice imposed on those internees as an outsider, the Christian church failed to suffer with the internees. These were difficult words to hear when your whole life was being torn apart, businesses ruined, families split, and amidst arguments about how much protesting would be right, and more basically, how you stood up for yourself and others as people created by God and, under our constitution, with equal rights.[84]

I will again quote Rev. Kitagawa in his self-criticism:

> The evacuation order was unquestionably a defeat for the forces of justice. All the Christian virtues -- humility, longsuffering, forgiveness, self-sacrifice, magnanimity and tolerance -- were to be practiced by the victims . . . while the oppressors, the majority of whom were at least nominally Christians, were not to be blamed for their organized robbery.[85]

Mary Tsukamoto, having remembered the message that the church preached to her, asks herself. "After all I had gone through and when I had an opportunity to speak, when people asked me to tell them the story, why didn't I have the courage to tell the truth?"[86] Her question is rightly placed. By Christian love she was silenced. She was too numbed to feel angry. This testimony casts a serious historical question to the global church, which in Japan, Germany, Italy, as well as the USA went along with the major currents of nationalism and did not stand for justice during WWII. The action of the church resulted in many scars and hurts which took many years to surface from those Christians, Jews, and other minority groups who suffered under oppression.

Mary Tsukamoto concludes her story having realized that she needed to become angry enough so that she can take action for "the *yonsei* (fourth generation) kids and for their children and their friends and all the generations that are coming."[87] Amen and amen.

Conclusion

The stories of the Japanese American women who experienced internment showed a need for the church to really understand and envision the call to strive to serve all the peoples from all nations. Problems of racism, colonialism, nationalism, and all the evil that prevents Christians from answering the call should be seriously faced within the church's theology and praxis. Only then can the church become salt and light in the overwhelming power of structural evil which many times works through governments. It is then crucial for each congregation to be open to start listening to stories: stories that give us clues to what theological issues we must address, and what social stands must be taken in our communities. At a practical level, experiments such as the Asian/Asian

American/American Women's Cultural Exchange which I mentioned in the opening section can be recommended.

In planning the place for the true exchange which would give safe and warm surroundings for the women to tell the true stories, the leaders of the groups would profit in learning feminist therapeutic methods. In the Asian cultures experience of trauma and displacement may be seen as retribution and shame to the suffering family. These persons come with feelings of shame and defeat to the group. Sensitivity is required of the leaders.[88] The program would first provide a support system among the women who are involved. There should be agreed trust among the women. The purpose of the storytelling is healing. Laird summarizes Spence's thesis that "the purpose of therapy should not be to rediscover and work through the traumas of the past, but to reconstruct a self and a life in the form of a narrative of the whole."[89] This should apply to the church program, which is not strictly a counseling session but a whole person interaction. To read (listen to) the stories as a living text, the readers (listeners) need a hermeneutical perspective.[90] Christian commitment to justice for all and to love one another can provide a basic hermeneutical horizon above every other horizon. By listening and understanding the stories, women will meet one another in a new transformed relationship. The leader(s)-therapist(s) of the program should be sensitive to this Christian perspective.

Another sensitivity to intra racial relationships among so called Asian women and Asian American women is required of the leader(s)-therapist(s). There are diversities in socio-cultural and historical background among these women. Collier thinks that "their only real link is the racism they encounter in the larger community."[91] In what other setting can women from enemy nations which waged racist wars against each other have an exchange other than in the church? All these women as women live in the different degrees of sexism in societies also. Women should feel free to tell stories and respond to each other's stories. In order to do this, leaders must be informed, sensitive to the diversity of cultures, and committed to peace-making.

The purpose of this healing group exchange will be accomplished when the women may be able to attain "incorporation" stage or "resolution" stage where these women can affirm both Asian and American identities.[92] They may be able to balance between the

Confucian (and Eastern Christian) technique of inner reflection and contemplation and Western articulation of speech to create their stories. The women will enjoy each other as whole persons and each other's resources for abundant life. Together they will claim the power of healing from Jesus for themselves and their children like the Syrophoenecian woman. Together they will overcome the societal abuse imposed on them for such a long time in history.

After such a support system is firmly established, this type of program can become a locus of ethnicity awareness and training for the larger church. Women of cultural historical backgrounds other than the "Asian/Asian Americans" should be invited to test the true inclusiveness of the group. I intuitively think that women in general like to make friends with each other, and like to keep the friendship if possible. Then through global women's exchange, there may be hope for a more inclusive church, deeper understanding of Christian *koinonia* of love and suffering, and more participation in partaking of "the good news" of peace in this war-fragmented world. I thank Asa for her courage and the sparkle of hope that she ignited among her friends by telling her stories.

Chapter Two

The Significance of the L.A. Uprising and James Cone's Black Theology:
Concentrating on Issues of Culture and Identity in U.S. Minorities

Jae Myung Lee

Introduction

When the L.A. riots that occurred on April 29, 1992 in South Central Los Angeles ended, leaving 44 dead, 2,000 injured, and $1 billion in losses[1], all Americans, as well as the world, had to address the reality of racial problems in the U.S. In fact, despite some ongoing racial troubles, black-white relations were considered to be improving until the L.A. riots uncovered the hidden chasm. Prior to the L.A. rioting, no one had imagined that there could be such extreme confrontations as the L.A. riots in the U.S. However, through the tremendous disturbances in L.A., Americans realized that the riots were an indisputable proof that uncovered the tremendous depth and breadth of hostility that remains among the races in the U.S. Furthermore, they began to recognize that the economic inequality or unbalance between the classes was no less important than political injustice in racial relations in the U.S. In other words, the L.A. riots did not occur simply because of political reasons, but it were occasioned by the intertwining of political injustice and economic inequality.

It would be possible to write a "fiction" of the L.A. riots focusing on racial conflict either between Blacks and Whites or Blacks and Korean Americans. However, unless the economic plight of the urban poor, intertwined with the racial oppression in the U.S., especially in L.A., is considered, the true nature of the L.A. riots would be distorted. In other words, in order to find out the cause and significant meaning of the L.A. riots, we must analyze the structural character of American society in relation to racism. With an accurate analysis of the social, economic, and political structure of American society, we may answer the questions: What did the L.A. riots mean to African Americans and, also, to Korean Americans? Who were the victims, and what made them victims? Why did the incident occur, and what can American minorities do to prevent future incidents? In order to answer these questions, the following shall be discussed. First, we shall discuss the validity of articulating the L.A. riots as the result of the racial tension between African Americans and Korean Americans. Furthermore, the role of the mass-media and the police shall be discussed in relation to the distortion factor influencing the L.A. riots. Secondly, we shall discuss economic inequality in the U.S. as a real cause of the riots. Thirdly, the significance of "black power" shall be discussed in order to reflect the meaning of the L.A. riots for Korean Americans. Finally, the issues of culture and identity shall be discussed as a solution for racial tensions and as a suggestion for the survival of all minorities in the U.S. centering on the theology of James Cone.

1. The L.A. Riots & African and Korean American Relations

The L.A. riots were regarded as a racial conflict between African Americans and Korean Americans. An incident in which a Korean grocer, Soon-Ja Du, was put on probation by a white judge who convicted her of killing Latasha Harlins, 15-year-old black girl (suspected of shoplifting a bottle of orange juice) aggravated the relationship between the two races and was pointed out as a main feature in the L.A. riots. In addition to this particular incident, two other factors have often been identified as contributing to the African American rioters' intentional looting of Korean American stores.

First, the exploitation of African Americans by Korean merchants was indicated as one reason. It is charged that the excessive economic desire of Korean American business people led them to "choose" the black community to take economic advantage of, while others usually avoided beginning businesses in predominantly black communities.[2] In other words, by establishing stores in ghetto areas, according to blacks, Korean merchants exploited poor black neighborhoods. It was not, however, the greed of Korean American merchants alone that brought calamity upon them. Although it was true that Korean Americans owned the majority of stores in South Central L.A., Korean Americans did not intentionally penetrate the black community in order to make good money. Rather, it was the obvious "economic necessity"[3] in those areas which presented Koreans with an opportunity to open their stores there. In other words, Korean Americans were willing to risk the overhead of managing their markets there. Also, it is a simple geographic fact that when the riots occurred, the closest natural targets were the Korean American stores. Hence, regardless of any specific racial relationship with blacks, any who were there at that time would have been victims of looting as the Korean Americans were. In this sense, the L.A. riots were "a grotesque case of being the wrong entrepreneurial group at the *wrong place at the wrong time*."[4] A second fact to remember is that it would be difficult to deny that from few years ago before the L.A. riots, there were racial tensions between blacks and Korean American shop owners mainly because of a deficiency in mutual understanding of cultural differences. Blacks complain of Korean Americans' impolite mentality in treating them as potential shoplifters, and Korean Americans complain of the blacks' proneness to shoplift. This kind of racial tension could potentially happen between any other race groups as well. To understand this tension better we need to think about the different histories of immigration regarding African Americans and Korean Americans. Put simply, African Americans' ancestors first came to America as slaves and so were not treated as human beings, while most Koreans came to America to seek out better economic opportunities. Due to this historical background of immigration, for blacks the most urgent interest was being treated as dignified human beings, whereas for Korean Americans it was achieving economic stability. In terms of theology, "liberation" for African Americans primarily means freedom from racial oppression, while for Korean Americans, liberation primarily means freedom from econo-political oppression.[5] We notice that the differences of culture, experience, and history can lead people into different lifestyles. In other words, because racial tensions between blacks and Korean Americans resulted from the lack of mutual understanding of each other's history and lack of communication, it is simplistic to claim that racial tension between African Americans and Korean Americans was the sole reason for blacks' looting Korean-owned stores.

Distortions by the Mass Media and the Police

What, then, made the L.A. riots seem like a racial conflict between African Americans and Korean Americans? Here, we need to think about how the mass media failed to present the full picture. The opportunism of the media should be recognized. It is not surprising that journalism is always interested in portraying the "dramatic images" of a situation, regardless of whether reality is sacrificed. Without exception, television created two major distortions in regard to the L.A. riots. One was a distortion of the image of African Americans as criminals who were prone to be violent and enjoyed "vicious fun,"[6] as indicated in the repeated showing of the video wherein a "white" truck-driver, Reginald Denny, was drawn out from his truck and beaten by "blacks." The second distortion involves Koreans. By repeatedly showing the images of Korean Americans' arming for self-defense on television and in newspapers without context, the media distorted the racial tension between blacks and Korean Americans as "the central feature of the riots."[7] With those images, implying the violent character of both minority races, the media camouflaged the very racial violence of the white dominant society which caused the L.A. riots. Elaine Kim was surely right when she put the distortion in this way:

> The tensions among people of color are rooted in racial violence woven into U.S. history for the past 500 years and evidenced today in a judicial system that can allow men who beat Rodney King to escape conviction. . . . The so-called black-Korean problem is a decontextualized manifestation of a much larger problem. . . . [It] masks a deeper racism in this country.[8]

Furthermore, the police's sluggish response to the situation has been indicated as a cause for the widespread nature of the riots. However, when we think about the implication of the "sluggishness" together with the police's "unreasonable" cordon to "prevent destruction from spreading north to Hollywood and Beverly Hills"[9] (relatively wealthy neighboring regions) and ignoring whatever happened in South Central in L.A. (the poorer regions of the city), we can assume that permitting continued violence was a strategy for controlling minority race relations by a majority power. In other words, the police (or the U.S. government) decided that the situation required a "scapegoat" to bear the rages and complains of blacks about racial injustice and economic inequality. In this sense, Korean Americans were a scapegoat for the racial and economic injustice of America, not just the natural victims of a riot.[10] What can we recognize from this race-controlling strategy? It is a camouflaged tactic of the oppressors which is intended to divide the oppressed permanently. Why do oppressors desperately want to divide the poor minorities? It is because, as Cone rightly indicates, oppressors also know that the most effective way to keep the oppressed under control is to divide them, keep them apart, have them fight each other, or at least share views that make them suspicious of each other. As long as oppressed peoples remain ignorant and suspicious of each other, they will remain open to believing what oppressors say about the others and thus will not build a coalition movement designed for the liberation of all.[11]

2. The Economic Cause Intertwined with Racial Injustice

What then was the real cause of the L.A. riots? It is often said that the Rodney King verdict was the main cause. It is evident that for African Americans the Rodney King case was a "litmus test" by which the true nature of the will of the American judicial system toward African Americans could be proven. Also, most African Americans hoped that it would be different from the unjust past.[12] In this regard, for blacks, the "not guilty" verdict and acquittal of the three police officers who beat Rodney King meant that their human rights were again completely overridden by the white-dominated judicial system. Thus, it was possible to make the quick conclusion that it was this outrageous verdict which made African Americans so furious and instigated them to riot. However, although the unjust verdict worked as a spark for the occurrence, racial injustice was not enough to cover the whole cause of the L.A. incident for two reasons: first, all minorities were involved with the riots; second, the crowd's primary lust was not for "blood" but for taking "property."[13]

What can we evidently assume from these facts? Nothing can be clear without considering the economic situation of inner city inhabitants, blacks and other minorities in the South Central L.A. area. What is the relation between race and class oppression in American society? It is important to note that, in a highly capitalist society such as the U.S., both are deeply connected, and their victims inevitably overlap. As James Cone states,

> An exclusive focus on racial injustice without a comprehensive analysis of its links with corporate capitalism greatly distorts the multidimensional character of oppression and also camouflages the true nature of modern racism.[14]

Put bluntly, black people, who have been oppressed by the racism of white society, are also oppressed by the capitalism of white society. For instance, under capitalism African Americans still fall victim to crime (such as drug dealing and gang warfare) because of their devastated economic situation. In this regard, it is very important to consider the economic situation of African Americans who live in South Central L.A.

The economic problems in South Central Los Angeles were serious.[15] In political history the "urban renewal" programs have failed to renew the urban areas which have been neglected in their plight of poverty.[16] Two causes have been pointed out for the deepening of urban poverty. One is the movement of the middle class into suburbs, and the other is the decline of the manufacturing industries in big cities.[17] The relentless flight of the middle class from city to suburb destroyed the sense of unity between the two classes and left the urban poor more destitute, both economically and psychologically, than ever.[18] The economic divide was much more serious than the racial divide in that it would be related to the future relations of the next generation of both blacks and whites.[19] What was more serious was the destruction of the sense of being united as a community. It is noteworthy that the economic egoism of middle-class Americans created in African Americans the sense of being segregated from the American community as a whole.[20] Observing the grave contrast between South Central L.A. and Simi Valley in L.A., it is hard to expect from either group any kind of communication or interrelationship as though they were one community who lived in the same area of the country. The separation signifies a terrible divide in this country between what is "your land" and "my land."[21] In a sense, the riots were the "price of neglect,"[22] for ignoring the urgent economic situation of the urban poor and refusing to take responsibility for that community.

That the areas destroyed by riots closely matched the economically devastated zone in L.A. can be seen as evidence for the reality of urban poverty and the anger of the poor in America. Their violence was a desperate plea for attention to be given to their neglected problems, to their plight of extreme poverty.[23] In short, the L.A. incident was a class riot protesting those who had by those who had been too long neglected by government and the middle-class capitalists.

3. Weakness of "Black Power" in the L.A. Uprising

Although the desperate feeling and the fury of African Americans are understandable, their distorted violence cannot be validated. Here, we ought to indicate a weakness of black power concentrating their focus exclusive on the political aspect and on self-affirmation in their struggle for liberation. It is indisputable that in his theology Cone has concentrated too much on the socio-political struggles of black people for liberation from racial discrimination in white dominant American society. And it is hard to deny that the excessive passion drove him and his followers to be blinded to other kinds of oppression that exist in the same society. In other words, that exclusiveness allowed the African Americans to regard themselves as the only victims or oppressed in the U.S. and as having the right to oppress others. This bias of black power results in an absurd justification for poor black people to oppress other minorities as shown in the L.A. riots. It was certainly an "irony" for one minority group to regard themselves as having the right to emit its furies on another minority group "in the name of civil rights."[24]

If African Americans treat other minorities unjustly as whites have treated them throughout American history, it would signify that their consistent and desperate claims for liberation from racial oppression are no more than a demand for the replacement of the oppressors' positions by themselves. African Americans must realize that they could never gain their freedom in an effort detached from other oppressed peoples' struggles for freedom or rights in America. It is because, as Cone rightly points out, the struggle for freedom is not an isolated endeavor but a "common" work, and so "there will be no freedom for any one of us until all of us are set free."[25]

On the other hand, it should be indicated that a one-sided focus on political power has neglected the economic oppression or the seriousness of economic situation under capitalism. Many of us, including blacks, may appreciate a partial political achievement in that there have been black mayors and black bankers as a result of the success of the civil rights movement. However, the more we concentrate on the political arena, the less we can recognize what the civil rights movement has missed. It is evident that "black power" has focused exclusively on the socio-political struggle, neglecting the economic aspect. The fact that the cities in which African Americans have dominant political power are in devastated economic situations indicates this exclusive emphasis of black power. The political success of African Americans achieved by black power could not improve their economic plight. In other words, despite their political power, the benefits of economic development have not been evenly shared.[26] From an economic perspective, it is right to say, the civil rights movement might turn out to be one of the worst things that ever happened to us. The dream of Martin Luther King has become a nightmare because all it had done is make white businessmen richer and make us poorer.[27]

Furthermore, the fact that there were not just a few blacks among the middle class who fled from the inner city to the suburbs implies that even black power missed the economic egoism which human nature inclines to. This is a strong reminder that "skin color alone is no longer a reliable guide to blacks' political attitudes"[28] under the typical ill-influence of capitalism mingled with economic egoism. It is noteworthy that Cone himself perceives this human nature in relation to economic lust later.

There are very few differences between black and white capitalists when viewed in the light of the consequences of their behavior for the poor. When profits are more important than persons, disastrous results follow for the poor of all colors. It does not matter whether blacks or whites do it.[29] Cone's indication is very significant in that he himself, who has strongly emphasized black power in the affirmation of the value of blackness while ignoring human nature's common inclination to injustice, acknowledges the other kind of oppression, especially in relation to the capitalism of modern society.[30]

4. Culture, Identity, and Black Theology

Nevertheless, we should not discard the strength of "Black Power" or the significant value of James Cone's black theology. In this chapter we shall discuss valuable insights given from black theology as a solution for racial tensions and a way of survival for minorities in the U.S. where multiethnic cultures are dominant. As we have discussed, in the American society where capitalism and racism are closely intertwined, it is necessary that the way of cooperation among all minorities for survival should be in connection with race and class simultaneously. Here, we need to think about what the L.A. riots mean to Korean Americans in relation to the issue of identity.

The L.A. riots stimulated Korean Americans not to ignore the identity crisis as if it is merely personal matter. In fact, most Korean Americans, who were born in the U.S. or who had never doubted themselves as Americans, have an experience of identity crisis through their childhood. At least one time in their lives, they were asked "Where did you come from?" or "What are you?" by "other" Americans, and the question made them terribly embarrassed. Before the L.A. incident, those questions could be regarded as a usual experience of immigrants. However, after the L.A. riots, Korean Americans recognized that the "other" Americans had their stereotyped image of Korean Americans as "diligent work machines"[31] in question. And because their intention was to ignore the Korean Americans' identity as Americans, those questions should not be underestimated any longer simply as a personally shocking (yet possible) experience that could happen to any U.S. minority. On the contrary, their doubt should be accepted as a challenge to test the Korean Americans' identity and as a denial of the validity of Korean Americans' existence in America. In a sense, that kind of treatment is an indisputable proof of non-acceptance of Korean Americans and also of all minorities as "pure" Americans. In this regard, it is not excessive to consider it as the evidence of failure of the "Melting Pot" strategy.

Through the experience of the Los Angeles riots, most Korean Americans, who had believed in the possibility of the integration of diverse races, realized that there was no possibility of the "Melting Pot." Rather, what they found was an unstable mix, not an integration. After the L.A. disturbances, what remained were the particles of the razed "Melting Pot" myth. For Korean Americans, who had dared to leave their home country dreaming the better life represented in the slogan "American Dream," it was too hard to give up the belief in the "Melting Pot," for it had been regarded as a kind of a guarantee for the realization of the "American Dream." Furthermore, Korean Americans realized that if there was any possibility of achieving the American Dream, it would not be actualized through racial integration. Rather, they recognized the real situation of America in which racial discrimination and inequality are at stake. Therefore, any kind of political or economic dissatisfaction could ignite a racial explosion.

What Korean Americans seriously experienced through the L.A. incidents was the sufferings from the disadvantages that accompanied the politically powerless minority.[32] On the one hand, they found themselves to be politically helpless, since they had ignored the necessity of political participation and had not organized any political associations. On the other hand, those who found themselves feeling culturally inferior to the majority of America educated their children to grow up to become perfect members of white society by encouraging them to use English rather than Korean even at home. Many of them, consequently, had discarded all aspects of Korean life-style and had replaced them with American ways of living not only in their external behavior but also in their internal mentality.[33] In other words, they intended to raise their children to become like white Americans. However, the L.A. experiences destroyed these sorts of trials at Americanization along with their economic accomplishment. It changed the way of thinking of Korean Americans regarding their Korean identity with the particularity of Korean culture in America, a mixing pot of diverse cultures. For minorities, it is important to realize the necessity of having one's own ethnic identity in order to survive in America.

Here, we as a minority need to be reminded of the meaning of integration in the white dominant society. Why should minorities reject the idea of integration? Why should the concept of integration be rejected in favor of struggle for identity? It is because, under the socio-political circumstance of the white dominant society, what "integration" means is nothing more than advocating the assimilation to the culture of the white majority which enslaved blacks and treated other minorities as perpetual foreigners. True integration does not mean being assimilated to a dominant culture while ignoring one's own identity. In this regard, only when integration signifies an appreciation of the particularity of each culture, and hence, allows all people to respect each other without any sense of superiority or inferiority, can integration really be racial cooperation and not racial "assimilation" or cultural "absorption." For this reason, to have self-affirmation of one's own identity is most urgent and essential to all minorities for the right to live as people with dignity in the American society. Hence, people with self-affirmation of identity refuse to acquiesce to any kind of humiliating or vicious "labeling" of their human dignity. On the contrary, because they have a certain self-determination to live their lives, they struggle for the realization of their humanness rather than servilely acquiesce to the given situations. Cone summarizes the character of living with self-identity as not living according to "what ought to be," but living according to "what is."[34] The loss of identity or self-affirmation results in the cultural "flunkyism" of minorities.[35] This "flunkyism" is likely to create absurd barriers in dialogue among minorities. It prevents minorities from cooperating altogether. What made Cone feel "strange" with the paradoxical attitudes of minorities in the U.S. can be interpreted as a sort of flunkyism. In other words, it is not difficult to witness that each ethnic group always makes a big deal of "the smallest and most insignificant" differences from other minorities in dialogue with them, while each group shows the efforts to overcome "horrendous barriers" with the white American majority.[36] This cultural flunkyism might have been in James Cone's mind when he indicated the relationships among the minorities of U.S.:

> No groups have been more divided and suspicious of each other and yet have the most to gain by mutual support and solidarity than have U.S. minorities. There have been few occasions of working together, but many occasions of indifference and hostility.[37]

The power to overcome cultural flunkyism can be derived from the sense of self-esteem. Cone was right when he pointed out that all minorities must overcome the sense of "self-hatred," "the worst crime" instigated by the white racist.[38]

In addition, however, we must be careful about insisting on our self-affirmation or identity in isolation from others. We need to think about the validity of our own culture or experience always in relation to other cultures and experiences. Although we agree that theology is "a product of its social environment and thus in part a reflection of it,"[39] our agreement ought to be no more than a necessary appreciation of the "Sitz im Leben" in relation to the history and culture of the oppressed in doing theology. Because experience cannot be the only source for theology, the emphasis on experience should not mean exclusiveness. In other words, we need to admit the uniqueness of different cultures and experiences and learn to appreciate their different ways of understanding and expressing God. For instance, "God is rice" in Minjung theology of Korea while "God is black" in black liberation theology. From the experience of black people, the blackness of God represents that the most urgent theological task is the self-affirmation of black people as dignified human beings due to the racial oppression of the white dominant society.

Because blacks have come to know themselves as black, and because that blackness is the cause of their own love of themselves and hatred of whiteness, the blackness of God is the key to our knowledge of God. The blackness of God, and everything implied by it in a racist society, is the heart of the black theology doctrine of God.[40] Likewise, to express God as rice signifies an inevitable requirement for human life under the econo-political exploitation of the Korean dictatorial government. This means that the Korean situation requires recognition that the economic problem is the crucial factor for doing theology. Tong Hwan (Stephen) Mun introduces the conception of God in Minjung theology;

Pap(rice) is heaven.
As you cannot go to heaven alone,
So pap is to be shared.
Pap is heaven.
As you watch the stars in heaven together,
so pap is to be shared with many.
Pap is heaven.
As you take pap into your mouth,
you receive heaven in your body.
Pap is heaven.
Ah, Pap is

for everyone to share.[41]

For this reason, the uniqueness of existential experiences and struggles of an oppressed minority cannot be qualified as having a dominant right to ignore the experience and struggles of others. Rather, we need to recognize that the difference requires the appreciation of others. Cone reminds us that in the struggle for freedom everyone has to be careful "not to make their particularity the exclusive focus."[42] Thus, the uniqueness has a creative value only when it enables its people to transcend their existential limitation and to accept others' uniqueness so as to strive together for their ultimate goals. This is what was in Cone's mind when he mentioned "universalism."[43]

Conclusion

The increasing pressure from the economically desperate situation of blacks and other poor minorities was the most decisive cause of the L.A. riots. In a sense, it is clear that the L.A. riots were a class disturbance and occurred as a protest of the urban poor against being neglected for a long time by the U.S. government as well as the affluent. In the L.A. riots, the economic cause is closely related with racial discrimination in the American society. By ignoring racial and economic injustice, all minorities involved in the L.A. incident must not allow the white racists and the wealthy to think that they can control the lives of minorities in order to get whatever they want from them.

What then should minorities do about this situation? Where do they go from here? "We feel abandoned. The Korean business owners will not just let it happen again. We call ourselves 'city soldiers.' We're well-prepared," a Korean American suggested.[44] Could preparation with force be a real preparation for the future for minorities? As we witnessed the minority controlling strategy in the distortions created by the mass media and the police, we need to realize that conflicts among minorities only increase the antagonism toward each other. Divisions among the minorities would only be beneficial for their oppressors, while unity would be good for minorities themselves. In this regard, the future will not be guaranteed by racial conflict but by racial harmony accomplished through appreciation of cultural particularities of each race.

Realizing the importance of our cultural identity and the necessity of political participation are critical lessons that all minorities must acquire from the experience of the L.A. riots. We must recognize the features of the multiethnic culture in American society. That is, we need to have a realistic understanding of the social character of cultural diversity. For minorities, trying to achieve the American dream while discarding their own identity and ignoring the cooperating relationship with other minorities could accomplish nothing desirable. In this regard, all minorities must reject being treated as perpetual foreigners and instead affirm their own identity. Mutual cooperation can be possible by understanding each other's history. Without an understanding of our histories, Korean Americans and African Americans, it seems, are ready to engage in a zero-sum game over the crumbs of a broken society, a war in which the advancement of one group means deterioration for the other.[45]

Therefore, they must begin dialogue with each other, mutually sharing their stories of sufferings.[46] With mutual understanding of each other's history of suffering they have to learn how to overcome the sufferings and then find the way to harmonize their historical and cultural diversity and to support each other in order to live as dignified people in America.

With their identity not imposed by their oppressors but realized by themselves from the recognition of the particularity of their own cultures, all oppressed minorities can realize the necessity to recover their rights. They must organize themselves in order to gather their potential power to regain their rights. They, then, can actively respond to the demands of the oppressed world for greater justice. Without realization of this, any other effort to rebuild their lives is doomed to fail again. All minorities must realize that what they have to do for their future and for their children's future in America is to recover their self-affirmation, their own identity. It is because their children cannot help but to live as belonging to one of the minority groups regardless of their self-affirmation as perfect Americans, they have to know how they could live as Asian Americans, African Americans, and so on. This idea is neither neo-nationalism nor a strategy for racial separation. Rather, it is a politically realistic idea in the socio-political situation of America where various races do and should live. Furthermore, cooperation among minorities should be carried out in the economic field as well as in the political field. It is noteworthy that the improvement of economic inequality can make an advancement in race relations. This is the most valuable lesson from the L.A. incident given to all minorities, whether they think of themselves as the victims of racial and economic oppression or not.

Chapter Three

"My Father is Japanese, But I Have My Mother's Last Name"

Henry W. Leathem Rietz

My family situation has always seemed normal to me. My mother was born in Germany and emigrated to the United States, eventually settling in Hawai'i. My father was born in Hawai'i to parents who had immigrated from Japan. I was just like many *hapa-haole*[1] boys growing up in Hawai'i in the 1970's and early 80's. I have often wondered, however, if anyone else shared a similar situation. What is different about my situation is that while my father is Japanese,[2] I have my mother's *haole* last name.

Among Japanese people, a family's name is one of its most prized possessions. The family's name is the vessel which conveys honor or shame across the generations. Honor is ascribed to people on the basis of the actions of their ancestors through the family name. People's actions, however, can also bring shame to their ancestors, to those who bear the family's name. Therefore, the protection and preservation of a family's name is important to an honorable Japanese family.

So was the case of my father's family. My father's mother had an honorable family name. There were, however, no sons to carry on the name. Therefore, as the oldest of three sisters, it was my grandmother's obligation to marry a man who was willing to accept her family name, a *yoshi*. Her marriage to my grandfather was *shimpai*, "arranged." After they were married, it was expected that the couple would take her family name, but her husband's father would not permit it; he wanted his own family's honorable name to be preserved. When my father was 21 years old, both of his parents passed away. As the eldest son, he assumed the duties and responsibilities of running the family's soap factory and of raising his younger brother and sister. Soon after his parents' deaths, his maternal grandmother approached him urging him to abandon his father's family name and to assume his mother's. My father refused.

The problem of preserving my grandmother's family name was seemingly resolved when my great-grandmother arranged a marriage for her youngest daughter; finally a *yoshi* was found. But as fate would have it, they had no children. So great-grandmother arranged to have one of the *yoshi*'s nephews adopted by the couple. A male progeny with the family name was ensured, despite the fact that he did not have the family's "blood." When the adopted son reached adulthood in the 70's, my father's nieces were pressured to marry the man who bears the family name in order to restore the family's blood to the name. All refused. Such is the extent to which an honorable Japanese family will go to preserve the family's name.

In 1966, my mother became pregnant with me. This situation posed a dilemma for my parents, since my father's family did not know about their relationship. For my father to marry a *haole* woman would bring shame and dishonor to his Japanese family. But my father, being an honorable man, proposed to my mother, offering to sell his property and move with her to the mainland. My mother, however, refused. She would not allow him to abandon his family. My mother, who grew up in Germany during World War 2, was orphaned as child, and later lost her only brother. Most of her extended family perished either at the hands of the Nazis or in the senseless Allied bombing of Dresden. She, who had no family, understood the importance of family. She, a *haole*, knew to sacrifice her own feelings for her family.

Since my father's family did not know about my parents' relationship, my birth was also a secret. My father's family did not know anything about me, they did not even know that I existed. To them, my father had no children.

I grew up in a four unit apartment building on the island of O'ahu, about a fifteen minute walk from Waikiki Beach. On our street, which was only one block in length, there lived people from various ethnic and cultural heritages; Japanese, Chinese, Filipino, Portuguese, *Haole*, Korean, and Samoan. It was a typical neighborhood in Hawai'i. Our landlord and her family, which spanned three generations, lived in two of the apartments. They were Portuguese and *Haole*. We lived in the third apartment. The last apartment was occupied by a professional couple.

He was a *haole* from Connecticut and she was a Japanese woman from Maui. I lived in this apartment building until I left home for college in Iowa when I was eighteen.

Growing up I received many culturally mixed messages. Some of the cultural messages originated on the mainland and were imported into Hawai'i through various media such as television, movies, and magazines. These images of the dominant *haole* culture of the United States were reinforced by our landlord and her family. They were members of the American Legion. The American flag flew in front of our apartment building during every holiday. Their ideal was John Wayne. He was the tough, brave, strong American man. In comparison to John Wayne, I, as a Japanese boy, seemed to be small, weak, and timid.

Elsewhere the messages were different. Whenever I went to the beach or other places where tougher kids congregated I often felt a sense of fear. "Eh, *haole* boy. Wat cha' you lookin' at?... Eh bra', you got one problem or wat?..., heh, *haole* boy, I talkin' to you. You like beef or what?" Because I was *haole*, I was often harassed. Because I was Caucasian, I feared being hurt.

At school many of my friends were of Asian ancestry, especially Japanese. Most of the girls that I was attracted to were Japanese. I often wished my brown hair was black and straight. I felt odd when roll was taken in class and I was one of only a few students with a *haole* last name. I wished I had a Japanese middle name like so many of my friends. After school, many of them went to Japanese Language School. I always wanted to go to Japanese Language School. Every year, Japanese families celebrate Boy's Day by flying over their house a flag of a carp for each son in the family. I always wanted to have a carp fly over our house.

My parents did not marry. A few years after I was born they had a falling-out and their relationship became strained. They, however, maintained a friendship for my sake. Throughout my entire childhood I saw my father virtually every day. My father came by every afternoon. He ate dinner with us and spent the evening with us. Each night, before we went to sleep he would drive home. Growing up, I never felt insecure because of my birth. My friends eventually heard my story. I never kept it as a secret from them. I was never ashamed of my situation.

Although I was never ashamed, I did find it difficult growing up 'without' relatives. I had no family heritage that I could claim. Or maybe, more accurately, there was no heritage that would claim me. The community of Hawai'i is small. Somehow, in some way, everyone's paths cross. When people meet for the first time, the conversation often turns to their extended families. Inevitably people discover that they went to school with each other's third cousin or that their sister worked for someone they knew. People are connected by their extended families. People's identity derives from their family name. Families have traditions. Some tail-gate at University of Hawai'i football games every year with their aunties, uncles, and cousins. Others picnic at Kapi'olani Park, or maybe Magic Island. Others gather hundreds of people for big *lu'au* celebrating the first birthday of every child born to the family. My father and his family pound *mochi* the Saturday before New Year and celebrate the *Obon* festival at the Buddhist temple every summer. I never participated in the traditions of my father's family.

The most difficult thing about my family situation was not knowing what to do in the event of an emergency. For example, I often wondered what I should do if my father would become sick and hospitalized. Should I visit him in the hospital and risk exposing the secret of my existence, risk bringing shame upon my father? What would happen if he should pass away? Should I attend his funeral? I eventually resolved that I would not visit the hospital and I would not attend his funeral. I would honor my father's life by not attending the services for his death.

Growing up I longed to meet my relatives. I wished I could get to know them. I wished they could get to know me. But I did not know whether they would accept me into their family or whether they would reject me because I was *haole*. Through conversations with my father I learned that my aunt and her family lived less than five miles from my apartment. My uncle lived about fifteen miles away. I knew the names of all my cousins. I knew where they went to school. I knew where they worked. In fact, I had friends who were friends of my cousins. I had seen my aunt walking on the street. I had been to my uncle's business. Once, when I was at the State Farm Fair with my father we bumped into his cousin; I quietly walked away. My father almost did not attend my high school graduation because he might meet someone he knew. I once escorted a friend to her sister's wedding. One of my cousins was the girlfriend of the best man. At the wedding, I sat at a table with the sister-in-law of one of my other cousins. Growing up I had met some of my relatives. None had ever met me. For all they knew, my father had no children.

When I was a junior in high school, I began to date a girl who was of Chinese ancestry. She was the second of three daughters. She came from a family with a very honorable name. Since the family had only daughters, there was no male heir, no one to carry on the family name. Her parents were from an aristocratic family in Northeast China and they had witnessed the brutality of the Japanese invasion of China during World War II. They had fled from the communists in 1949, eventually emigrating to the United States in the sixties. Although they were 'strong' Christians, they were very Chinese in their thinking. They believed that their Christianity reinforced their Confucian heritage. Her parents opposed our relationship and they cited various reasons for their opposition. I did not come from a "Christian" home. My grades were poor. I wasn't "doctoral material" (her father was a professor and they wanted all of their daughters to go to medical school, or at least earn a Ph.D.). The actual source of their opposition, however, was racial. They did not like the fact that I was not Chinese. And, to make matters worse, I was not only *haole* but also Japanese.

Throughout most of our relationship, which lasted through college, I was a secret. We had to be discrete when we went out, "lest one of her parents' friends sees us." I never attended any of her family's parties, though they would often fix me a plate of food to eat in my car. At these parties, her parents would introduce her to "desirable" young Chinese men. Over time they slowly began to make concessions to our relationship. They allowed me to work for them, doing the yard work, painting their house, and repairing a second house they rented out. All the while they kept my relationship with their daughter a secret from their relatives and friends.

The rejection of my girlfriend's family was painful to me. I longed to be accepted into an extended family. I longed to be connected with a heritage. I resolved to meet all of their criticisms. My grades went from C's and D's to straight A's. I started going to church. I learned phrases in Chinese and I read her father's books. When I went to college, my studies included Chinese philosophy and I set my sights on earning a Ph.D. My girlfriend even made known to her parents that if we were to get married, I would be willing to take their family name. I was willing to become a *yoshi*.

In the end our relationship did not last and we broke up soon after graduating from college. Eventually, I married a *haole* woman from the mainland, Susan Leathem. For most of my life I had experienced alienation from my Japanese heritage. In an Asian American context, I was always conscious of how *haole* I was. I had struggled to be accepted by and connected to an Asian heritage, a struggle I had always lost. Now, living on the mainland and being in a relationship with a *haole* woman, I began to discover different aspects of my identity. In order to succeed in a *haole* context, I found myself adopting *haole* strategies of relating and *haole* expressions of identity. While I was able to function in a *haole* context, I did not feel comfortable. I did not 'feel at home.' My *haole* persona felt like a three-piece suit on a local boy who spends most of his free time at the beach. While the suit may appear stylish, it felt awkward and constraining, nothing like the tee-shirt, shorts, and slippers I was accustomed to. Living in a *haole* context, I began to recognize how really Japanese I was. I began to face the challenge of forming a *hapa* identity to integrate both heritages rather than to assimilate one into the other or to accept one at the expense of the other.

The challenges of constructing a *hapa* identity became even more complicated as I moved from forming my own identity to participating in the formation of my family's identity. In the spring of 1995, Susan and I were expecting our first child. It was then that I became convinced that the secrecy pervading my family must end. I could not bring a child into a world in which she did not exist. *Kodomo no tame ni* is a Japanese phrase which epitomized the ethics I had learned from my father and which he, in his own way, modeled honorably for me his entire life. Kodomo no tame ni. For the sake of the children. Now I was becoming a father. It was now my responsibility to give my daughter a heritage, an identity. So I asked my father on behalf of my daughter for something that I could never ask for myself. I asked my father that he make our existence known to his family. Over the years I had known that my father wanted to introduce me to his family. Though we had never spoken about it before, I had sensed the pain he felt because he could not acknowledge me publicly. He was as much a victim of the situation as I. Over the years, we each silently had endured. And now my father bravely did what

I am sure he had always longed to do, but could not do, not for himself. He told his family about us, about me. *Kodomo no tame ni.*

A month after Maile, my daughter, was born, my father brought us to the family columbarium at the Soto mission, to the ashes of my grandparents. We brought flowers and offered incense. There, Pa introduced us to his parents. The next month my parents were married. The wedding service was performed in same Shinto shrine as my grandparents'. A friend of my mother's and I were the only witnesses.

My father's family was surprised by the news that my father had a son, and now a grandchild. Despite how small the island is, they never knew that my father had a son. My cousins received me warmly and welcomed me into the family. My father's cousin, the one I had avoided at the Farm Fair, invited us to a family party in his home where even my father's matriarchal aunts seemed to accept me. My father's uncle, the brother of my grandfather, gave me a key chain with the family's mon, the family's crest. Now, to everyone we meet, my father proudly introduces me as his son and Maile as his "*haole* granddaughter." The only person who could not recognize my existence, who could not accept me, was my aunt, my father's sister. The news that my father has son devastated her, and their relationship. The image of her brother, the one who had taken care of her and honorably looked out for her all these years, shattered. The man who had accepted all the responsibilities as the oldest son of a Japanese family, who tended the family altar, who represented the family at the funerals of the relatives of all the people who came to his parents' funerals, who provided wise counsel and leadership, the man who modeled what it really means to be Japanese to the family, the man who brought honor to the family, that man had now, in her eyes, dishonored the family. To her, my existence brings shame on the family name. She cannot see that my father is indeed an honorable Japanese man.

I am saddened by my aunt's reaction, but the hurt I feel cannot not approach the pain my father experiences from the rejection of his sister. For a Japanese man, whose identity is derived from his family, to be estranged from his sister is like being estranged from himself.

While I am hurt by my aunt's rejection and while I am angered by the pain it causes my father, I cannot self-righteously condemn her reaction. As a *hapa haole*, I embody a loss of the Japanese culture, a threat to Japanese heritage. In these ways, my existence is a greater danger than merely bringing shame on her family name. The process of forming my own *hapa* identity involves integrating seemingly contradictory elements from both of my heritages. Furthermore, as a *hapa haole* living on the mainland for almost a decade, I too feel the threat to my Asian identity. Being part *haole* living in a predominantly *haole* context, I struggle with the temptation to assimilate rather than integrate. It is too easy for me to "pass" as another *haole*, if not in appearance, at least in demeanor. So I combat that temptation, at times with the instinct to preserve my Asian heritage at all costs.

My desire to protect my Japanese heritage even affects who I am as a father. A part of me feels a sense of loss that my daughter Maile, who is only one quarter Japanese, has blue eyes and blond hair, and does not have Asian features. I am saddened that she doesn't have a strong *hapa* appearance, that she doesn't look like me. Despite all that I have experienced, I still harbor fears that some day she will marry a *haole* man from the mainland. Although I am sure that I will fully accept him into our family and love him, I probably will mourn the increasing loss of our Japanese heritage and culture, a loss which becomes greater with each successive generation. Will my children know what it means to be part Japanese? Will they preserve some of our Japanese customs and take pride in their Japanese heritage? Will they remember their ancestors? Will they bring honor to their family name?

Appendix

Brief Reflections on Hawai'i's Cultural Diversity and Early Christian Ministry among the Japanese Immigrants

The dynamic interaction among diverse cultures now existing in Hawai'i is part of a process which began over a hundred years ago. Hawai'i's local inhabitants, the *kama'aina*, tend to categorize all people of European ancestry together as "*haole*," and sharply differentiate between the various groups whose ancestors came from Asia or the Pacific Islands. According to the 1990 Census report, the largest ethnic group in Hawai'i consists of people of Japanese ancestry, followed closely by those of European ancestry. However, these two groups combined still comprise less than half of the entire population of Hawai'i. Thus, no ethnic group constitutes a majority in Hawai'i.

While ethnic and racial discrimination do exist, there is a sense among the *kama'aina* that everyone, in addition to their specific ancestral heritage, shares in the broader local Hawaiian culture. The people of Hawai'i understand themselves as comprising one large family, an '*ohana*'. This concept of '*ohana*' is distinct from the ideal of a "melting-pot" which is common on the mainland United States. The "melting-pot" image promotes assimilation of differences into the culture of the majority, rather than preserving the particularity of the individual heritages. In contrast, the concept of Hawai'i as an '*ohana*' embraces a diversity of ethnicities and cultures. This diversity reflects the individual *kama'aina* families which increasingly include people of various ancestral heritages through intermarriage. This diversity of heritages ultimately is embodied in the children of these families. The situation in Hawai'i, both on a macro level as well as on the level of individuals, indicates that a rich diversity of heritages need not result in fragmentation nor in homogenization.

Hawai'i's present ethnic diversity has its roots in the plantation economy which dominated the islands during the nineteenth century. The ancestors of many of Hawai'i's *kama'aina* were brought to work as laborers on the sugarcane plantations a little over a hundred years ago. These first generation immigrants were forced to learn to adapt to their situation, living and working with others who spoke different languages and who held different customs and traditions. At the same time, many of these immigrants hoped to one day return to their homeland, so they also struggled to maintain and preserve their own cultural heritage.

Along with other early groups of immigrants, the Japanese who were brought to Hawai'i shared in the tensions to integrate on the one hand and to retain their cultural identity on the other. The situation is made even more complicated by the Christian mission to the Japanese immigrants whose religious backgrounds were predominantly Buddhist and Shinto. While arrangements were being made to import the first contract workers from Japan, preparations were also being made to provide a Christian ministry to them.[1] From the very beginning, the Christian ministry to the Japanese immigrants was provided primarily by Japanese ministers. In 1884, the Hawaiian Board of Missions contacted the Hawaiian Consul in Japan and requested that a Japanese Christian worker be sent to Hawai'i. Among the first group of Japanese immigrants who arrived in Honolulu on February 8, 1885 was a Japanese preacher by the name of Shinichi Aoki. Aoki arrived equipped with Japanese translations of the Bible and it is said that he led the first Christian worship service among Japanese immigrants at the immigration station. The Christian ministry to the Japanese immigrants was begun by a Japanese immigrant in Japanese.

While many Japanese immigrants remained Buddhists and Shinto, some became Christians. During the early years, Christian ministry among the Japanese in Hawai'i was continued in large part by a number of Japanese ministers and laity who were born in Japan. Over the years, it became apparent that many of the Japanese immigrants would never return to Japan. Accordingly, some of the Japanese ministers began to understand their ministry to include helping members of their congregations integrate and permanently settle in Hawai'i. For example, the Reverend Takie Okumura, who was born and educated in Japan, wrote;

> I felt most keenly the need of removing the causes of all lawlessness and immorality among the Japanese - the spirit of drifters and the frightful scarcity of women. I thought that the best way of combating these causes would be to encourage permanent settlement and building up of home in Hawaii. If not, no social or evangelical work could be a success.[2]

Okumura believed that a key to the Japanese success was education, and in 1896 he opened the Okumura Home, a dormitory which enabled Japanese children to attend public school. At the same time, however, Okumura was also concerned that the youth be proficient in the Japanese language, so in the same year he established a Japanese language school. The students thus were able to receive an English education in the morning and a Japanese education in the afternoon.

Okumura's vision of integration into the larger culture and preservation of the distinctive Japanese identity is still visible today in the sanctuary of Makiki Christian Church in Honolulu.[3] As plans for the sanctuary were being drafted in the early 1930's, Reverend Okumura remembered the Otakasaka castle in the province of Tosa where he grew up and he proposed that the new sanctuary be modeled after a Japanese castle. Criticisms were raised that a castle has militaristic connotations inconsistent with a Christian church. Okumura countered such criticisms by saying, "the castle in feudal Japan was a stronghold to maintain peace and order in the country."[4] One of member of Hawaiian Board, Dr. Theodore Richards, commented on Okumura's argument, saying "Unlike most Japanese who tend to throw overboard everything Japanese and imitate all things American when they become Christians, you try to preserve the good heritage of the Japanese and Christianize it."[5] Among the architectural features of the castle-like sanctuary are 164 ceiling panels of Japanese fruits, flowers, and vegetables. Some of the panels illustrate Japanese poems or proverbs. On the roof of the sanctuary are two gilded dolphins, the equivalent of the ichthus symbol in feudal Japan. Okumura's ministry, symbolized in this sanctuary, provides an interesting example of how integration into a new culture, and even into a new religion, does not necessarily require complete abandonment of one's ancestral heritage.

The experiences of early Japanese Christians in Hawai'i is just one story among many. All of the early immigrants faced the challenges of integrating with one another while at the same time maintaining their own distinct heritage. Many were faced with the additional challenge of adopting a new religion without abandoning their cultural identity. Similar challenges continue to be faced as new groups of immigrants arrive in Hawai'i. For the *kama'aina*, the challenges have changed and much of the focus is on preserving their cultural heritage. Now, a few generations removed from their ancestral homelands, those homelands have become foreign to them. They are now foreigners in their own ancestral homelands. Many of their parents intermarried, and so they are charged with preserving not just one, but several heritages. These embodiments of "multiculturalism," *hapa* as they are called in Hawai'i, are challenged to construct their own identity, drawing on unique combinations of heritages while at the same time being distinct from the individual heritages, often on their own.

Ancestry of the Population of Hawai'i: 1990[6]

Ancestry group[7]	Persons	Ancestry group	Persons
Total[8]	1,108,229		
European	253,481	Asian	574,938
German	102,883	Japanese	262,113
English	71,569	Filipino	176,370
Irish	65,587	Chinese	96,293
White	13,442	Korean	28,887
		Okinawan	5,998
Portuguese	57,125	Vietnamese	5,277
Pacific Islander	175,066	Afro-American	23,864
Hawaiian[9]	156,812		
Samoan	14,971	Puerto Rican	16,432
Tongan	3,283		
		American Indian	14,835
		Not reported	55,494

Chapter Four

Tracking the Spirit of the Vietnam Veterans Memorial

Peter Thiam Chai Chang

Introduction

The Christian gospel is the good news of peace from God to humankind. But has the institutional church been a catalyst and epitome of liberation and reconciliation for a world ravaged by oppression and strife? The church bears a chronicle that incriminates her creeds and implicates her in some of the worst human tragedies. She has failed and continues to fail to live in the exuberance and empowering spirit of liberation and reconciliation. Instead she is held paralyzed by a perceived barbarian siege by those outside her "Roman walls." The church herself needs liberation and reconciliation, and that emancipating and healing spirit will necessarily come from those outside the "Roman walls." In espousing a "theology as tracking spirit"[1] in popular culture, one takes an essential step towards identifying and acknowledging the liberating and reconciliatory powers of those "outside" the walls, those spirits whose contributory values towards peace have so long been denied and "paganized" by the ecclesiastical "moral establishment." This recognition will debunk the church's self-deceitful sense of spiritual monopoly and must necessarily lead to a reclaiming and re-reading of God's general revelation in the fullness of all creation.

For my part, I have chosen Maya Lin's architectural works as a subject for "tracking the spirit" in popular culture. Lin's designs, and in particular her involvement in the Vietnam Veterans Memorial (VVM) project, have exuded a powerful spiritual dimension that is seldom acknowledged in religious circles. I found in her design and her personal conduct in this highly controversial VVM project a powerful display and interplay of liminal, integrative, emancipative, and conciliative forces.

These forces were not always discernible because most of them were the effects of unintended consequences, of wild improbability, and unconventional happenings. What started off as intended low-profile memorial art turned instead into art engulfed in heated controversies of racism, sexism, and political ideology. This paper has three primary sections: analysis of the controversies surrounding the VVM project, analysis of the VVM design, and a concluding theological reflection.

1. Vietnam Veterans Memorial: The Project

Maya Lin was a student of twenty-one at Yale University when she submitted her design for the Vietnam Veterans Memorial. Although her entry prevailed in the competition, it became the subject of a heated controversy. Lin tried to defend the integrity of her idea, but in the end her vision for the memorial would be compromised. It was not until the memorial itself was completed that the power and subtlety of her thinking became clear. Lin created an American icon, a memorial that has become an integral part of American popular culture and is destined to be a key chapter in the history of American public architecture.

There are three aspects of the project that deserve separate and closer analysis: the improbability of the event, Lin's encounter with sexism and racism, and the corresponding political fallout.

Improbability of the Event

Like the war, the Vietnam Veterans Memorial project was littered with controversies from the conception of the idea through the process of design selection, and to its final construction. On hindsight one is astounded by the complexities of the interlocking events and amazed at how it finally came to realization. Here is how one of Lin's fellow architects recounted these extraordinary events:

> For the United States, at the height of its military and economic world domination, to lose a war against an insurgent peasant army was virtually unthinkable. For a country dispirited and bitterly divided by this war and its disastrous conclusion to undertake to erect, at private expense, a major national monument to its fallen soldiers was unlikely and still more unlikely is to elect to locate

> this monument on the central triumphal axis of its national institutions and collective memory. For the commission to design the monument to be awarded to a very young, unknown architecture student, a woman, and, what is more, an Asian American woman, was unprecedented. For this design to be realized over the vehement, vociferous, and on some regrettable occasions, vicious opposition of some of the most influential politicians in the land, was astonishing. And then for the complete work of art -- a work predicted to be divisive, unpatriotic, coldly abstract -- to become one of the most influential and beloved monuments in the United States, the center of a virtual cult of remembrance - that is the wildest improbability of all.[2]

The memorial construction has not resolved the war controversies, but it has for now put a cap on a series of implausibilities in America's Vietnam war saga. Defying convention in all its absurdity the mighty were strangely bowed in humility. As one "tracks" across this painfully improbable history, one cannot but acknowledge that there is an "invisible hand" at work in drawing these historical events into a culmination at the VVM. America was not humbled by brute force; America was confounded by an "invisible hand," a spirit that brought the mighty to its knees. What is this spirit?

Lin: Youth, Racism, and Sexism

There is no doubt that Maya Lin, the individual, was the strongest single factor that sent shock waves rippling through the VVM debates. Lin's "otherness" as a young student, a woman, and an Asian American triggered savage outbursts of vituperation from conservative hard-liners. And race was undoubtedly the central issue: "How did it happen that a young Asian American woman was permitted to make a memorial for American men who died fighting in Asia?"[3] Lin, who was born and raised in Athens, Ohio, never considered herself anything other than an American. She was now forced to come to terms with her ethnicity and its impact on the design competition. Lin reflected, "It took me a year to realize that there were a lot of problems behind the scenes because I was

Asian . . . The competition was anonymous . . . It has always been a question in my mind as to what would have happened if names had been allowed." That "spirit" had secured Lin, a woman of "oriental extraction," to be the author of the winning design, was a shocking and "dis-orienting" experience to many involved in the project. The "spirit" has conspired and forced America to face and reconcile the seeming contrariness of East and West, male and female, youth and experience. But first the initial shock and viciousness of the reactions had to be endured before reconciliation could begin. Lin was accused of being a cunning little Asian girl capitalizing on her sex and race: "Everyone is worked up about this poor little girl who is getting kicked around by the Secretary of the Interior. The press has turned her into a Cinderella."[4] Lin was called an "idealistic, uncompromising kid," "female - as a child" and a "gook." Was Maya Lin any relation to Ho Chi Minh?[5] Lin, for who she is, touched a raw nerve in America's wounded pride and troubled conscience. She personifies the reincarnated spirit of Vietnamese female war victims for the simple fact that anyone who looked like Maya Lin in Vietnam could have been raped and slaughtered by an American soldier. Lin haunted the American conscience as if they had to re-fight the war once again, this time in the shadows of their consciousness.

Lin stood her ground with a maturity and tenacity beyond her age and experience. She did not let her youth, gender, and race became an her issue. Instead she stayed focused upon her design and allowed herself to speak only on the design. Jan Scruggs,[6] who described Lin as a "genius," has this to say of her, "Lin has an artistic temperament, and she really stood by her guns to make sure that her memorial design was not tampered with." Scruggs admitted, "It was very important that she did that, because throughout the entire controversy that surrounded the memorial, she really believed in her design; she really knew that it was going to work." And "the strength of her own conviction carried us through quite a few conflicts." Lin left her youth behind, and this marked her coming of age.[7] As a result of her courage and strength, Lin became a heroine and a model to youth, women, Asians, and other minorities. She has shown that youthfulness does not necessarily belie maturity. Professionally she marked herself as a pioneer in the architectural world, which remains a male domain. And she has elevated the profile of Asian Americans into the mainstream American public discourse. In recognition of her momentous contribution towards the reshuffling of American consciousness, Lin was invited to design the Civil Rights Memorial at Montgomery, Alabama, in 1989 and a sculpture commemorating the one hundredth anniversary of the admission of women into Yale University's graduate school in 1991.

Lin and the Political Fallout

With the political controversies of the war remaining largely unresolved, the VVM Fund committee in 1979 was resolute that the project should be sheltered from further political wrangling and opted for private funding to ensure minimal governmental intervention. The VVM design program specifically emphasized that "the Memorial will make no political statement regarding the war or its conduct. It will transcend those issues." The hope was that "the creation of the memorial will begin a healing process."[8] But can a controversial historical act of war be so simply neutralized by an act of art? Could a troubled consciousness be ushered into a healing plane by installing a monument without first a passage of redemption?

The design program predetermined Lin's intent that the memorial would be apolitical. Lin wrote: "The design was not going to make a judgment about 'why' or 'why not,' about 'did you serve or not serve.' It will not take sides, neither glorifying nor profaning the war." As a structure, the memorial says nothing directly about the controversial issues related to the war, the differences and conflicts of values and meanings that divided families and separated friends. Lin simply wanted to acknowledge and highlight the lost of lives in the war and to allow those who suffered the loss to have a space for healing and reconciliation. And for all intents and purposes, the jury regarded Lin's design as the one that "most clearly meets the spirit and formal requirement of the program."[9]

The sincere intent for neutrality in the VVM was deliberately distorted. Lin's focus on the lives lost was interpreted as a "glorification of defeat." The design was deemed "unheroic," lacking patriotism and nationalism, and not affirming the legitimacy of the Vietnam War. Lin was attacked as "leftist" and "communist." Her choice of black marble was interpreted as representing the color of "Vietcong pajamas." Was the V-shape of the walls the protest "peace" sign?[10] The central position of the VVM in relation to the Lincoln and Washington monuments was read as a rebuke to its neighbors and as an implicit critique of the whole trajectory of American history, leading from Washington and Lincoln towards the disastrous war in Vietnam. In these Lin had to face the brunt of political heavyweights such as Perot and Buchanan. The government joined in the fray, threatening to stop the project altogether. Finally, through a series of counter-proposals and reluctant compromises, the design was accepted.

True to Lin's conviction, the completed memorial radiated a powerful spirit of reconciliation and healing. After a baptism of fire, the memorial now has a "life" and voice of its own. Many who visited the site were profoundly impacted by that experience. The instant waves of popular public acceptance silenced its political foes. President Reagan, who would not attend the memorial inauguration, later visited it after the millionth visitor. The VVM opposition was largely won over if not muted. The reconciliation came through after a painful passage of redemption that was marked by some ferocious accusations and vicious opposition. The nation as a whole made peace with the VVM and in some ways with its Vietnam saga. To discern the reconciliation within the human soul, we need to look into the power of the design itself.

2. Vietnam Veterans Memorial: The Design

The VVM has been widely acclaimed as a provocatively unconventional work of art, and its concept acknowledged as simple yet very direct, abstract, and subtle, like Taoism. The monument will be analyzed from three perspectives: the wall's relationship to the landscape, the wall and the names, and the wall's interactive quality and healing power.

The Landscape

The immediate impression on visiting the memorial is its spatial harmony with the surroundings, exhibiting a sensitive blending and hugging of the existing landscape. The themes of wholeness and integration permeate the memorial's form and concept. But there is also a brief and succinct acknowledgment of its violent historical context.

> Walking through this park, the memorial appears as a "*rift in the earth,*" a long, polished black stone wall emerging from and receding into the earth. Approaching the memorial, the ground slopes gently downward, and the low walls, emerging on either side, growing out of the earth, extend and converge at a point below and ahead.[11]

Lin explains the "rift": "I wanted to work with the land and not dominate it. I had an impulse to cut open the earth . . .an initial violence that in time would heal."[12] The initial violence or cut in the ground signifies that in war, the violation is as much a wounded cut in the soul of humanity as it is an injury to nature. In the "cut" Lin highlights and draws out the pain of the war. "First the pain must be reckoned with then only can the healing begin," Lin said. As one moves downwards into the center of the wall and "into the pain," the gentle and gradual descent serves to ease that pain. Symbolically the "cut" is bandaged in and nursed by nature, and in nature's time and space a healing will come about.

> The thick granite walls, each two hundred feet long and ten feet below the ground at their lowest point, gradually ascending toward ground level, effectively act as a sound barrier, yet are of such a height and length so as not to appear threatening or enclosing. The actual area is wide and shallow, allowing for a sense of privacy, and the sunlight from the memorial's southern exposure along with the grassy park surrounding and within its walls contribute to the serenity of the area.[13]

The design clearly seek to embrace and enclose the turmoil of the war within a sanctuary of tranquility and peace. The recession into the earth is a haven of serenity where wounded souls can find a private space for personal reckoning, healing, and liberation. The essence of the wall radiates a feminine spirit that always seek to protect and nurse the wounded. There is a significant maternal touch to the healing process.

> The passage itself is gradual; the descent to the origin, slow; but it is at the origin that the meaning of this

> memorial is to be fully understood. At the intersection of these walls, on the right side, at the wall's top, is carved the date of the first death. It is followed by the names of those who have died in the war in chronological order. These names continue on this wall, appearing to recede into the earth at the wall's end. The names resume on the left wall as the wall emerges from the earth, back to the origin, where the date of the last death is carved at the bottom of this wall. Thus, the war's beginning and end meet. The war is complete, coming full circle, yet broken by the earth that bounds the angle's open side and contained within the earth itself.[14]

One sees a dialectical interplay of opposites, the juxtaposition of brokenness and oneness. The wall is disjointed by the earth, yet the monument finds its completeness in the earth's containment. The names represent human history, and the break in its chronology represents the fragmentation of humanity. But this fragmentation is enveloped and contained by the earth, a powerful symbol of nature's embrace of human brokenness.

> The memorial's construction involves re-contouring the areas within the walls' boundaries so as to provide for an easily accessible descent, but as much of the site as possible should be left untouched, including trees. These should remain a park for all to enjoy.[15]

That interplay of earth and stone, nature and construction, further reinforce the recognition that all human work must necessary find its context in nature. The gentleness and grace in which it descends into the ground and the minimal interference on the surroundings reflects the designer's natural sensitivity.

In the landscape and the contours of the monument, one sees the constant juxtaposition of opposites: the cut and the containment, the turmoil and its serenity, the synthetic and the natural. In so a way, the VVM forces upon its beholder a dialectic experience of reckoning and reconciliation, of pain and healing, of fragmentation and holism. This continuous interplay of limimal and integral forces eventually brings forth emancipation. "Perhaps if we stand long enough and re-visit the wall enough times, we can begin to find ways to live together with our social, cultural, philosophical and religious differences," Lin wrote.

The Wall and Names

> Walking into the grassy site contained by the walls of the memorial, we can barely make out the carved names upon the memorial walls. These names, seemingly *infinite in number, convey the sense of overwhelming numbers while unifying those individuals into a whole.* For this memorial is meant not as a monument to the individual, but rather a memorial to the men and women who died during this war as a whole.[16]

The overwhelming and seemingly infinite list of names stuns the beholder to the immense human cost of the war.[17] Lin's monument does not seek to cover up that cost but to face it; "to overcome grief, you have to confront it." She explained: "An honest memorial makes you accept what happened before you overcome it. When you touch a name and the pain comes out." Healing comes after the pain.

> We the living are brought to a concrete realization of these deaths. Brought to a sharp awareness of such a loss, it is up to each individual to resolve or come to terms with this loss. For death is, in the end, a personal and private matter, and the area contained within this memorial is a quiet place meant for personal reflection and private reckoning.[18]

The monument is at the same time a place of public gathering and a space for private reckoning. Names are etched on the marble walls to signify the individuality of each death and to allow the living to personalize their grief. All the names are inscribed on one monument stone symbolizing their oneness in a collective historical consciousness. The placing of the individual in the collective is a recognition of each person as an integral part of the whole -- that one's pain and suffering is a shared, collective experience.

The reflectivity and tactility of the wall effectively engage visitors in profoundly therapeutic acts of communion, as so many have testified through words and deeds. One veteran, who was scanning the list of names, suddenly saw his face reflected in the polished stone and realized that "it was a memorial for all of us."[19] The beholder becomes a part and participant of this historical moment. The countless rituals of touching, taking rubbings of names, and leaving behind messages and mementos attest to the human intimacy of the memorial.[20] Its extensive and in-depth psychological therapeutic value is well attested to, as this poem testifies:

The Wall has a long reach...
longer than its length...
higher than its height...
The Wall can reach into your soul...
I swear to you, my Brothers...
When you touch that Wall...
Your long lost Brothers...
Will reach into your soul with healing...[21]

The suffering of the Vietnam veterans will continue for a long time, but under the wall, "you could pick your head up again; you could believe that you had finally come home."[22] The VVM has now come to be known as the Wall, and a "wailing" wall, a place for crying, releasing of grief, of healing and of bringing to closure a painful past. It is only through the grieving process that we can truly come to understand our common bonds of humanity and transcend our differences and begin to heal ourselves.

Interactive Concepts

Spirit languages have been used to describe the VVM as if the monument has a "life" of its own. The VVM serves as a medium of communication and point of connection for the living and the dead, the present and the past. It draws the beholder into itself and releases him/her back into the world. "The memorial is composed not as an unchanging monument, but as a *moving composition* to be understood as *we move into and out of it.*"[23] Favoring an interactive, personal approach to interpretation, Lin added that "I try not to editorialize on history but to document it. In that respect I'm not political. I would never tell someone how or what to think." So the monument is open to the reading of those who come carrying their own historical perspective. "For me, the VVM requires the kind of art that can communicate with you almost immediately and not be referential. The second you start intellectualizing, it's lost. It's the difference between telling people what to think and enabling them -- allowing them -- to think."[24] This open-book approach to the VVM opens the history of the war to varied interpretations.

As a result the meaning of the monument has changed with time and the political climate. The VVM has proven that the character of the monument can be transformed through history, it can be given new meaning, and it can allow different kind of responses to pass through its space. Lin cited the history of Tiananmen Square as an example of how the meaning and spirit of a space changes from generation to generation. She questions the notion that a space is neutral and that a space is fixed in time. Lin sees the ownership of meaning resting not with the designer but with the political and social reality of the time. The VVM is in a living dialogue with the spirit of its time.

The VVM has become a key quasi-religious symbol in what sociologist Robert Bellah has termed America's civil religion.[25] It has become a quintessential American icon. In an issue of Superman comics, the man of steel battles an arch villain before the VVM, exclaiming "I won't let you desecrate this Wall."[26] The National Park Service reported it to be the most visited site in the nation's capital, with over a million visitors a year gazing their own figure on the marble walls.

3. Theological Reflection

In her multiple "otherness" Lin wrestled with liminality, being made aware of her dislocation "in-betwixt-and-between" and her banishment to "the limit."[27] She did not "become" marginalized; she discovered her marginality. This painful discovery is part of many young Asian Americans' self-development. On account of her "otherness" Lin became a victim of the center. Yet in this ostracism, and perhaps precisely because of it, Lin drew the strength and spirit that enabled her to produce such powerful works that bear the voice of the limimal. By the margin she stood her ground, for women, for youth, and for the ethnic minorities she represents. Lin's monument also reflects an initial aura of marginality and detachment. Lin works with what is essentially depersonalized, industrial information -- names, dates, enrollment figures, simple facts -- merely to "present facts." This produces in the beholder a strong initial sense of alienation from the information. The names and numbers possess an autonomy, inaccessibility, and power that dominates the powerless beholder as the individual is unilaterally provided with selective, disembodied, objective information.[28] Yet against this alienating dynamic Lin's monument formulates and invokes a type of response. The forms invite an extended, tactile, personalized engagement with the "facts" that over time might mitigate the authority of the information.[29] In this regard one sees in Lin's works a move towards a holistic vision, with a "penchant for the integrative"[30] with nature, history, and culture. The embrace of the VVM on its surroundings, the walls' gradual intrusion into the earth, and the earth's containment of the walls reflect the spirit of Lin's integration with nature. At the VVM, the sunken, circular chronology of names depicts the war as decisively and therapeutically over and closed. At the same time the walls upon which the names are inscribed rise up to point outward at the Washington monument and Lincoln Memorial, "to create a unity between the nation's past and present." Lin symbolically seeks to bring to closure the traumas of the war and integrate and locate the war in America's holistic history. But VVM is a work that transcends its specific American historical subject matter and attains a broader spatial representation of key modern human experiences. The etched names and the reflective walls draw the beholder into the monument. It heals the souls of the wounded, and reintegrates the fragmented lives of the individual.

The interlocking of Lin's limimal sensibilities and integrative vision sets a drive towards liberation.[31] The VVM becomes a place of reconciliation and emancipation from the historical trauma and pain of the war. And it has also powerfully become a symbol of the break out from dominative forces of mainstream America. If there is a primacy of liminality alone, or of integral vision alone, then it is far less likely that these two dynamics will come together in dynamic interplay with emancipation.[32] In Lin one sees a definitive coming together of all these three characteristics of the "spirits." The accentuated "otherness" is harmonized in "conciliation" which in turn brings about liberation to the souls of the marginalized. I would say that the VVM has provided America with a "stylized mobile form" that interplays the three traits of liminality, integrative reach, and emancipatory concern, to enable us to know that we have encountered a distinctively spiritual dimension in the VVM.

Historically, monuments, like high places, altars of grassy turf, and offerings, were often identified with stiff-necked self righteousness, with hypocrisy.[33] But Lin's wall heralds a new era of monument spirit, a spirit of humility and lowliness. The VVM is hidden beneath the ground signifying humility, and awareness of one's frailness and struggle. It reflects the Asian psyche of internalization, where one tends to bring the problem into focus in the heart. Yet it is not totally subdued -- in a quiet and non charismatic composure, is speaks a prophetic message. "I am not into excess. I limit my language. But that does not mean I strip it bare. If you do something simple, is it necessarily austere? Can't something simple be very rich, very warm?" Lin wrote. If the strategy of socially critical art is to represent, reproduce, or intensify the conditions and experience of authority and alienation in the hopes of stimulating resistance, then Lin's monuments are definitely not critical. But if socially critical art could be construed as following an opposite strategy to provide alternative experiences of freedom, imagination, and intimacy in the hopes of unleashing desire as a weapon against repressive authority, then Lin's monuments might be regarded as potentially transformative.[34] Lin has used a backhanded, unconventional way to bring about transformation.

Lin in her demeanor and style, with her few words, has been able to show inner conviction and strength. Lin has shown that resistance, protest, and agitation can be done in the most staid of ways -- through gentleness and firmness of character, and through innate monuments. What Lin has accomplished is to bring a usually detached discourse into the public square, into the park and into the wider consciousness of America. The success of the VVM inspired an exact replica of the wall, called the "Moving Wall," a mobile monument transported throughout the country to spread the liberating and reconciling spirit of the wall.

Conclusion

Lin is a humanist whose life and work shares the language of Christian liberation and reconciliation. I have been inspired by the manner Lin and her works confronted the dominative forces of racism and sexism. Lin and the VVM have been used as a vehicle for reconciling and liberating the wounded and the oppressed. The church needs to look beyond herself and be empowered by the "unchurch" spirit working in the world. Who is this "unchurch" spirit? This is the spirit of Jesus Christ who freely chooses to manifest his spirit-self in all of God's creatures and creation. This liberates me on a quest to reclaim and to "track the spirit" in aspects of my Asian heritage and culture that will reinforce and complement my Christian faith.

Chapter Five

Pilgrimage and Home in the Wilderness of Marginality:
Symbols and Context in Asian American Theology

Sang Hyun Lee

Introduction

There was no particular problem with my life in this country when I thought of myself as a foreign student from Korea. All I had to do was study hard and get good grades. But when I began teaching in a small town in the Midwest with the prospect of living my entire life here, something disturbing began to emerge in my consciousness. However long I stayed in this country, I seemed to remain a stranger, an alien.

And this condition of being a stranger appeared to have two dimensions: the experience of being in between two worlds, the Korean and the American, belonging to both in some ways, but not wholly belonging to either. The other element in my feeling as a stranger was the sense that I as a non-white person may never be fully accepted by the majority of the dominant group in this country.

It is not that there are no experiences of a positive nature for Asian immigrants. Acts of human kindness expressed across racial ethnic lines, the warmth of sunny days, and other ordinary blessings of life abound in this land. However, the pervasive and relentless reality of the cold glances and gestures of disdain and rejection from the American public at large sadly clouds over the positive experiences and finally gets an Asian person to admit in the depth of his/her soul: "I don't belong here. I am a stranger!"

This predicament of marginality is vividly expressed in a poem by Joann Miyamoto, an American-born Japanese American. Here is an excerpt:

When I was young
kids used to ask me
what are you?
I'd tell them what my mom told me
I'm an American
chin chin Chinaman
You are a Jap!
flashing hot inside
I'd go home
my mom would say
don't worry
he that walks alone
walks faster
people kept asking me
what are you?
and I would always answer
I'm an American
they'd say
no, what nationality
....
but there was always
someone asking me
what are you?

now I answer
I'm an Asian
and they say
why do you want to separate yourselves
now I say
I'm Japanese
and they say
don't you know this is the greatest country in the world
now I say in America
I'm part of the third world people
and they say
if you don't like it here
why don't you go back.[1]

A ten-year old Korean American girl summed it up this way in an oratorical contest in Orange County, California: "In this country I feel like a stranger. If I returned to Korea, I would be a stranger there, too. But then who am I? I hope someday I will know the answer to this question."[2]

It is then with people like Joann Miyamoto and that twelve year old Korean American girl -- that is, in the context of marginality -- that the Asian American church is called upon to live out its Christian faith.[3] And the Asian American church has been asking for some time now: How do we as Christians live in this bewildering predicament of in-betweenness and in face of the painful alienation in the American society? What is the Christian meaning of living one's whole life as a stranger?

What I propose to do in this lecture is mainly twofold: first, I want to give some specificity to the term "marginality" as used in reference to the Asian American experience; second, I will look at two historic Christian symbols -- namely, pilgrimage and home -- and show how these symbols are given particular expressions by the Asian American context and also how these symbols continue to challenge, widen, and correct the life and work of the Asian American Christians.

1. Marginality as Forced Liminality: The Context of Asian American Theology

The classic discussion of marginality by sociologists Robert E. Park and Everett Stonequist in the 1940's already recognized the existence of two elements in marginality: namely, in-betweenness and non-acceptance by the dominant group. A marginal person, according to Stonequist, "is poised in psychological uncertainty between two (or more)social worlds, reflecting in his soul the discords and harmonies, repulsions and attractions of these worlds, one of which is often 'dominant' over the other." Such a person, further, "emulates and strives to be accepted by a group of which he is not yet, or is only peripherally a member.[4]

One of the many criticisms of Stonequist's work by subsequent researchers has been that he did not emphasize sufficiently the factor of exclusion by the dominant group in the marginalization of minority people. It has been pointed out, for example, that marginality results from a hierarchical relationship of groups in which "a resistance is offered by members of the non-marginal and dominant group, to his (the marginal person's) entry into the group and the enjoyment of its privileges." It is due to the dominant group's resistance, in other words, that "the individual in a marginal position possesses characteristics (those gained from the process of acculturation) which would 'ordinarily' give him a higher status, but which do not."[5] The "resistance" by the dominant group as at least one of the causes of a non-white person's marginality, however, was already present in Stonequist's discussion. And the value of Stonequist's analysis is that he clearly saw the presence of both in-betweenness and non-acceptance by the dominant group as components of the marginality experience.

Some anthropologists, on the other hand, use the term "marginality" to refer primarily to the experience of "in-betweenness." It was the Dutch anthropologist Arnold van Gennep who spoke about the transitional period in a *rite de passage* as marked by "margin" or "limen" (meaning threshold in Latin). The anthropologist Victor Turner developed further the idea of liminality in his many influential studies of the changes in traditional societies. Turner analyzed the liminal period of in-betweenness as a transitional condition of being out of the usual structure in people's lives -- a creative condition in which a experience of *communitas* can occur.[6]

Now, the liminality or in-betweenness is clearly an essential part of the Asian American experience. Asian Americans are caught between two worlds. But their liminality exists in the context of the non-acceptance by the dominant group.[7] Their liminality is a liminality that is made permanent by the barrier of the dominant group's non-acceptance. In such a situation, the creativity of liminality cannot flourish, nor can any fruits of the in-between experience be brought back productively into the structure. Such liminality, then is a frustrated and suppressed liminality, and the people caught in it are deprived of completing the process of human becoming. By the term "marginality," then, we shall mean a forced and permanent liminality -- an in-betweenness that is suppressed, frustrated and unfulfilled by barriers that are not in one's own control. This definition of marginality, I believe, enables us to recognize a potential creativity of liminality in the Asian American experience without ignoring the negative factor of racism in the American society.

Our discussion thus far also enables us to point to an important difference between the experience of white European immigrants and the experience of non-white immigrants such as Asian Americans. The experience of an immigrant from Europe can usually be explained in terms of the so-called straight-line theory of assimilation. That person will arrive, experience a period of in-betweenness, and with an increasing acculturation, "structural assimilation" would follow since that a European immigrant would not experience non-acceptance. That person will become "one of us" to the dominant group in America.[8]

But the straight line assimilation theory does not apply to non-white immigrants. A Korean immigrant, for example, may speak beautiful English with a name like Peter, Nancy, or Michael. But when that person walks down the Main Street, he/she is still a stranger, a new arrival.[9]

I have been in this country for over thirty-eight years. When I am away from campus, people still ask me "Where are you from?" I answer, of course, "Princeton, New Jersey." But they ask again: "No, no, where are you from?" "Princeton, New Jersey" is hardly ever sufficient in my case. Small reminders like this occur for Asian Americans day after day, week after week, and year after year, and decade after decade. And eventually you get it. You get that they don't think you belong here. Race sticks for Asian Americans as it does for other non-white persons in this country. They are indeed "strangers from a different shore," as the Asian American historian Ron Takaki puts it.[10]

Asian Americans, however, do not personally feel a sense of marginality to the same degree. The rule is that the more they adopt mainstream white America as their reference group and want to belong to it, the more they will be personally conscious of what mainstream white Americans think of them -- namely, of their marginality.[11] We shall return to this point.

To summarize what I have been saying thus far: All processes of change have three stages: ending, transition period, and reaggregation or return to structure.[12] Asian Americans are a people who left a world and are going through transition. They now need to be realigned, reestablished in a social structure. And the white America is reluctant to be that social structure. They are allowed in -- but only to the edges of this society. Asian Americans, in short, are trapped in the wilderness of in-betweenness needing a structure to return to.

2. Historic Christian Symbols and the Asian American Context

What I want to do now is to ask the question: what are the important faith-responses, both in word and deed, of the Asian American churches to their marginality? I will deal with this question by lifting up two symbols -- pilgrimage and home -- that are important in the Asian American church and by discussing their particular meaning in the Asian American context.

My discussion assumes two principles. First, the living Christian symbols exist not in abstraction but in concrete contexts. And new contexts can bring out certain fresh meanings of symbols that may not have been sufficiently recognized before. Second, the historic Christian symbols are not just reappropriated and reinterpreted, but they continue to critique, challenge, and deepen the Christian church's faith responses.

I am reminded here of the image of water as it is used by Taoism as in *Tao Te Ching*.[13] The ultimate reality, this book says, is like the water that makes its way down a stream. Water yields to and is shaped by the contours of the stream bed, by the stones and rocks it encounters. But the water that yields also has a shaping power. In the long run the stream and everything in it is reshaped by the gentle force of the water. The historic Christian symbols live on by yielding to ever new contexts, but in a most fundamental way those symbols reshape and mold the life and work of Christians in their particular contexts.

3. Pilgrimage in the Wilderness of Marginality

The image of the Christian believer as a pilgrim who does not absolutize any one place or idea but is always ready to leave the present situation toward a God-promised goal has been important for the Asian American church.[14] The way Abraham obeyed and left home when he was called, "not knowing where he was to go," and the way he and his family sojourned in the wilderness as "strangers and exiles," seeking the true "homeland," "a better country," "the city whose builder and maker is God" -- these images from the letter to the Hebrews have been deeply meaningful to many Asian American Christians.

Most Asian immigrants of course do not come to America consciously thinking of themselves as pilgrims. They usually come here for very mundane reasons -- for a better education, for a better financial future, and the like. And these dreams are fulfilled for some of them --

sometimes beyond their expectations. The Christian pilgrimage, however, does emerge as a compelling image as Asian immigrants invariably face their uprootedness that results from emigration. They come to America scarcely prepared for the consequences of leaving home. In addition, they as a non-white people encounter the cold glances of disdain from the American public. So after a number of years in this country a crisis of sorts develops. In the secret places of their minds Asian immigrants ask themselves: Did we make a mistake? Is there any meaningfulness in living as strangers? Most of them dare not voice these questions loudly because surrounding them in the living room are their own deeply Americanized children for whom home is nowhere but in America. And studies have shown a strong tendency on the part of most Asian immigrants to shrink away from the cold winds of marginality and to cling to the cozy comforts of their ethnic enclaves at the risk of bringing about a dangerous isolation from the larger American society.[15]

It is in this context of having problems of leaving home and really arriving in America that the image of the Abrahamaic obedience to God's call has been invoked in the Asian American church. The challenge is to see the Asian immigrants' de facto uprootedness as an opportunity to embark on a sacred pilgrimage to some God-promised goal and, therefore, to believe that a life as strangers and exiles can be meaningful. One of the hymns written by a Korean immigrant pastor has the following first stanza:

> Obeying when he was called, leaving home by faith,
> Abraham made altar wherever he wandered.
> We are all Abraham; let us learn of his faith;
> Through our faithfulness to God, may God's own purpose fulfill.[16]

We must pause here, however, and ask whether or not the above appropriation of the pilgrimage symbol has a sufficient regard for the particular context of Asian Americans. I myself have written and preached about the Asian immigrants' Christian calling to be pilgrims, but have now for some time been growing a bit suspicious as to whether or not such talk goes far enough in taking account of the full import of Asian Americans' marginality.[17] For Asian immigrants, to enter America or to make it their reference group is asking for trouble -- namely, to become consciously aware of their marginality. Therefore, it is not adequate to call upon the Asian immigrant Christians to become pilgrims and to enter into the American society as if their doing so would be the same as it would be for white European immigrants.

What then is the particular meaning of the Asian Americans' pilgrimage into America? Why should they be asked to do something that is bound to bring them trouble? Beyond and above the secular goal of "making it in America" by getting a piece of the American Dream, what is the Christian reason why Asian Americans should at least once in a while leave the comforts of their ethnic enclaves and mix with the majority people in America at the risk of becoming marginalized? In thinking about this question, a passage from H. Richard Niebuhr's *The Meaning of Revelation* continues to have for me a hauntingly irresistible quality to it. Niebuhr writes:

> He (Christ) is the man through whom the whole human history becomes our history. Now there is nothing that is alien to us. All of the wanderings of all peoples and all the sins of men in all places become parts of our past through him. . . Through Christ we become immigrants into the empire of God which extends over all the world and learn to remember the history of that empire, that is of men in all times and places, as our history.[18]

Speaking from his perspective of radical monotheism, Niebuhr regards all parts of the world and all aspects of human history as the realm of God's activity and thus sacred though finite. It is a responsibility of a faithful Christian, then, to make a pilgrimage to every part of history and to every place of the world and to include them in his and her remembering.

But what does it mean to make every part of human history our own for Asian Americans in America? I would like to suggest that to get at the specific implication for Asian Americans of what Niebuhr is saying here we need to pay a more direct attention to Asian American Christians' own experiences of making pilgrimage into America.[19]

The tragic events of 1992 in Los Angeles, I believe, are particularly instructive. The initial reaction of the Korean immigrants in Koreatown was one of surprise: How could this happen in America? they asked. These Korean immigrants were mostly living in ethnic self-confinement and had not really entered the American society. What happened to them on April 29 can be said to be a coerced entrance into the American realities: a painful lesson in their own and other minority groups' marginality in the American society. What resulted was awareness, in other words.

Awareness then led to sympathy and solidarity. The first and the younger second generation Korean Americans suddenly forgot all of their generational conflicts and joined together in relief work and marched together in a peace demonstration. A Korean American young woman told me that the pain she felt at the sight of other Koreans' suffering told her that she was a Korean after all. Korean American and African American churches and church leaders came together in various ways to worship, to share each others' experiences, and to discuss the ways of helping each other in their common struggle for justice and human dignity. Being consciously at the margin of the society gave them the capacity to become aware of others at the margin; this capacity was also a capacity for solidarity. To put it in Victor Turner's language, having become aware of their alienation from the American society and thus in a sense freed from the dominant social structure, Korean immigrants became consciously liminal and thus open to *communitas* experience.[20] Whatever else it may mean to become pilgrims for Asian Americans, it does mean to become self-conscious strangers and thereby to become capable of solidarity with other strangers.

All this suggests that creative and redemptive events occur at the in-between and often despised margins of this world. Margins can be creative centers, in other words. Is it any accident, then, that we find the following words in the letter to the Hebrews?

> So Jesus also suffered outside the gate in order to sanctify the people through his own blood. Therefore let us go forth to him outside the camp, bearing abuse for him. For here we have no lasting city, but we seek the city which is to come. (13:12-14)

In this passage pilgrimage theme and redemption theme come together. "Outside the camp" is where Jesus began his redemptive project.[21] And it is the pilgrims who know that "here we have no lasting city" and are willing to follow Christ to the margins that participate in Jesus project. And these pilgrims are not alone but have Jesus as "the pioneer and perfecter" of their faith. In other words, something more than sheer human courage is going on here. There is behind all this an intentionality of God's own self, God's own journey, and God's own project.

4. God's Household for the Strangers in the Margin

To be pilgrims and self-conscious strangers at the margins, then, can lead to an experience of *communitas* and solidarity. But they cannot stay in such ecstatic moments indefinitely. Asian American pilgrims, as all mortal humans, need a hospitable structure for belonging. They need a home.

And, as many people know, in the Asian American community, it is the ethnic church that has played a greater role in meeting this need for belonging than any other institution. The church is the home or at least a home away from home for many Asian immigrants and their succeeding generations.[22]

It is interesting to note at this point that according to the biblical scholar John H. Elliott the "home for the homeless" is precisely the way I Peter in the New Testament conceives of the essential nature of the church as the eschatological community itself. According to Elliott, the good news offered by I Peter to the socially marginalized Christians in Asia Minor was "not an ephemeral 'heaven is our home' form of consolation but the new home and social family to which Christians can belong here and now," "a supportive circle of brothers and sisters." And "status here is not gained through blood ties nor by meeting social prerequisites; it is available to all classes and races of mankind as a divine gift."[23] They remain despised strangers in society; but in the *oikos* or the household of God, everything has changed. They are "the elect of God." "But you are a chosen race, a royal priesthood, a holy nation, God's own people. Once you were no people but now you are God's people; once you had not received mercy but now you have received mercy" (2:9-10).

What the symbol the "household of God" or the "home for the homeless" stands for receives a powerful expression in the Asian American church. The Asian American church is one place in America where Chinese Americans, Japanese Americans, or Korean Americans feel that they are somebody. As Asian Americans come together in their ethnic churches, sit next to each other, worship together, eat together, and just be together, they experience an inversion of status, turning upside down the way they are viewed in the society outside.

In this way, the church as the household of God takes an ethnically particular form in the Asian American context. But the Asianness of the Asian American church is nothing to apologize about; ethnicity in this case can be an instrument of the church's redemptive function. When Asian Americans are marginalized and made homeless because of their ethnicity, how can a church be a home to them if it did not affirm and celebrate the dignity of their particular ethnicity? As the Japanese American theologian Roy Sano puts it, "liberation *through* ethnicity" and not "*from* ethnicity" has to be an essential function of the Asian American church.[24] The symbol "the household of God," then, has to be contextualized in this way in the Asian American context of marginality.

For the second and later generations, their particularity as Asian Americans takes the form of an in-between ethnicity, a hyphenated synthesis that is neither just Asian nor just American. The first generation immigrants also experience an in-betweenness, but their rootedness in their homelands and the strong first generation church provide them with much comfort. But the later generations often feel alienated both from their parents' first-generation church and community as well as from the American society. In other words, neither the Asian community nor the American quite accept them for what they are.

The Asian American church as a household of God must become a place where the second and later generation people are accepted as they are -- neither just as Asian nor just as American but as a new synthesis of the two with an integrity all of its own.[25] In the Asian world, they are often criticized for not being Asian enough; while in the American society, they are looked down upon for not being American enough. In the household of God, they shouldn't have to be enough anything -- except to be what they are and to have faith in Christ. The in-between colors have names as one Korean American woman put it. She said:

> I thank God for making the rainbow, the rainbow with beautiful primary colors and lots of in-between colors.

> When we mix red and yellow, we have orange. . . . Yet orange is not red, orange is not yellow. Orange is another color with its own name and its own color. I am the "in-between." In-between colors have names, too.[26]

Another way to look at the particularity of the Asian American ethnicity is to point to its fundamentally dynamic and open character. The Asian American identity and ethnicity is not an eternally fixed reality; it is in the making. And the making of this something new requires the creative energies inherent in the in-between, liminal condition of Asian Americans. One of the essential tasks of the Asian American church then would be to free up the creativity of the in-between people by affirming them for what they are. The household of God, in other words, has to be a place where Asian Americans can dream dreams. Gaston Bacherlard has noted that home or house is a place "that protects the dreamer, allows one to dream in peace."[27]

The Asian American church then must affirm all the particularities of Asian Americans in their new emerging ethnicity. But to be a true embodiment of the household of God, the Asian American church also has the challenge to become ever more inclusive -- both internally and externally. The one area where most of Asian American churches have a long way to go in becoming a true embodiment of the household of God has to do with the place of women. Asian American women are marginalized not only in the American society but also within the Asian American community itself. Much of the economic success of many Asian immigrants is due to the inordinate amount of labor provided by women at business places. But women do not enjoy the same status and privileges as men either at home or at the church.[28]

What Asian American women, especially the first generation, are up against is the whole Confucian metaphysics with a conception of household in which women exist primarily to serve men.[29] The household metaphor, therefore, is ambiguous for Asian American women. The Asian cultural ideology about women needs to be purged and corrected by the reality of the biblical household of God. And the church as a household needs to be presented as a liberating household in which the usual ideas of women are turned upside down. Liberated from their double marginalization, it should be noted, the creative energies of Asian

American women's two-sided in-betweenness or liminality can be set free -- their liminality as women and their liminality as Asian American.[30]

The symbol of the household of God also challenges the Asian American church to become ever more inclusive in its external relations with other peoples and other churches. To affirm the Asian American ethnicity in all of its particularities, we saw above, is an essential dimension of the Asian American church as church. However, the ethnic particularity must not be absolutized. Whenever this absolutizing happens, the demonic consequences of idolatrous ethnocentrism would only be perpetuated again -- this time in its Asian American form. The Asian American church, in short, has this most delicate and difficult calling to affirm its ethnic particularity over against racism and at the same time to resist the temptation toward self-enclosure and constantly to move beyond itself toward others. To be as home in the household of God, in other words, is to be at home in such a way that one does not fear the margins -- that is to say, one never ceases to be a pilgrim.

To sum up: The two historic symbols of the Christian faith -- pilgrimage and home -- manifest their original power in new ways when they are appropriated in the Asian American context of marginality. Pilgrimage for the marginalized people means the willingness to face up to one's marginality and to join with other strangers in the margins. But it is precisely their pilgrimage or their freedom from the idolatrous centers of the world that prepares them for an experience of the reality of the household of God which God is building for all humankind. Pilgrimage and home, then, necessarily go together. This can only be so because, in the final analysis, pilgrimage and home are connected by a story that is God's own story.

5. God's Own Story

In conclusion, then we ask: What is God's own story in which pilgrimage and home have their foundation and unity? What we have been saying in this paper suggests an answer which we can only mention here without elaboration. God is also a pilgrim who left home. Not that God was not perfect from eternity but rather that God wanted to repeat God's inner life of loving community now in time and space.[31] But God's own world did not welcome God. God was not accepted by the idolatrous and absolutized centers of this world, and became stranded in the wilderness of marginality. So the marginalized pilgrim God began God's project of building the loving community in the margins of the world. This project will be a struggle because it is carried out in the margins. But this project cannot fail because it is God's own project.

And also because this project is God's own, it is a project and a story which all of God's creation, regardless of their race, are invited to join in. To do so, however, means that they first become pilgrims and embrace their own wilderness in their own ways. The Asian American theology in the context of marginality, in short, is an invitation for all to meet in the margins as fellow strangers and to stand by each other in solidarity as they join in God's own joyous struggles to build the household of God where all of God's creation can come and be at home.

Chapter Six

Postmodern Politics of Difference and Asian American Identity

Wonhee Anne Joh

By the rivers of Babylon --
there we sat down and there
we wept
when we remembered Zion.
On the willows there
we hung our harps.
For there our captors
asked us for songs,
and our tormentors asked for
mirth, saying,"Sing us one of the songs of Zion!"
How Could we sing the Lord's song
in a foreign land?
(Psalm 137: 1-4)

As a Korean American woman I have often been infuriated by the subtle challenges/demands to prioritize either my gender or ethnicity over one another.[1] For Asian American women it becomes clear that racial and gender identifications are often experienced as opposition. The strategies we use to deal with multiple categories of identification across lines of race, class, gender and sexuality can fail to acknowledge the contentious framework in which Asian American women are forced to negotiate identity politics. We are often asked to choose our allegiance between our gender and our race.[2]

It is urgent for us to re-examine where it is that we stand in terms of race relations. Our identity politics of difference must be grounded in our commitment to recover the selves in us that have been erased and/or distorted. The debate raging amongst many feminists over essentialism and anti-essentialism may be paralyzing rather than empowering as we struggle to claim the many ambiguities of being Asian Americans. The essentializing of Asian American identity is yet a different way in which racism pervades cultural politics. Racist dynamics function much the same way as sexism in our society; in this regard it is crucial for Asian Americans to take note of Franz Fanon's observations. In his criticism of colonialism he was adamant that a new order was necessary . . . a movement in which the social structure of the old oppressive system would not be reproduced. He claimed that the new order would have to avoid assimilation to the dominant culture's disposition which would effectively render the new movement as only a caricature of the old oppressive order. The new movement should be alert to uncritical nativism or racialism that would appeal to essentialize notions of precolonial identity. Fanon believed in the necessity of a movement constantly engaged in the changing dynamics of the institutions of rule.[3]

The two chasms of navel-gazing and navel-erasing are the matrix in which many Asian Americans find ourselves. As an Asian American feminist theologian I often receive ambiguous feedback from others: I am either held in suspicion of making an issue out of my race, am assigned an honorary white status, am an embarrassment to my ethnic community who firmly adhere to the theory of assimilation, or am subject to racial erasure.

Although identity politics place feminists on a very low rung of the intellectual ladder, women of color doing identity politics are often placed lower. Moreover, the most painful realization occurs when we become aware of the role that garners most attention and validation -- that of watchdog who keeps white feminists honest about their own theories. Asian Americans are sometimes relegated to secondary category of racial "otherness" when it comes to race relations. Our experiences of racism are cast as less absolute, less meaningful than the black/white binary relationship that dominates racial discourse in the United States.

Our politics of identity in a North American context must begin by claiming our ambiguous identity and naming this ambiguity as the site in which Asian Americans may constitute radical embodied identities. It is necessary for our communities to actively hear one another and to recognize the richness of the complexity that make us who we are as

Asian Americans. Moreover the many conversations engaged with the notion that Asian Americans face an identity crisis due to the generational gap between first-generation immigrants and second generations are in the long run quite detrimental because they dismiss the complex web of power dynamics which permeate the micro- and macro-relations. As Lisa Lowe states

> The reduction of the cultural politics of racialized ethnic groups, like Asian Americans, to first generation/second generation struggles displaces social differences into a privatized familial opposition. Such reductions contribute to the aestheticizing commodification of Asian American "cultural" differences, while denying the immigrant histories of material exclusion and differentiation.[4]

From malicious, insecure people who want to put me in my place, in a way of speaking, and from well-intentioned good folks who assumed I must be a foreigner, many people have asked me and continue to ask me repeatedly this question of my origin, "So, where are you from?" This question continues to make me think of my identity because I have never felt comfortable with my responses, nor were my responses ever satisfactory to me. At this point in my life I respond with "How far back do you want me to tell you?" Implicit in this common question asked to many who are people of color is the belief that unlike German or Irish or other European immigrants, we are somehow not really American, no matter how much we assimilate. I have often been left to feel that I will, without a doubt, be a "stranger from a different shore" as Ronald Takaki puts it.[5] Not foreigner, yet foreign. At times rejected by my own immediate community, Koreans, Americans, feminists . . . other times needfully retrieved. I have been both useful and useless, always suspicious and always under suspicion.

The complex and often ambiguous feelings of belonging/not belonging and yearning to belong and the distaste for the yearning all seem to stem from the simple desire to both be part of a social community and to be accepted as who we are individually. How we best live with and among many diverse selves without being annihilated by the dominating social group has been raised by many feminists and between feminists. I have as a hyphenated person, Korean-American, often been caught in the push and pull of where my allegiance may be placed. Am I a Korean or an American? Am I Korean American or feminist? *Immigrant Acts* correctly observes the salient space of Asian American identity which is continually shifting, multilayered, and contested by both "inside" and "outside" the Asian American community. I would align myself with Lisa Lowe in that the stress should be put on heterogeneity, hybridity and multiplicity in the characterization of Asian American culture as we engage in identity politics. This space is given different names according to different groups: la frontera, marginality, third space. This space of in-between is what Homi K. Bhabha calls the "Third Space." In his much welcomed articulation of this Third Space he writes that this Space is

> . . . *the indeterminant space of subject(s) of enunciation* . . . though unrepresentable in itself, which constitutes the discursive conditions of enunciation that ensure the meaning and symbols of culture have no primordial unity or fixity; that even the same signs can be appropriated, translated, rehistoricised, and read anew . . . It is significant that the productive capacities of this Third Space have a colonial or post colonial provenage. For a willingness to descend into that alien territory -- where I have led you -- may reveal that the theoretical *recognition of the split-space of enunciation* may open the way to conceptualizing an international culture, based not on the exoticism or multi-culturalism of the diversity of cultures, *but on the inscription and articulation of culture's hybridity.*[6] [italics mine]

I am convinced that this fluidity, this suspension of being "in-between," is a unique space in which distinct Asian American entities may continue to emerge and constantly transform. This "hybrid" space is one in which we find ourselves both Asian and American, neither Asian nor American, it can be the site in which creative diverse selves may live in community.

A politics of difference encourages a dialectic neither repressing difference nor privileging identity. Politics of difference struggles for the rights of oppressed groups to seize the power of naming difference itself, and as Iris Marion Young writes, politics of difference explodes the implicit definition of difference as deviance in relation to a norm, which freezes some groups into a self-enclosed nature. Difference now comes to mean not otherness, exclusive opposition, but specificity, variation, heterogeneity. Difference names relations of similarity and dissimilarity that can be reduced to neither coextensive identity nor non-overlapping otherness.[7] It is this subjective plurality that encourages people to express ever-changing identity and difference. The self which is not fixed or complete is in constant process of becoming.

The dynamics of race, gender and class are all interwoven in a complex web of covert and overt oppression. The process of forming a sustainable subjectivity is one that is fraught with complexities of not only gender but of race and class. Similar to many other groups of women of color, Korean American women derive their identification from both ethnicity and gender. We often find ourselves swimming in ambiguity when our ethnicity is pitted against our gender identity by people who cannot grasp such a multi-layered dimension to our identity.

As a woman who "came to her own" through white feminist movement and later through creative works of women of color, I am often pushed into a position of being the Anglos' misperception of the Asian female as the victim of victims, or aligning myself with Anglo feminists sometimes at the expense of my Asian/Asian American brothers and sisters. Yet, my sense of belonging is not reciprocated even by the liberation oriented white community or by the Asians overseas. Somehow, Korean Americans and in general Asian Americans are often easily displaced, and dismissed.

Even the most well meaning people in the academy are able to quickly ease their conscience by often times lumping all Asian and Asian Americans in one supposedly homogeneous lump; however, they fail to grasp and distinguish the differences between Asians and Asian Americans. I believe this is their racism. Essentialism can be the benign face of racism and sexism. Either they do not want to admit political/social implications of our presence in this country, North America, or they find it easier to play their paternalistic role with our brothers and sisters across the ocean. Perhaps it is our proximity in this country that is threatening to them.

Although the white feminist movement has changed very much since the 1980's, there is still a certain unconscious or even conscious blindness to the construction of female subjectivity in some feminist works. I find that most of my energy is spent in deconstructing white hegemonic feminist discourse along with patriarchy.[8] The white feminist movement has struggled for the subjectivity of Anglo women while leaving aside the complexities involved for the non-Anglo woman as she struggles to claim her subjectivity in the midst of white men, white women, and in the midst of her own people.[9] The experience of white women's oppression as synonymous with all women's experience has received much critique and thus undergone some changes. However, the effort should not be in attempts to smooth over such differences but rather, as Judith Butler writes:

> the rifts between and among
> women over the content of the term [women] ought
> to be safeguarded and prized, indeed, that this
> constant rifting ought to be affirmed as the
> ungrounded ground of feminist theory. To deconstruct
> the subject of feminism is not, then, to censure
> its usage, but, on the contrary, to release the term
> into a future of multiple significations,
> to emancipate
> it from the maternal or racialist ontologies to
> which it has been restricted, to give it play
> as a site where unanticipated meanings
> might come to hear.[10]

In our on-going identity formation, our "difference" has played a substantial role. It is important to understand and embrace the postmodern celebration of "difference." Nevertheless, we should do this along with constructive criticism springing from our commitment to justice for Asian Americans. Our politics of difference must be grounded in our commitment to recover the selves in us that have been erased and or distorted. Insofar as identity is a social construct, Asian American identities have been under erasure from the beginning of our history in this continent.

As Trinh T. Min-ha asks, "How do you inscribe difference without bursting into series of euphoric narcissistic accounts of yourself and your own kind? Without indulging in a marketable romanticism or naive whining about your condition?"[11] The two chasms of navel-gazing and navel-erasing are the matrix in which many Asian Americans find ourselves. Instead of attending to those who have been oppressively rendered "other" or "different" in the past, postmodernism's celebration of "difference" has ironically functioned to erase group difference why maintaining specificity for the oppressed groups. Gary Okihiro writes that

> The view from those sites (margins, la frontera, third space) . . . affords a clearer perspective on the mainstream, its location, ambiguities, and contradictions. Although situating itself at the core, the mainstream is not the center that embraces and draws the diverse nation together. Although attributing to itself a singleness of purpose and resolve, the mainstream is neither uniform nor all-powerful in its imperialism and hegemony . . .the mainstream derives its identity, its integrity, from its representation of its Other.[12]

In our society the dominant discourse tries never to speak of its own name. As Russell Ferguson argues, its authority is based on absence. The absence is not just that of the various groups classified as "other," although members of these groups are routinely denied power. It is also the lack of any overt acknowledgment of the specificity of the dominant culture, which is simply assumed to be the all-encompassing norm. This is the basis of its power even in the promising post-modern conversations. Asian American feminists, for example, are given authority only when we speak about Asian feminism, not about Asian American feminism. As much as postmodern thought assumes the posture of liberation, it has too easily glossed over embedded structures of oppression and failed to adequately mind accountability and justice. Without falling into the trap of falsely glorified essentialism, it is critical to recognize at the same time the dilemma Jane Gallop poses:

> I do not believe in some "new identity" which would be adequate and authentic. But I do not seek some sort of liberation from identity. That would lead only to another form of paralysis - the oceanic passivity of undifferentiation. Identity must be continually assumed and immediately called into question.[13]

In our politics of subjectivity and difference, the concept of "difference" has at best allowed certain minority privileges and at worst bought in the pluralism of indifference which does not struggle against but rather inadvertently sanction the existing status quo.[14] Moreover, the role of defining "difference" has most often been the privilege of those in power, in the dominant position. Hence, through "difference" most marginalized people have had their realities constructed for them. The difference is handed over with one hand and taken away with the other.

> There is a tendency in more sophisticated and elaborate gender standpoint epistemologists to affirm an identity made up of heterogeneous and heteronomous representations of gender, race, and class, and often indeed across language and cultures with one breath and with the next to refuse to explore how that identity may be theorized or analyzed, by reconfirming a unified subjectivity or "shared consciousness" through gender.[15]

The concept of unity and diversity begs the questions: where is the feminist standpoint in theorizing about differences among women? In terms of politics of difference? Who is the feminist "Self" and the feminist "Other" even while the discourse espouses multiplicity, heterogeneity, self-less-ness, fragmentation, interrelationality? Difference from what or whom? Who is defining difference? Who is comparing difference? When I was growing up as a Korean American, in order to be accepted in this society, I could not afford to be different. The importance of assimilating into the white culture of North America was the constantly impressed into my psyche. I was told in many different ways that anything to do with my Korean-ness was inferior and negative and *different*. The key to survival in this country was to destroy the

Korean in me. The price of being accepted and surviving in this country was through mutilation and destruction of our memory as Koreans, as Asian Americans. However, now that the West is hungrily devouring difference, it is to my loss that I am not different enough. The "culture vultures" of this country would have an easier time accepting me now if my name was "Bright Destiny" rather than Anne. People such as myself are most often in a no-win position. Our identity is one that has to constantly negotiate and renegotiate vis-à-vis the dominant culture. The dominant group tells us that to be accepted into the dominant group we need to be like them. (Asians have to be more like whites; women have to be more like men.) However, when we do and expect to be accepted, we are turned away because they say we are different no matter what. Whereas the rules stay the same for many others, they keep changing for the oppressed. I have for a long time, lived with the contradictions of simultaneously being an insider and outsider and having the burden of explaining, proving, and representing/misrepresenting. In the postmodern conversations that celebrate our differences we should also keep our critical minds alert. The promises of postmodernism should not be embraced without critically examining its implications and presuppositions.[16] As Trinh T. Min-ha notes,

> Planned authenticity is rife; as a product of hegemony and a remarkable counterpart of universal standardization, it constitutes an efficacious means of silencing the cry of racial oppression. We no longer wish to erase your difference. We demand, on the contrary, that you remember and assert it. At least, to a certain extent. Every path I/i take is edged with thorns. On the one hand i play into the Savior's hands by concentrating on authenticity, for my attention is numbed by it and diverted from other, important issues; on the other hand, i do feel the necessity to return to my so called roots . . . The difficulties appear perhaps less insurmountable only as I/i succeed in making a distinction between difference reduced to identity-authenticity and difference understood as critical difference to myself.[17]

By engaging in identity politics Asian Americans are able to voice ourselves before we are voiced and to creatively and critically argue for our specific location and articulation of our hybrid heterogeneous identity. Furthermore, because identity politics finds its strength and staying power from a receptivity to cultural differences,[18] it is crucial to not only claim our unique space but also to keep our critical minds open to possibilities of what it means to be in such a unique position. Korean Americans are in a unique position. Instead of seeing our standpoint as a dilemma to be overcome, it would be to our empowerment, if we learn ways to fully live an embodied self-identity. The ambiguity caused by this dualistic challenge can be resolved by claiming this very space which we find ourselves. Jung Young Lee envisions this hybrid identity as

> The holistic understanding of a marginal person . . a new marginal person is a person living in-beyond. The essence of being in-beyond is not a by product of being in-between and being in-both; rather, it embodies a state of being in both of them without either being blended . . . to live in both of them without being bound by either of them.[19]

This "Third Space" embraces a *both/and* way of thinking; however, it is also something different from both. It is a unique space. Our space of "in-betweenness" is a site, a space of radical possibility, a space of resistance. The dialectics of both/and have offered ways for rediscovering and reconstructing Asian American feminist subjectivity. Our marginality is the site, the space, in which radical freedom can be claimed. It is a site pregnant with myriads of possible radical transformations. It is within and through this space that we can live a life of resistance filled with life-giving promises and subversive hopes. This hybrid space brings together both dislocation and the radical challenge of reconceiving the American space and Asian American identity as we engage in politics of difference. Our marginality should become the site which we embrace because it is one which will nurture our visions and sustain us in our journey of resistance. As we claim our voices, as we tell our stories, we need to be keenly attuned to who is listening and what they are hearing, and what we are saying.[20] Likewise we must not speak only about our pain, our victimization, and powerlessness but dare to speak of resistance, radical hopes, and radical challenges for change.

Theological Reflections

In order to do this we need to make a distinction between that marginality which is imposed by the oppressive structures and that marginality one chooses as site of resistance -- as location of radical openness and possibility.[21] Jung Young Lee also stressed marginality as the space filled with possibility for radical transformations. He contents that "centers are created within margins; margins are also created inside of centers."[22] He further writes that

> In-between boundaries form a marginal condition. Marginality, therefore, is more than a boundary itself; it is many boundaries encompassing two or multiple worlds. In marginality, the two or multiple worlds are brought together and depart from each other or others. Neither world is independent, but exists in relation to the other and opposite . . . hence marginality is a condition that offers opportunity for creativity.[23]

It is necessary for our communities to actively hear one another and to recognize the richness of the complexity that makes us who we are as Asian Americans.[24] It is through the gifts of remembering, re-collecting and hearing each other that we begin to reconstitute and connect our fragmented selves into a sustainable identity. Asian American theology must constantly engage in decontructing and constructing alternative understandings of theology. Moreover Asian American theology must emerge out of our fears, struggles and the bitterness that have become lodged in our hearts.[25] While keeping a wary eye on the potential of postmodernism to at times be apolitical, the emerging Asian American "diaspora" theology must also hold hands with both postmodernist theology and postcolonial theology. Asian American theology must be able to articulate the many multilayered and often complex realities of our resistance and struggles in North American context.[26] It is necessary to embrace the multiple voices of our diverse communities not only within but also outside as well. This theology must be grounded in the margins, and must speak from the margins.[27] The memories of our sharply fragmented lives are ways through which resistance can be fueled. These collective shared memories of Asian Americans are what should become the life-giving hope enabling the construction of Asian American subjectivity. It is these memories which challenge and re-work pre-existing frames of identity for Asian Americans. Segovia is adamant that integral to such a theology of the diaspora is the "myth or narrative of origins: the re-collection, re-construction, and re-telling of the passage or transition from the one world to the other."[28] Therefore, even for Asian Americans the central theme is that of a journey. We must articulate and live our theology from out of our belonging to that hybrid, diverse, multi-layered salient space in which we move, live and have our being.

This hybrid space brings together both dislocation and the radical challenge of reconceiving American space, one and the same in a single imaginative act. Segovia articulates not only for Hispanic/ Latino communites but also for other communities existing in the margins when he writes

> . . . the everyday life emerges as deeply divided: overridingly hostile, but calling forth struggle and resistance; fate and inescapable, yet constantly arousing hopes of and strategies for change and reformation; ultimately resigned and yet endlessly defiant.[29]

The challenge for Asian Americans then is to garner wisdom and courage to travel between and through many boundaries, and multiple communities without exoticizing oneself and/or becoming paralyzed in the false push and pull of "loyalties." This hybridity is the creative space in which the Asian American subjectivity can be fully embodied unapologetically. It is the ground which gives way for the creating of a shared dwelling place: a home.

Chapter Seven

Identity Formation During Identity Crisis :
Reflection on the Significance of Religio-Existential Aspects of Identity Formation

Timothy D. Son

Introduction

Identity formation is ultimately concerned with discovering the religio-existential significance of one's existence. In the face of constant change, one seeks for a meaningful paradigm of unchanging continuity on which one longs to dwell and construct a sense of self-identity. On a psychological level identity formation is concerned with maintaining what Erikson called the "sense of self-sameness" or "self-continuity." The quest of discovering "who I am" and maintaining that sense of self-identity is certainly a lifelong process. No single incident or single experience could give a holistic definition of "*who am I.*" The sense of self-identity, rather, can emerge only through the processes of internalization and integration of conflicting aspects of human experiences throughout the life cycle. Discovering of self-identity, therefore, is an on-going process through which a person seeks to maintain a sense of "who one is" not only against unpredictable future uncertainties but also in the face of constant changes in the present.

Many psychological studies have been done on the subject of identity formation. Jean Piaget described it from the perspective of cognitive intellectual development. Piaget asserted that a child's sense of self-identity develops as he or she moves through various developmental stages from what he called the egocentric "preoperational stage" to the inter-relational "formal operational stage." In the former stage, Piaget said that a child has a narrow myoscopic vision of "who s/he is" only in terms of his or her immediate needs and impulses. Then a child begins to see the need to cooperate with others on an equal basis reciprocally and to learn that not "everything" evolves around for his or her "egocentric" interests. Piaget named this differentiating period the "concrete operational stage" through which the later and more mature level of developmental stage, called the "formal operational stage," is achieved. At this latter level, the child no longer understands others in relation to his or her egocentric impulses but seeks to assimilate the roles and images which others think as important.

Kohlberg also described the human development process in terms of moral development. Kohlberg saw that a person achieves a higher sense of self-identity as s/he engages in more integrated and sophisticated moral judgments. In Kohlberg's view, as a person attains higher levels of moral development, s/he tends to decentralize from "egocentric" and "immediate individual problem-solving perspectives" to more societal and even principle-oriented moral praxis. Analyzing hypothetical moral/ethical situations, Kohlberg incorporated philosophical aspects into his view of the process of human development and thus went beyond the Piagetian cognitive realm. Piaget and Kohlberg as well as Loevinger, Maslow, Erikson and many others seem to agree that in order for a person to develop a mature sense of self-identity, s/he needs to be liberated from a "pre-social, physiological, egocentric and biological survival" orientation. They all agree that a mature self more freely engages in"interpersonal, self-conscientious, and autonomous" actions in relationships with others in his or her psycho-social environment.[1]

To be sure, contributions that have been made by such studies are important, and no one should overlook the significant results of their studies. Nonetheless, these studies spend much time, in my opinion, in describing the psychological, moral, and behavioral characteristics of each stage without devoting sufficient attention to the transitional processes between each stages. Such questions as what does authentically happen during this transitional period as a person strives to discover autonomous sense of self-identity have not been discussed significantly. How does a person resolve his or her conflict in the face of constant changes and paradigm shifts? Is identity development predominantly a psychological phenomenon which needs to be evaluated empirically with a scientific mind? Can it be described in any other meaningful ways from philosophical and religious perspectives?

Considering these questions allow us look at the identity formation more as a dynamic process rather than a set of static psychosocial phenomena. A person constantly seeks to improve his/her relationship with an ostensibly ambivalent psychosocial environment. At the same time, s/he also longs for inner security and peace of mind by establishing some sort of inner principle to which s/he dearly adheres. If we look at identity development more as a dynamic process of "becoming," we may better understand the mysteries of identity formation in both psychological and religio-philosophical perspectives of human development. For to understand "who I am" demands an ontological explanation to a question "*what does it mean to be fully a human being?*" To be fully a human being, moreover, is to search for a more concrete sense of self-identity through ongoing processes of becoming. This is plausible since a person seems to spend more time during transition than at any one stage in the developmental process.

My intention in the following, therefore, is to discuss how a person develops a sense of self-identity even during transition. What authentically does happen during this transitional period? In order to discuss this question meaningfully, we need to distinguish psychological aspects from philosophical aspects of human development without polarizing the two. We need to perceive the relations between the psychological and the philosophical aspects as necessary elements in the process of human development which the creative human spirit seeks to integrate during identity formation. Since a person exists as a psychosocial and cultural being, we also need to discuss a relationship between identity formation and (cultural) tradition. For identity formation is by no means a private affair. In so doing, we also need to discuss some motivational factors of such psychological and philosophical functions of human mind to being and becoming fully oneself. In conclusion, I will suggest several educational implications for enhancing a healthy identity formation process.

1. A Present Difficulty: Modern Understandings of Religion and Human Beings

Why is it difficult for us to have an integrated view of human development with explanations from both psychology and religio-philosophy? It may be because of the fact that today's modern and post-modern mentality is a product from the 19th century Enlightenment philosophy. The claims of objective science have no difficulty of being accepted as credible criteria and thus are received blindly as the only reasonable and valid ways of knowing truth. Such a secularized consciousness tends to push aside any possibilities for meaningful discussion on the religion and religiosity of human persons.

As Peter Berger has stated, most modern people think about the reality of life and its significance in terms of scientism, which restricts the scopes of their investigation. Within a scientistic frame of mind, there is hardly any room for religion or any religious quest for the supernatural.[2] Out of such a framework of consciousness, people give emphatic affirmation that the ultimate worthwhileness of human life dwells in the natural world alone. Berger calls this tendency "secularity."[3] Secularity opposes any notion of religious supernaturalism or an intrinsic religious dimension in the process of searching for one's self-identity.

Religious circles have, on the one hand, reacted vigorously against notions of scientism, but on the other hand slowly begun to assimilate into the cultural ethos of secularity by anchoring the ultimate significance of human life to the domain of the natural world. The fundamental difficulty lies in a polemical situation in which religious persons cannot fully accept supernaturalism because it is not only contrary to the secular understanding of reality, but also is insensitive to the secular valuation of human life. Yet they cannot reject it either, for they cannot abandon the authority of their religious tradition, which has provided mystical (and yet concrete) spiritual experience and meanings at times of existential void. Caught between secularism and mysterious supernaturalism, religious minds have not been able to evade pervasive influences of their culture, and they have finally become secularized. The triumph of the modern secular spirit over the old religious vision and tradition is clearly seen in the following remarks by Langdon Gilkey:

> "The task for twentieth-century Catholicism calls for the reinterpretation of the transcendent, the sacred, and the divine -- the presence of God to men -- into the worldly or naturalistic forms of modern experience rather than in the supernaturalistic forms of Hellenic and medieval experience."[4]

It is no surprise, then, to see that with such secularized criteria, empirical psychology has become the normative way of explaining the wonders of human development. The prevailing tendency is that human beings are understood primarily as "bio-psychological" beings (Skinner, Piaget, Freud) environmentally determined according to their psycho-social and cultural surroundings. Consequently, the religious and existential dimension of human development has largely been ignored, and when not ignored, then understood either with scientific reductionism in an effort to make it more comprehensible, or with the incomprehensible explanation of speculative philosophies. Why not explain human development process with religio-philosophical views? This has simply not been possible, since such explanation would not be empirical enough. Consequently, empirical scientific studies have focused mainly on manifested psychological phenomena and psycho-relational behaviors concerning a particular situation of human development. The psychological data are then analyzed with empirical language of "cause and effect." There is hardly any mention, however, of how the creative human spirit accommodates the threats of existential void and meaninglessness between the stages during the transitional process.

The psychological description of developmental stages is no doubt a very useful and tangible tools for understanding the paths of human development and identity formation throughout the life cycle. Yet its success is not without cost. While it clarifies many dubious wonders of human behavior, its explanations remain significantly within static stage descriptions. It describes well the state of being someone in a given psychosocial environment, but it does not say much about the process of becoming -- for example, from an egocentric person to a more integrated person. This dynamic aspect of human development is, in my opinion, perhaps equally important in our effort to understand the process of human development and identity formation. In spite of prevailing modern secularism, we must consider our own religiosity and religious experiences in order to gain a deeper level of understanding of the holistic process of human development. Without a proper understanding of our religious and existential dimension, we may not do justice to our effort to understand human beings who are not only socioculturally and environmentally related but also religiously bound in spirit to transcend their locality and finitude. After all, each of us is not only a biological being with corporeal body but also a spiritual being with a creative mind and spirit to go beyond the horizon of creaturely finitude. The essential question is whether or not we can appropriate meaningfully such a polemical relationship between natural (scientific) and supernatural (religio-philosophical and existential) in the process of identity formation.

2. Dual Aspects of Identity Formation

Identity formation as an on-going process inherently contains dual aspects -- the external which corresponds to the demands from one's psychosocial environment and the internal which seeks for meanings and purpose at times of existential crisis. The former "external" aspect helps us consider the importance of psychosocial context in the process of identity formation. For example, a person who is undergoing cultural transition constantly seeks to assimilate the various demands and forces created by the new external culture, so s/he tries to imitate certain cultural behaviors, particular gestures, different fashion styles and communicative skills. Yet s/he soon experiences a limitation or "gap" between his or her "idealized" self-images and his or her own actual level of performance to attain those idealized images. Psychological evaluation usually focuses on behavioral and relational pathologies of a subject within the framework of the function of ego, i.e., in its maneuvered defensive mechanism. At a deeper level, however, a person's struggle is more philosophical and religio-existential than psychological. In the face of an existential void, s/he may ask "what does all this mean to me?" or "is it really necessary for me to emulate others, and if not, what can I do?" and so forth. Unless a person names invisible causes of his/her own frustrated situation as well as gives meanings to that existential void with a sense of purpose, s/he is not likely to succeed in resolving conflicts by discovering inner principles or conviction. The inner principles or conviction not only are independent from the external demands but also give freedom from mere "anxiety" (angst) and frustration.

Robert Kegan in his *The Evolving Self* also recognizes this dual aspects of identity formation. He defines identity formation as a continuous evolving process of the "meaning seeking" person who is constantly resonating back and forth between what he calls "identification and integration." Kegan contends that a sense of self-identity evolves from within a person as s/he differentiates other objects and persons from him or her (i.e., identification process) as s/he seeks to incorporate "identified" differences into a meaningful coherent schema of interpretation (i.e., integration process).[5] Throughout the book, Kegan makes an implicit distinction between psychosocial reality and religio-existential aspects of identity formation.

In the face of constantly changing reality, a person experiences marginal situations where the sense of his/her being "who s/he is" is potentially threatened. The external demands imposed upon oneself by one's socio-cultural environment influence significantly the manner of one's socio-relational behavior. Yet every assimilative behavioral decision that is made by a person is concerned ultimately with philosophical interpretation rather than psychological self-evaluation. This duality between "external" and "internal" is then an inevitable and inseparable aspect of human identity formation. For the process of identity formation deals with not only how one can best fit into the patterns of socialization structure prescribed for its members, but also whether such conformity is desirable in light of inner moral/ ethical and philosophical convictions. In short, what can be argued is that there is something more than "functional" psychological aspects of identity formation processes.

What is the "other" aspect that we need to consider? We need to discover what Erik H. Erikson called "the sense of self-sameness or (inner) continuity" in the face of many different local environments and psychosocial liminality.[6] We need to discover something coherent throughout the ups and downs of our lives. For the roles we play (in which we have a sense of "being") change constantly depending upon the demands of the psychosocial environment at different times. Yet we discover that the sense of self-sameness or (inner) continuity of persons stubbornly protests against the external demands of culture, society, and even cultural ideology. Such an inner sense of self-identity is rooted deeply in the soil of our existence beyond the level of psychosocial environment, perhaps into the level of religious existence searching for the ultimate significance of our existence. Although Erikson does not make this religious notion explicit, nonetheless, the implications are evident when he wrote that:

> "Of all the ideological systems, however, only religion restores the earliest sense of appeal to an Ultimate Provider, a (religious) Providence."[7]

What becomes clear in the process of discovering one's identity is that unless one is aware of the religio-existential identity, the holistic sense of "self-sameness or continuity" may only be partially understood. And that religious dimension of one's identity is perhaps best seen during the transitional process of becoming when one encounters the threats of an existential void. It is during this transitional process that the meaning constitutive process (which integrates both religio-philosophical and psychological aspects) of identity formation can be better seen as including necessary dual aspects of human developmental processes. As psychological studies can demonstrate the changes of personality in relation to the external environment, so can philosophy reveal the existential aspects of the creative work of human spirit during this process of transitional becoming.

3. The Process of "Becoming" in Identity Formation

Identity formation, in general, emerges more as an inner philosophical principle or conviction rather than as a psychological effect in relation to an environmental cause. In the initial stage, the sense of self-identity is constructed passively when the images of self are being mostly attributed by significant others through associating certain images with names which may correlate a child's visible personality traits or behavior to that of particular characteristics of animals. Because a child during his/her early stage of identity formation longs for affirmation to satisfy the feeling of being accepted by significant others, s/he tries to conform to certain prescribed roles. During this early stage, the formation of one's self-identity is largely dependent upon the "otherly" sources in the external psycho-environment.

As soon as a child grows further and enters the adolescent period, s/he begins to test the authority of his/her former psychosocial traditions. It is during this period that a young adolescent begins to question the validity of what was previously given or attributed. Often during this time, it is common for young teens to disagree, disobey, and rebel against rigid institutional structures or the status quo. Young teens experience much frustration because what used to be appropriate seems no longer to hold its validity in the face of contradictory multiple variants. Consequently, anxiety and inner instability set in as older children and youth confront the need to reevaluate their formal traditional views and values in the light of newly emerging contingencies. Erikson argues that these "inner anxieties" and "conflicts" contribute significantly to the manners in which an individual becomes more of a distinct personality.[8]

This time of adolescent confusion is the transitional process of becoming a more mature and autonomous individual; it is also a time of "crisis." Erikson describes this transitional period as "a turning point, a crucial period of increased vulnerability and heightened potential, and therefore, the ontogenetic source of generational strength and maladjustment."[9] The adolescent mind in this process of "becoming" is, according to Erikson, a mind of the moratorium, a psychosocial stage between childhood and adulthood, and between the morality learned by the child and the ethical responsibilities to be developed by the adult.[10]

Existentially speaking, this is the crucial time between the processes of "from being to becoming a new being" must be confronted by youth. It is out of this transitional process of becoming, the autonomous and independent sense of self-sameness and (inner) continuity can develop. Such sense of self-identity arms a person with a well-balanced character of trustworthiness and consistency against all possible conflicting variants and threats of external psychosocial forces.

At this point, it may be helpful to lay out what we have discussed about the processes of identity formation. It can be generally described as following:

Identity Formation Processes

BEING →	*BECOMING* →	*NEW BEING*
*What is given; attributed roles, names, and social functions;	*Attesting the former values and norms;	*Internalized & owned sense of self-identity;

Attributed Identity	Searching Identity	Owned Identity
*Temporal and contingent;	*(Re)evaluation of the "given" images about the self;	*Consistent and continuous;
*Dependent and passive to the external condition	*Ambiguous mixture of activity and passivity;	*Independent and active;
	*Identity transition	*Inner principle and freedom from external constraints

The success or failure in discovering the "owned" sense of self-identity largely depends upon how a person integrates and internalizes numerous conflicting variables into a meaningful coherence during the transitional process of becoming. Much of its enduring willpower during this transitional process is determined by his/her former psycho-relational legacy -- how a person was treated by his/her significant others during childhood. The potential of a positive and trusting attitude toward one's environment stem from an early sense of "trust" and the feeling of "being loved." Without such somatic conviction -- the sense of trust of oneself and others during the transitional "becoming" -- a youth is less likely to resolve the transitional process of identity crisis successfully and positively. Without the sense of self-autonomous "will" with purpose and confidence, a youth would feel helpless in seeking to fill in his/her existential void with mere role-plays and assimilation sporadically without concrete purposes. The consistent experiences of being loved and cared for during the early childhood, however, engender a strong sense of "hope" and "will" to be self-confronting and autonomous against the various uncertain situations. A fidelity to a deep inner "I-ness" can remain constant and continuous despite the external forces that the social matrix imposes upon a person to assimilate. The irrevocable sense of self-sameness and continuity, therefore, settles into the deepest part of a person, perhaps within one's religio-existential dimension.

4. The Meaning-Seeking and Creating Process during Transition and the Role of Tradition in the Identity Formation Process

The transitional process of "becoming" in identity formation illumines a potential possibility for a more holistic existence in the pathway of human development. In the face of an existential void, a person searches for meaningful solutions no longer in terms of an "I-and-the world" relationship but moves into the possibility of the void, or "becoming nothing." In the void, the authoritative claims of empirical psychology reaches their boundary as a person's internal existential struggle becomes metapsychological and philosophical -- the question is now no longer how to assimilate but why and for what purpose one needs to modify one's belief. For a person must seek the ontological significance of his or her existence beyond the realm of empirical science. As James Loder recognized in his *Transforming Moment*, when a person is thrown into the void, s/he has a higher possibility for religious experience encountering what he called "the presence of the Holy"(or God).[11] In the presence of an imminent void, an imaginative vision and a new understanding about oneself emerge as inner convictional principles.

The searching for ontological significance with a heightened potential for a religious encounter does not emerge *ex nihilo*. For the emerging sense of self-identity intrinsically constitutes a person's past psychosomatic experiences with significant others and the external world. Thus in understanding the meaning-seeking and creating process as a constitutive part of identity formation, we must consider what kinds of psychological influences one's psychosocial legacy can exert upon the existential attitude of the meaning-seeking person during the transitional period. As Erikson and other attachment theorists recognize, the psychosomatic experiences during early childhood leave significant effects on a person's latter personality development. The existential struggle for developing a sense of inner security during the transitional process is not only a continuation but also reminiscent of person's primordial struggle for maintaining psychosomatic security in the absence of his/her caregiver. According to Erikson, out of a person's early experience between "trust vs. mistrust" and "autonomy vs. shame and doubt," the sense of self-identity is constructed (either positively or negatively) as a distinctive personality during the latter period of the life cycle. Even in ways of imagining God, a person's psycho-relational legacy of the child-parent relationship is a key factor.[12]

What becomes more apparent in our discussion is a need to recognize the indispensable relationship between psychosocial (including early psychosomatic) experience of the past and religio-philosophical aspects of the transitional present in the process of identity formation. For a person's psychosocial and relational legacy prepares metapsychological and philosophical ground for existential struggles during the transitional process of identity crisis. While a concrete sense of "self-sameness" and "inner continuity" emerges more as an inner religious and philosophical conviction, nevertheless, the patterns of the former relational experience in relation to psychosocial environment provide the foundational metapsychological context for this religio-existential struggle in various crisis situations. The early psychosomatic experiences of affirmation provide courage and will to endure during meaningless situations with the persistent sense of hope in the process of meaning creation.

During the transitional process of identity searching, a meaning-seeking person struggles to establish a "worthwhile" sense of self-continuity by incorporating former experiences into his/her present conflicting situation in a personally relevant way. At the same time, a person also seeks to interpret his/her early psychosomatic conviction synthetically in light of new meanings in order to form meaningful coherence and an inner religio-philosophical self-conviction. This synthetic process of "meaning creation and interpretation" is essentially a symbolization process. A struggling person in his/her ontological and existential void enters into a mysterious symbolic relationship with particular objects, individuals (whether historical or fictional figures), or unusual events. In this process, a person recalls the symbolic significance of his/her own symbols which reveal meanings in a transitional situation.

In Judeo-Christian tradition, for example, the ritual practice of "breaking bread and drinking wine" has become the symbolic event for commemorating the continual presence of Jesus Christ. When the disciples and the early Christians participated in this particular ritual (holy communion ceremony), they sought to recreate the divine presence of Jesus. In reproducing symbolic acts of "breaking" and "drinking," the disciples were able to recall the concreteness and significance of their Lord's claims in the midst of an existential void brought about by the absence of their Master's bodily presence. By entering into a symbolic relation with the sacred reality to which symbolic ritual as well as their symbolic objects point, the disciples were able to rededicate their full commitment for the cause of their inner religio-philosophical conviction. For some other Christians, the Cross as a symbolic object also bears conventional significance through which they can discover and interpret the various present situations since the Cross as a symbol reveals new meanings during the times of an existential void.

A meaning-seeking person as ontological/existential acting subject likewise relates to particular memories or experiences of events (or persons, or objects) in an effort to search for symbolic significance in order to resolve his/her conflicts by discovering the logic of meaningful coherence as inner conviction in the face of multiple conflicting variants. Such meaning-seeking and creating activity is universal for all thinking persons since the "symbolic" (objects, persons, or ritual practices and events) contains the common denominator of all the ways of giving meaning to (conflicting) reality.[13] In attempting to understand the phenomena of change, people have sought to resolve their existential conflict -- such as the absence of Jesus Christ -- by performing certain acts of a specifically imitative character in the present so that the symbolic meanings of the past could either be recreated or their efficacy made available for present use.[14]

In this meaning-seeking and creating process, psychology is concerned with ultimate reality as it longs for the ultimate source for what Schleiermacher called "absolute dependency." Whatever is discovered and internalized as an "absolute" inner conviction then becomes the symbolic source for a person's aspiration and hope in the continuous process of ontological/existential becoming. This process consequently alludes to the significance of metapsychological and philosophical aspects of human existence in the process of identity formation. For a person seeks the ultimate meaning of his/her present struggle against the threats of an existential void by discovering an irrevocable sense of self-sameness and inner continuity through entering into a symbolic relationship with particular cultural, religious, and psychosomatic symbols.

In this transitional process, a person not only draws the sources of symbols from tradition (either psychosocial or cultural and religious) but also attests to the authoritative claims of tradition and its validity in the emerging existential crisis situation. Instead of simply accepting the sedimented symbols of tradition, s/he now seeks to re-interpret the symbolic significance and its credibility for the sake of continuing his/her meaningful existence in the on-going process of identity formation.

It may be helpful now to consider a concrete transitional situation of identity formation. I have encountered many Korean American youths who are in the process of an identity crisis situation. Many of them try to find some coherent self-images which may ensure the sense of self-sameness or inner continuity during their struggle. In the process of cultural transition, they are frustrated not knowing how to assimilate into a new cultural paradigm without totally giving up their former cultural tradition. In a radical cultural transitional process from a former authoritarian culture to a new achievement-oriented society, many of them experience great anxiety because they find that what used to be normative and proper is no longer valid in a new cultural context. Passive silence and obedience are no longer perceived as desirable, but regarded instead as disadvantageous or inferior to a necessary image of self as confident and assertive. The needs for self-expression and assertiveness are essential in a new socio-cultural context, but the Korean Americans do not have clear guidelines to acquire these qualities. Without proper theoretical guidelines, many young Korean Americans struggle to integrate many conflicting variables in their lives. Young Pai, a professor of the University of Kansas, has observed these phenomena quite vividly in the following chart.[15]

Different Cultural Values for Self-Identity: A Comparison between Korean and American Cultural Tradition

Korean Culture (Collectivism)	*American Culture (Individualism)*
*Human as a part of nature -- (Implicit passivity in relation to nature)	*Human as a supervisor of nature -- (Active explorer of nature)
*Ingroup regulation of behavior	*Individual regulation of behavior
*Interdependence	*Self-sufficiency

*Subordination of personal goals to goals of ingroup	*Ingroup and personal goals are unrelated
*Ingroup harmony is important	*Self-expression is encouraged, even if confrontational
*Sense of common fate with ingroup	*Personal fate (less dependent on ingroup)
*Ingroup is center of psychological field	*Person is center of psychological field
*Ingroup is extension of the self	*Self is distinct from ingroup
*Shame control	*Guilt control
*Obedience and silence as virtue	*Self-assertiveness and expression
*Authoritarian/hierarchical relation	*Horizontal/egalitarian relation

In the process of searching for one's own identity, many young Korean Americans experience great difficulty because their former tradition is diametrically opposed to the new cultural values and paradigm. This process of transition often becomes too overwhelming to internalize the conflicting cultural values and external forces in the process of cultural assimilation. This is inevitable among the Korean American youth who experience a radical sociocultural, relational, and ideological ground shift between their ancestral tradition and the new American culture.

The crucial area of transition which often hinders healthy identity formation in Korean Americans is their formal tendency to construct their identity in relation to their in-groups or tribal affiliation instead of their individual achievement and performance. This poses a serious problem for Korean Americans, because they often feel that they must give up everything that they are, which they believe involves total sacrifice and radical change of their whole life style and paradigm, without much time for reflection and internalization. This is by no means an easy task, nor is it a task which can be resolved in a relatively short period of time.

In general, the more faithfully a person adheres to his/her former socio-cultural tradition, the more difficulties s/he will experience in the transitional process of re-discovering the significance of his/her former tradition as well as accepting its authority. Many important aspects of cultural values, principles, and beliefs are already engraved in tradition and have become already a constitutive part of who a person is. In this socio-cultural context, a person is more a part of tradition than the tradition is a constituent part of individual identity. "What s/he is," in fact, is influenced by tradition. Even in the traditioning process of re-interpreting the validity of one's own tradition, a person is a part of tradition. The continual influence of tradition is kept alive either by retaining what is meaningful to a person or by discarding what is considered irrelevant or contradictory. The continual efficacy of tradition still continues even when a person replaces the discarded elements with the novel features and symbolic meanings derived from other sources. Although ideas and symbols of the past may lose their appeal in a certain period or situation, this should not be final, for such traditions may regain their validity and significance at another time in a different contingent historicity.

As a meaning-seeking person seeks to re-interpret the significance of traditional claims, s/he must remember that tradition is not something that stands against him/her but is always a "part of his/her interpretative process."[16] In many cases, tradition not only stands as the content and the subject matter which need to be inquired about, but also is the ideology itself by which the ways of interpretative modes of a person are influenced. From this perspective, a meaning-seeking and creating person belongs to a particular socio-cultural and philosophical tradition with a certain set of prejudices. Tradition has a determinant power upon a meaning-seeking person in the process of becoming.[17]

In the case of persons who struggle to assimilate into the norms of a new tradition, one of their important tasks is to bring themselves as well as others to an explicit awareness of this historical affinity of "belongingness." For such awareness may prevent us from blindly accepting the values and claims of tradition as "absolute," i.e., normative to be maintained at all costs.

Tradition is, however, not only an accumulation or historical deposit of the past but also reconstruction of the meanings of the past into the present situation for the meaningful existence of all its members. In this light, the authoritative claims of tradition can be modified in a new context and differentiated in the light of an emerging contingent historicity. A person may decide to reject some of the previous cultural paradigms or to maintain or even to enhance some other aspects of tradition. Whatever decision is made, a person's desire for change and modification is still somewhat within the formative power of tradition. In this sense, as Rosenak contends, tradition contains both the past and the present and is, therefore, capable of shedding ontological light on new situations and, at the same time, absorbing their perceived individual meanings into a collective term. Rosenak seems to believe that in the meaning-seeking and creating process, tradition does not always function either as legitimation of, or as impediment of change in a polemical separation, but the new meanings emerge as a result of synthesis in a dialectical relationship within the old (tradition) "through its metamorphosis or reshaping."[18] This intrinsic relationship between a person who is constantly seeking for new possibilities of "becoming" and tradition in which a person belongs is inseparable, for tradition functions as the modality for this process of *becoming*. Understanding one's self-identity is, therefore, not a private individual affair apart from tradition. Nor can it be a fragmentary understanding of the present in isolation from the past. In order to maintain a meaningful existence with others, a person not only needs affirmation from his/her own socio-cultural tradition, but also needs to find socio-cultural continuity from the past.

Tradition, whether old or new, provides ontological ground for the meaning-seeking and creating human person to discover the legitimacy of seeking the acceptable criterion for symbolic interpretation (as well as relevant psycho-social data) within its cultural boundary. Yet, identity formation is not only a discovery of the patterns of one's psychosocial phenomena in relation to others, but is also a quest for the religio-philosophical meanings of one's existence in the ever-changing world. In the transitional process of becoming, a person seeks to maintain a sense of self-sameness and inner continuity by maintaining the symbolic core meaning of the former tradition as a part of his/her inner personal principle. From this perspective, the validity of tradition and its authority undergo also a dynamic process of becoming to be reinterpreted and reappropriated in every new contingency. This traditioning process often becomes an inherent part of the identity formation process of a person who experiences transition as an indispensable aspect of human development.

Conclusion

We discussed above an increasingly apparent problem in recent psychological investigation of the human development process. The problem, as it has been recognized, is a modern tendency to overlook the importance of religio-philosophical aspects of the process of identity development. Under the prevailing influence of modern secularism, we have tried too hard to explain the mysteries of the creative works of human mind primarily in terms of empirical psychology as effect-responses to unresolved infantile desires. Consequently, a polemical tension between psychological interpretation and religio-philosophical interpretation is difficult to avoid.

A modern person today would not be satisfied if the explanations of many wonders of human mysteries in the process of identity formation are given in unscientific ways with dogmatic assertion of religio-philosophical interpretation. At the same time, the mysteries of the creative works of human mind seem to demand philosophical, phenomenological and even religious explanations concerning the purpose, value, and meaning of a person's existence in the process of becoming "who s/he is." For the unchanging sense of self-sameness and inner continuity cannot be attained only by means of psychological assimilation to the patterns of socialization. In the inevitable face of an existential crisis, a human person makes a mysterious shift through a symbolization process into a metapsychological and philosophical dimension of existence.

A modern problem which is polemical in nature, however, still persists between to those who insist psychological interpretation is the absolute means of understanding developmental phenomena, and those who refuse to give full authority to psychology and thus recognize a need for different explanations about developmental phenomena other than empirical psychology. While psychology understands the meaning-creating process primarily as the distortion of elementary meaning connected with infantile wishes and desires, philosophy (especially phenomenology) understands the symbols -- myths, rituals, and beliefs -- more than as fables merely created out of the regressed infantile desires, but it sees them as a particular way in which a human person places oneself in relation to fundamental reality, whatever it may be.[19]

Such tension is already inherent in the post-Enlightenment modern society as our initial discussion of Peter Berger's recognition of the separation between "natural" and "supernatural" has suggested. What is deeply embedded in our mentality is a belief that "to be modern is decidedly not be medieval and religious; to be reasonable is not to be dogmatic; and to be free is clearly not to live under ecclesiastical authority." Such blind rejection of tradition as unscientific and oppressive cultural superego hinders people to appreciate fully the values of tradition, including its formative power to give new birth to meanings and cultural reformation. Today, the norms of tradition are felt to be oppressive and binding, demeaning of individual rights, dignity, and liberty. The normative religious tradition, especially, is not only seen as enemy of individual rights, but also as an invasion of personal privacy, violation of moral conscience, and reeking of old-fashioned dogmatism and bigotry.

The change and seeking for a new identity is understood by many people in a radical annihilation of the "old" tradition in the name of "new" and "progressive" humanization. The problems as they are identified suggest to us invaluable educational implications not only for bringing the "old" tradition and the "new" change together in the process of traditioning, but also for rediscovering the importance of religio-existential elements of tradition in the process of human development. I propose the following humble suggestions in order to help those who are in a process of transition to discover a sense of self-identity:

(1) A person needs to have a sense of historical rootage and conscience. We need to understand our past, that is our tradition, in order to have a vision for tomorrow. We need to teach our traditional values and beliefs to others not only by means of transmission but also by demonstrating in our actual moral/ethical lifestyle what we truly believe. For what we do educationally and how we live according to the convectional vision is reflected both in our words and deeds as well as in our lifestyles. Teaching tradition and the sense of historical rootedness means to translate with integrity the "principles" into concrete praxis and a set of clear particular norms. These norms can become symbolic sources for others in the process of symbolization when they experience transitional crisis.

(2) The task for religious educators is to encourage both the development of distinctive self-identity and the search for commonness

with others. Not only must we encourage our children to discover and appreciate their own individual and cultural particularity so that they come to feel at home with themselves as well as their ideals, but also we ought to guide them to enter into communion with others, freely giving and receiving of each other in mutual *koinonia*. We need to look seriously at establishing links between us by seeking similar values and commonality without sacrificing our own values and the distinctive sense of "who we are." In this process of seeking, we become involved in a constant process of soul-searching discernment that requires serious questioning, critical reflection, and constructive accommodation. This is, in its essence, the process of traditioning through interpretation and reinterpretation of our tradition.

(3) Based on our commonality, we also need to revive a concrete sense of community which shares common purpose and interest. In such a community, individuals are made accountable for one another at times of struggle when they seek genuine support and acceptance. The struggling individuals would find psychological and existential security within a caring community in their quest for new meanings, purposes, and a sense of self-identity. The process of discovering self-identity inevitably involves our longing for acceptance and inclusion on a psychological level. Therefore, we need to create a trusting and loving environment where a struggling person can feel at home and fully supported without being threatened. Such a faith community truly can function as a "mentoring culture"[20] which not only provides a qualitative faith experience that shapes personal character, but also leads a meaning-seeking person to self-surrender of ego in the face of void to the potential encounter with the Holy in the deepest level of human existence.

I am not arguing that the above suggestions hold the key for developing an ideal and secure sense of self-sameness and continuity for which we all strive. The quest of holistic self-identity should continue generation after generation. In a constantly changing world, the quest for the unchangeable in our being is an inevitable expression of our humanness and our deep anxiety of losing a meaningful sense of identity; it is also confession of our longing to be a part of the Eternal in and by which we may maintain the convictional inner continuity through all times. Yet we can face the persistent threats of meaninglessness and void of the unknown future with courage and hope when we accept our historical past as irrevocable evidence of the continuation of our "individual" and "collective" identity. Against the changing moments of continual process of becoming, searching for our own convictional inner-identity means, as Paul Tillich correctly observed, to have this courage not only accept to but also to affirm the finitude of ourselves in relation to the Ultimate reality which concerns us ultimately.

Chapter Eight

Quest for Self:
Stages in Identity Formation for Korean American Women

Inn Sook Lee

Introduction

"Reserved," "submissive," and "passive" are the western stereotyped images of Korean American women. Yet, a high percentage of these women are strongly motivated, highly educated Christians. Korean women were raised in a Confucian patriarchal culture, but as immigrants they have moved into a radically different cultural context. The personal conflicts involved in this experience have launched them on a lengthy journey toward a new definition of themselves. When women are torn away from their native culture[1] and suddenly placed in the western cultural milieu, they experience an acute conflict about themselves, caught between the two cultural ideologies. Confucian culture demands conformity and obedience to societal norms, while the western cultural ideology promotes individualism and personal success. The Korean women's encounter with the American women's feminist consciousness is a special source of identity disturbance. The women feel pressure to preserve their cultural heritage, and at the same time, to assimilate themselves to the western sociocultural value system for survival.

Having been raised in the Confucian cultural sphere, most of the first-generation Korean women were not allowed to develop themselves as what western feminists would regard as authentic selves with a true sense of self-worth. Now in a new environment, they are encouraged to search for self-realization and self-fulfillment. The old self-image and self-identity do not fit in the contemporary American society. The women feel that they must strive to gain proper respect in American society by cultivating new cultural and personal identities to reach the realm which is described by Rollo May as the "creative consciousness of self"[2] in which one can make one's own decisions and take the responsibility for one's own happiness. In order to discern the process in which Korean women form their clear self-identity after cultural transition, a research plan was designed and the collected data were analyzed. In this short report, the detailed theoretical explanations and the verbatim story sharing are not included.

A woman's identity is her concept of self as an individual, and this concept is strongly influenced by the image that other people have of her. Identity formation usually takes place during adolescence. During that period most young people discover a personal anchor point in an inner self-identity. Erik Erikson calls adolescence a "psychosocial moratorium."[3] When an adolescent discovers that niche, he or she will also find a sense of inner continuity and social identity that reconciles his or her concept of self with the concept held by the community. A person's sense of inner self and centrality points toward a feeling of wholeness. Wholeness, in turn, suggests the assembling of differing functional ideas of the self with a fruitful organization of diversified parts.[4]

When different ideological structures collide, they can create a sense of spatial centrifugal dispersion. This may result in a conflict between divergent self-images, a loss of personal centrality, a sense of confusion, and/or a fear of dissolution.[5] Such an unhappy state of mind can indicate a primary symptomatic upset. This upset may affect not only the development of one's personal self-identity, but one's cultural identity as well. Overseas migration or local intercultural conflict can cause such a dispersion or diffusion of identity.[6]

Sustaining a clear self-identity is critical because it is the basis of one's perception and judgment concerning all matters relating to that self.[7] Establishing a strong self-identity is particularly crucial for Korean American women who have experienced cultural and ideological transition and must survive as members of a double minority, as women and Asian. This study will discuss the following topics: Korean culture and women, Korean women in America, and Korean American women's search for identity.

1. Korean Culture and Women

The patriarchal cultural system has been the controlling power pattern in most societies throughout history and the Korean cultural system is no exception.

The Impact of Confucian Culture

The patriarchal cultural canons of Asian communities have largely confined women to their homes, organizing women's lives to serve others, especially males, at home. Korean women were required to obey their fathers before marriage, their husbands after marriage, and their sons in old age. In traditional dynasties, the women learn early in life to be quiet, submissive, and obedient under all circumstances. Many women, even in contemporary settings, learn these restrictions rooted in a Korean type of Confucian philosophy. Derived from classical Chinese sociopolitical thought, Confucianism was an ethical and moral system designed to govern all social relations in the family, community, and nation. It particularly stressed a rigid vertical order of human relationships based on age, gender, and inherited social status.

Some of the major Confucian dictums that pressured women during the Yi Dynasty (1392-1910)[8] were: women should be trained to serve others in the household; parents should arrange their daughter's marriage; a wife belonged to her husband's family after marriage; visits to her parents were almost nil; a woman usually was known by her husband's or son's name; women could not carry on a family line; and daughters could not legally inherit property from their parents.[9] If a wife did not bear a son, her husband was free to marry a second wife in hopes of having a male offspring to carry on the family line. A widow was not permitted to remarry, and even after her husband's death she had to continue serving her husband's parents for the remainder of her life. Society applauded women who adhered to and promoted these oppressive rules and dubbed them as "virtuous women."[10] The degree of adherence to these hard Confucian dictates varied considerably across class lines. Women in the lower classes and female slaves did not have to fully conform to all the rules. They were even free to go outside their homes to run errands.[11] Even in contemporary setting, the Confucian cultural expectations that exist at the base of the culture generate low self-esteem in Korean women and cause them intense inner conflict and negative effects on their psychological well-being.

Christianity, the Korean Cultural System, and Women

Contact with western ideas brought a great change in the traditional Korean cultural system. In the seventeenth and eighteenth centuries, many Korean scholars studying in Peking were drawn to Catholic Christianity. When they returned home they introduced its humanist concepts to their relatives and friends. The teaching of these scholars became known as Silhak or practical learning.[12] The Catholic ideas of human equality helped weaken the rigid Korean class system and the gender barrier. Scholars and Christian believers both worked for the improvement of women's status and organized activities for them in the churches. In the latter 1700s, Kang Won-suk organized the Catholic Women Believers Association, perhaps the first women's organization in the country.[13] Protestantism was first introduced to Korea in 1884 and played a major role in advancing women's status. Early female missionaries from the United States started many educational programs for women. In 1886, Mary Fitch Scranton of the Women's Foreign Missionary Society of the Methodist Episcopal Church founded Ewha Haktang [predecessor of Ewha Woman's University] in Seoul, the first modern school for girls in Korea. In 1899 the government even included a fund for girls schools in the national budget.[14]

The Japanese occupation of Korea, from 1909 to 1945, brought a major setback for Korean women's education. During that unhappy period, many patriotic organizations were formed, and women were active in them. But the roots of most of these groups were more political than educational. After the Korean independence from Japan in 1945, and the rapid spread of Christianity throughout the country, the idea of gender equality was more frequently advocated. The number of co-educational schools grew, and by 1955, 66% of the boys and 58% of the girls in primary school were studying in co-educational institutions.[15]

In the church, women participated in revival meetings, Bible study groups, evangelism, Christian women's associations, and church choirs. Protestant churches made a special effort to change the traditional Korean gender morality. They worked strenuously to promote monogamy and the general advancement of women's status. The church preached the idea of equality between husbands and wives, and the principle gradually took root in Korean society. Such changes were among the most important aspects of the cultural transformation of modern Korea, but the results of her efforts have been slow.

The Christian churches have grown rapidly in Korea, and in the 1980s, over 70 percent of their members were women. Nevertheless many important decision making positions in the church's organizations were seldom open to women. Some say that the mandate for women's equality in the church has been delayed for political reasons. For example, young pastors, because of ageism existing in the context, feel that they already have more problems than they can handle, working with the older men in their governing bodies. Because of this reality, they oppose the introduction of older women into the ruling structure since it may create an extra load for their leadership efforts. In any case, ageism, sexism, and other Confucian cultural influences are still very strong in Korean Christian life.

2. Korean Women in America

Immigration and Women

According to a 1987 study, nearly one million Koreans will reside in the United States by the year 2000.[16] Perhaps many women have immigrated because of the greater incentive to find freedom and career opportunities in a free country. The first group of Korean women to immigrate to this country arrived at the turn of the century to be the brides of Korean laborers who had earlier been recruited to work on Hawaiian sugar plantations. About seven hundred of these so-called "picture brides" arrived between 1903 and 1905, and approximately one thousand more followed by 1924.[17] Women heard exaggerated tales of wealth in America and came willingly. For all, coming to America meant risking marriage to a stranger in a foreign land. Yet for many, it was also an opportunity to escape from the economic hardships and social limitations commonly suffered by women in traditional Korea.

The second wave of Korean women immigrants to the United States were the wives of American military men stationed in Korea during and after the Korean War. Between 1951 and 1964, 6,423 Korean wives of GIs entered the United States, with approximately 1,500 more following each year during the 1960s, and approximately 2,300 more following each year in the 1970s.[18] By 1979, over fifty thousand cross-culturally married Korean women were living in the United States.[19] No words can adequately describe the struggle and pain these women encounter each day. Their sense of isolation and emotional turmoil come largely from the lack of understanding and compassion of the people around them.[20] Many are divorced and left alone with two or three children with no means of support.[21] Yet the transculturally married Korean women have made a great contribution to Korean ethnic communities and businesses by their patronage to these institutions.[22]

The third major group of female immigrants was composed of young girls who were adopted by American families after the Korean War. There were 66 percent more girl adoptees than boys, mainly because childless couples in Korea prefer to adopt boys.[23] Most interracially married or interracially adopted women have not had the personal background that would prepare them to have a workable self-identity in a new cultural milieu.

By far the largest group of Koreans living in America today has immigrated since the Immigration Act of 1965 (PL 89-236), which eliminated national origin as a criterion for immigration in the United States. These Koreans are identified as professionals, who are highly educated, urban middle class people and skilled workers. From 1965 to 1975, 93 percent of Korean immigrants had received their college education before they immigrated.[24] From 1965 to 1977, 264,000 Koreans entered the United States[25] and among them were more than 13,000 physicians, pharmacists, and dentists.[26] The 1980 US Census reported that the number of Koreans in this country increased from 70,000 to over 350,000 between 1970 and 1980. At the end of 1987 the total number had reached around one million with approximately 68 percent being women.[27]

Stress in Family Context

Many Korean women immigrated to America mainly because their husbands wanted more education or business training. Not surprisingly, these husbands have no great interest in changing their traditional male-dominant attitudes about family order and authority.[28] They seldom have intimate conversations with their wives, and do not compliment them or express warmth and affection toward them. On the other hand, the wives who have recently taken outside jobs and started actively helping to support their families are no longer prepared to accept without objection the old male-dominant family relationship patterns.

With men interested in maintaining their authoritarian role and women eager to affirm their newly adopted western egalitarian values, domestic tensions are growing. Korean men who have problems dealing with American culture in their workplace, usually with a lowered status, find it difficult to tolerate diminished status in their own households. Many Korean men suffer the status inconsistency.[29] Back in Korea, they were in positions in which they could respect themselves in their minds in a societal setting. Now in a strange land, they can only hold positions in which they can hardly have any self-respect. Many Korean men, who were teachers and held positions in governmental structures while in Korea, are now in a new setting, often working at manual jobs. This is one of the crucial stress producing points in Korean immigrant family settings.

Coping with the generation gap in immigrant families is another critical issue for Korean immigrant women. First-generation parents miss their homeland, so they try to become more Korean and put an increased emphasis on Korean ways of living. At the same time, their children are trying hard to succeed in school and gain acceptance in American society. Therefore, they want to become as Americanized as they can be. Thus, parents and children are going in opposite directions.[30] In addition, the parents speak Korean more than English at home, thus making it difficult for the family to maintain the basic communication channels necessary for healthy parent-child relations. Serious linguistic and cultural conflicts exist in Korean American families. Because Korean culture, like so many others around the world, is at heart very family centered, such painful stress in marital and family relationships is particularly disruptive.

An additional family stress involves the elderly grandparents in immigrant families who frequently feel neglected in a new cultural setting. They cannot satisfactorily talk with their grandchildren because of the language and culture gaps, and because their adult children are busy running their small businesses. These sons and daughters-in-law are also drifting away from traditional standards of respecting and caring for the elderly of Confucian family values. Therefore the elderly find themselves in the uncomfortable position of serving their children in a strange land. Such a reversal of accustomed roles is extremely difficult for the older generation to accept, and many Korean American families find themselves struggling to deal with the resulting tensions.[31] A large percent of the elderly women who live with their children prefer to move out of their children's homes and live in separate households.[32] The conflicting feeling existing within women themselves is hard to ignore, although some families are able to manage the situation quite successfully.

Tensions in Church and Community Settings

Korean women have been sacrificially active in their churches and other Korean community groups throughout their years in America. In spite of diverse language and value systems existing in the Korean community, first-generation immigrants still control most of their formal organizations. Many first-generation Koreans tend to be strongly nationalistic, traditional, and authoritarian. It is true that many contemporary men support their wives, who are working and developing themselves, by helping with housework. But they seem to wish to preserve persistent Confucian ideology on gender roles in the ethnic community life setting.[33] So, women usually must content themselves with supporting roles and rarely becoming officers or board members.

The church, which is a major social and psychological focal point for Korean immigrants, reflects traditional Korean values. In most church institutions, male leadership continues to be normative as it maintains its conservative, hierarchical, and male-dominant structural system. Women who are active in church women's associations usually spend most of their time preparing meals and washing dishes. Many respond to the situation with unresolved anger at being born a woman.[34] Some just leave the church community, longing for a sense of wholeness, dignity, and gender partnership in Christ elsewhere.[35] Some women simply resign from church posts after having the experience of receiving no contact for the meetings and also realizing that all the decisions are made without them.[36] Many women seem to resolve the situation by identifying themselves with the biblical symbol of the cross as a lifelong demand for suffering and self-sacrifice which they must bear in the Korean church setting.[37]

Because women have been kept out of structural responsibility in most Korean institutions, they have organized many separate women's associations and are making important contributions to the community through youth services and other social service activities. They are active in women's leadership training programs and work to promote their positions in community organizations. In so doing they are gaining much valuable experience as leaders.

Many women who are active as volunteers in the community also have full-time jobs outside their homes and have families to care for as well. A good many of these women have the full support of their husbands in their volunteer work, but some do so in spite of their husbands' opposition.[38] Most Korean women quietly carry out their double and triple responsibilities despite frustration and unhappiness with the limitations forced upon them. Others say they simply do not have time to even think about their problems.

The Korean Christian women derived their sense of self worth from their belief in Jesus Christ. They believed that Jesus supported women's humanity and dignity, and valued women as authentic and thinking human beings. That was the key point through which the women were able to sustain their strength both at church and in society.[39]

The 1.5 and Second Generations

Asian American sociologists have termed those who have immigrated with their parents between the ages of eleven and sixteen the 1.5 generation.[40] They are usually bilingual and bicultural. Many 1.5 and second-generation Korean American women are also beginning to participate in social service activities, although such activities bring them into frequent cultural and identity conflicts. They feel strong emotional ties to their parents, yet also long to assert themselves as individuals. Most of them eventually establish a strong self-identity after much painful struggle both at home and in society especially with discrimination and a sense of alienation.[41] They have had to find viable ways between complete assimilation into American society and re-immersing themselves in their Korean cultural heritage. Some do succeed in balancing the competing value systems. They become independent individuals, and still maintain warm relationships with their families. They have much tolerance of diverse cultural pressures, an adaptability to new situations, and much absence of prejudice.[42]

Vocationally, however, too many American-born Korean women still find themselves in low-paying, low-status jobs. They personify to some extent the traditional Korean image of the virtuous woman who is loyal, diligent, attentive to details, and a good subordinate.[43] But they are often compassionate toward other younger generation Koreans because they too have experienced the pain of growing up as minority children in a racist society.[44] Many Korean American second-generation women opt to major in the fields of psychology, law, and counseling, and that indicates their high level of interest in human service. Most younger generation women seem to participate in service activities with a more egalitarian spirit than their seniors.[45]

Many Asian American women seem to be making their way into important roles in American society, and hopefully the image of Asian women as passive and servile will not prevail much longer.[46] More Korean women are starting their own businesses and are becoming a substantial part of the American entrepreneurial system.[47] More schools are hiring Korean American women teachers, although their total number is still small. More Korean women are also being ordained as elders and ministers in American mainline denominations.

Stereotyping and Self-Image

The stereotyping of Asian women in American society relates closely to society's general discriminatory view based on gender and race. In the larger society, stereotyped images picture all women as physically, psychologically and intellectually inferior to men.[48] Asian women in particular are viewed to be weak, reserved, self-sacrificing, soft-spoken, submissive, passive, and dependent. They are commonly thought to be conservative, traditional, discreet, and emotionally suppressed. They are also considered polite, exotic, erotic, and doll-like. "Geisha" and "China doll" are common labels put on them by the dominant society.[49] It is recognized that it is harder to overcome pre-conceived images than just earning the approval through exercising individual capabilities.

When women try to break out of this fixed mold to live as authentic beings, many of their fellow Asians disapprove of them. To live as an efficient part of the society, women often have to become highly visible in public, and this is contrary and contradictory to Korean values of modesty and moderation prescribed for women.

Many Korean women seem to view themselves as dependent and identify themselves as daughter, wife and mother for their self-identity. They are dependent on communities and they live with ascribed roles, and believe that they were born into a highly structured relationship web. But many women who live in modern society live with a high degree of frustration and conflict, dealing with a strong yearning for self development.

Employment vs. Family Responsibilities

Most Korean women in the U.S. have been working outside their homes from the very beginning of their lives in this country.[50] They have played a vital role in building an economic base for their families and community, and have stood strong in holding their families together. In addition, the husbands of most of them expect them to continue their traditional roles of housekeeping, family nurture, and child rearing.

Unfortunately, in the American environment, many female graduates of good Korean universities can only find minimum level work as baby sitters or cleaning women because of language and cultural barriers. They work ten to fifteen hours a day, seven days a week. Yet amazingly, some still find time and energy to be involved in church work and community service. Even obtaining a high level of education in an American college or university does not guarantee immigrant women proportionately high earning power.[51] The possibilities of higher earning capacity should relate to an individual's educational level, but this is not so for Asian American women. Many women with college degrees must still take work as secretaries or office clerks.[52] Thinking that submission is the only way to hold their positions, many work double hours for the same low pay.

It is even more significant that as an Asian woman's educational level goes up, her earning power usually falls far behind that of a white woman with comparable qualifications.[53] This is especially true when the job is one that requires considerable contact with the public. This reality is a major reason why Asian American women choose to become small business entrepreneurs.

A recent study on the south side of Chicago targeted the business involvement of the working wives of Korean entrepreneurs.[54] One finding of the study indicates that the wives' work schedule outside of the home seldom modifies their traditional role in home and family or increases their husbands' help with household tasks. According to the same study, Korean working wives did more than 75 percent of the housework in their homes. These tasks were divided into four areas: grocery shopping, house cleaning, doing laundry, and cooking and dishwashing. It was found that only 4 percent of Korean husbands did a significant amount of dishwashing and grocery shopping.[55]

For immigrant wives the freight of the double burden of household duties plus long working hours outside the home is a continuing cause of domestic dissatisfaction. The problem is due to a combination of structural, situational, and cultural factors in immigrant life. Without a combined approach that deals with all these factors, a realistic solution to the problem seems unlikely. Many seem to wish to reorganize home care structure in such a way that all persons involved would take up an equal sense of responsibility for both child care and domestic home care. Yet, it is true that many women develop self confidence and self esteem as they gain economic capabilities on their own.

3. Search for Identity

Korean American women are seeking a workable cultural and personal identity in western society. As they seek self-actualization, they find themselves in a vise between the two cultures. In this context, the writer conducted a research project designed to examine the processes by which immigrant women resolve their cultural and personal identity conflicts. The research design included interviews with sixteen first-generation Korean American women. Twelve interview results were chosen for analysis.

The Research Design

As the research design for the present study, the qualitative method was chosen for it was deemed to be effective for an exploratory research.[56] The personal interview method was selected as the main vehicle for the data collection. The self-reporting method, such as an individual interview, was an intense process and seemed to be a viable and acceptable method for data collection for a social science inquiry.

The unstructured interview method was deemed to be more useful in studying the contents and categories of existing social psychological patterns. For the present research, the data collection was done through in-depth, unstructured, focused individual interviews. The study utilized the in-depth exploratory research process in order to collect the salient variables. The selected study participants were interviewed for the duration of one and a half to two and a half-hours per person. The unstructured interview allowed for considerable freedom during the interview process so that these sessions may approach the informality of ordinary conversation with the researcher guiding that conversation.

The interview contents were focused on the subjective experience of the interviewees in regard to their encounter with the second culture and the issue of the women's movement in the United States. The head topics included demographic characteristics, experience in childhood and adolescence, experience with identity conflict after the cultural transition, and incorporation and resolution of their psychological conflict and gaining of clear self-identity and peace of mind.

All study participants were college graduates, and all claimed to be Christians. Eleven women out of twelve said that they were Protestants, and one identified herself as an independent. In regard to age cohorts, the present age at the time of interviews, four women were in their 30s, four in their 40s, and four in their 50s. Occupation of the study participants varied; three were in independent sales businesses, two were church workers working in the church structure, two were professionals, four were full time graduate students, and one was a real estate broker. The age of immigration spread nicely from eighteen to forty-five; two women immigrated at age eighteen with their parents; the majority, nine persons, immigrated in their 20s; and one immigrated in her 40s.[57]

Years in residence in the United States ranged from six to thirty-nine years, median length being 16.5. One woman was single, nine were married with children, and two were married without children. The place of residence of the women varied as well; two women resided in California (one in Los Angeles, one in San Francisco), six in the State of New Jersey, two in New York, one in Washington DC, and one in Pennsylvania. (see Appendix B).

The interviews were done in the Korean language. Over four hundred fifty pages of interview transcripts were transcribed in English for data analysis and writing. Recording tapes were not used for interviews in caution that it might inhibit the participants with their free feelings of sharing. The results of the investigation are outlined below in terms of the stages of women's cultural and personal identity formation. Again, the verbatims from the interviews are not included in this particular article.

Cultural Identity

Korean immigrant women seem to experience five progressive stages in the formation of their cultural identity.

1. *Pre-encounter.* First, Korean immigrant women appear to experience a pre-encounter period in which they still feel comfortable in their original cultural context. In this stage the women generally retain their Asian cultural mentality whether they are in Korea or have already arrived in the new land. They also hold a positive view of western culture, even to the point of idealizing Euro-American values, including incidentals such as hair and makeup styles.

2. *Dissociation Consciousness.* A second stage of cultural identity formation is a post-immigration dissociation consciousness. In most immigrant situations, Asian wives are involuntarily disengaged from their accustomed home surroundings. They have immigrated mainly because their husbands wanted further education or job training. Thus, the involuntary nature of their separation from the homeland makes it much harder for them to cope with their new life. It must be recognized that a few women willingly seem to have sought out a type of cultural disengagement for the sake of self-renewal. They even have a feeling of excitement about being in a new environment and sometimes experience real acculturation, assimilation, and transformation.

For most immigrant women, however, dissociation and misidentification are not easy. They are cut off from their old ties, have lost their self-definition in the new society, and are disenchanted and disoriented because of the intense change in their predicament. Immigration has canceled the customary easy ways of defining themselves that their old environment had firmly supported. In the previous culture, they had easily identifiable positions. Since personal relationships were the base of Asian culture in their homeland, most women identified themselves in relation to a recognized institution, organization, or family name. In America, though, none of those structural connections are recognized.

Coping with employment related misidentification is particularly challenging. In the new culture a formerly respected school teacher may be reduced to working as a baby-sitter because of her limited language capabilities. This particular experience deflates her self-esteem[58] and makes her feel as if she had dropped back to the bottom of the social ladder into a kind of vulnerable limbo.

Immigrant women are also frequently disenchanted by the collapse for them of the so-called "streets of gold" myth of universal prosperity in America. One of their most upsetting realizations is the discovery that the golden American world they dreamed of never actually existed. There is also the equally disillusioning realization that their old pre-immigration Asian world too has become unreal for them. Its old meaning and value for their daily life are now useless in the new environment.

In this stage, immigrant women frequently suffer from an intense disorientation consciousness. They have found themselves on the other side of the globe. What was day has become night and what was night has become day. Food, water, culture and language have all been turned upside down. It is also true, however, that if these shocking realizations can be properly interpreted, they can stimulate a positive personal response. It is entirely possible for these hard experiences to lead women to look deeper into themselves, to form concrete plans for organizing their lives, to get on with supporting their families, and to go on living.

3. *Encounter.* The third stage of the search for women's cultural identity can be termed as the encounter stage. It is inevitable for them to feel cultural conflict when encountering a new culture. For most Asians, the hardest problem is mastering the new language. In the larger American society generally, a person's importance in a business or institution is measured largely by his or her ability at verbal articulation, whereas the Korean culture can be termed a "being culture," meaning that in the Korean sociocultural setting, if you are present, you count. Not long after starting work they begin to also feel the fierce winds of racism prevalent in American society.[59]

The sociocultural power structure harbors a deep indignation at the presence of minority persons in its ranks, largely because of racial and economic concerns. Asian immigrants, especially Chinese and Japanese immigrants, have suffered this prejudice for many years.[60] Immigrants must also face the frightening sense that in the eyes of the majority, they lack validity even as persons. They live in a time between dreams. They have lost their old cultural connections and have not yet discovered new ones. Unfortunately, this dangerous stage of immigrant transition usually continues too long. It takes time to unlearn all that had been learned in the past and rebuild a respectable persona in a new and largely unknown world. One woman told the writer that when she first started living in the US, she felt as if the bottom of her world had been pulled out from under her. To deal with their distress, immigrant women must spend much time alone to discover themselves and make concrete plans for their cultural rebirth.

4. Re-direction to Asian Roots. The next stage in the immigrant woman's cultural identity search is a redirection back to her Asian roots. When they experience distress in their relations with the majority culture, they naturally turn back to their ethnic community for support in spite of the sexism existing in that community. They need a sense of social belonging and recognition that they can find through activity in their Asian ethnic associations and churches. They donate funds to Korean art exhibits, to Korean churches, and to ethnic historical and cultural events. This generosity can be understood as a desperate reaching out for cultural identity, driven by deep psychological needs. Under such stress, women's survival and positive identity resolutions can be greatly aided by participation in strong support groups.

5. *Incorporation.* The last stage of the cultural identity search can be called incorporation. In this stage the immigrant woman finally emerges from her cultural confusion and begins moving toward a resolution of her cultural conflicts based on inner ideas and inner change. In this stage she begins to develop a working image for her new life and she has at least four patterns to guide her.[61]

Traditionalists want to live in ethnic enclaves more Asian than American. Integrationists choose to detach themselves from the Asian community and try as much as possible to blend in with Anglo-Americans in the majority society. Some people have called Asian integrationists "bananas" because on the outside their skin is yellow and their inclinations are white on the inside. Another grouping can be described as isolationists. They do not want to live as either Asians or Americans in this country, but would return to Korea if they had the opportunity. Finally, there are those who seek to live successfully as pluralists. They prefer acculturation, including social assimilation, and try vigorously to resolve the inherent cultural conflicts of Asian Americans living in a pluralist American society. In time they attain competency in American style living and affirm in themselves a true bicultural consciousness with a personal sense of mission and historicity

Personal Identity

Beyond the quest for defining cultural identity, there was the struggle for personal identity formation for Korean immigrant women. There also appear to be five progressive stages in this process. On data analysis the labeling of stages has been influenced by the theory on racial ethnic identity formation process identified by William Hall and William Cross in "Stages in the Development of Black Awareness."[62] In that scale, four distinct stages had been identified. Also an influence was William Bridges's transition theory, in which Bridges identifies three stages of the process of beginning a new life after a life transition.[63] In this present study, five progressive stages have been identified for Korean immigrant women in developing both clear self identity and achieving the state of peaceful self amidst a culturally and ideologically diverse environment.

One of the goals for the study was to investigate the process through which women develop themselves from the culturally codependent self to a free self to love and to be. The codependent self can be described as a depleted self in which they are not fully aware of their humanity, just living and doing their contextually defined duties, and hence, do not quite feel either a sense of happiness or fulfillment as an individual.[64] When a woman sees herself as a psychologically independent entity she would be able to feel free to love and free to be; being able to think, perceive, interpret, create, and be able to take an action as a person. Thus she would be able to feel a sense of serenity/happiness, and a fulfillment in doing what she wants to do, whether it will be a service to her family she loves, the church she is devoted to, or to the community projects she feels deeply committed to.

The description in this article is a short condensed version of the research findings, including neither theoretical explanations nor the life sharing verbatim. The five stages are described as follows. ***

1. *Conformity Stage: The Depleted Self* . Korean immigrant women seem to begin their personal identity formation with an impulse toward conformity with cultural and societal expectations. At this phase of the self-affirmation process, they are trying to fulfill their needs and wishes through other persons, particularly relying on their husbands' accomplishments in status, income, recognition, and a sense of well being. At this stage they feel comfortable if they can just do what others demand of them. The women in that cultural adaptation seem to feel concerned with what others may think of them, and usually are security-oriented.

The society and the cultural context praise and award women who just serve their husband and family under the influence of Confucian ideology of women, living their lives with goals of being good wives and wise mothers. Under this contextual sphere, it can be described as a woman living as a depleted self not being aware of her self as an independent self with hopes and goals in life of her own. Deep in the subconscious sphere, the level of anxiety seems to be high and their self-esteem low at this phase of women's development, although some try to tell themselves that this is the way it is and they cannot fight the reality. The women seem to have little respect for self or others, and they see the world as an unfriendly place.

2. *Conscientization Stage: The Awakening Self.* Next, most Korean women seem to experience conscientization about women's issues. During this period, they become aware that they have not been living as fully authentic human beings, from western/Christian sociocultural perspectives, with a full sense of wholeness and dignity. They realize that the standard processes of culture and society are not reliable aids for the development of their ego power and self-definition. Conscientization may occur either in Korea or America through actual life experience, through books and group discussions, and through observing the life patterns of others who are close to them or whom they admire.

The women are awakening to acknowledge where they are and what their lives are all about. They wish to look at themselves as persons with talents and gifts that were buried, undiscovered and unutilized. During this phase, although the level of pain is high, their anxiety level is lowered and self-esteem heightened.

3. *Encounter Stage: The Suffering Self.* Soon after conscientization, the women become open to a more profound sociostructural awareness. Some women try to go out into society and hold a position. Some suffer with the language and cultural barrier. Others discover that even when they do not have any problems with either language or skills to perform the job, responsible positions are not given to them. In her new and heightened sensitivity she realizes that societal and structural organizations have been unfair to Korean women and have exploited her. Living as double minority persons in western society, Korean women have felt that pushing against the stereotyped image of the Asian woman is like trying to move a mountain. Chinese American and Korean American women know that they have been exploited both in the German owned garment districts and Asian owned garment industries, and in other entrepreneur institutions.[65] At this stage in time they begin to engage in cultural analysis and sociostructural analysis. Some women feel that they lack resources to succeed in the larger society or to start a business of their own at this stage in their acculturation process. They feel they have been thrown out into a wilderness.

The women feel that they are not yet firmly stationed in this society and feel that they are lacking validation as full persons. A sense of confusion, a sense of being lost, and the feeling of anger are all parts of this stage. They feel, again, a low self-esteem and much anxiety on the prospect of their life in this society. Yet they seem to unconsciously know that they are on the right track in looking for their real selves and better understanding of their marginalized position in this society. Thus their self esteem is heightened and anxiety level lowered at this stage of development.

4. *Introspection Stage: The Evolving Self.* In the next stage, that of introspection, many women seem to conjure up the courage to be reborn. They seem to immerse themselves in self-discovery and strive for self-development. In this stage they give more attention to gaining individual autonomy and affirming themselves as authentic human beings. As such, they steadily recognize and develop the God-given talents and gifts that they have always possessed. In order to become better informed

and grow intellectually, women return to school and attend various types of seminars and personal growth conferences. They seek out support groups and discover that, after women's conscientization, such groups can be indispensable for their survival.

During this critical period in the process of forming positive self-integration, many Korean women take time to contemplate a rebirth in new perspective. They seem to process such critical elements as working on the evolving self from the suffering self of previous stage, and seem to engage in self analysis,[66] analysis of family relations,[67] grieving the losses, healing the wounded self within,[68] forgiveness and working through the codependent self.[69] In doing so, they seem to wish to contemplate the meaning of establishing boundaries[70] for themselves for self-integration, in order to become better partners in all relationships.

In this period, women make efforts to establish themselves as God-created authentic beings instead of seeing themselves as mere products of Confucian cultural expectations. Although this process is a difficult and painstakingly lengthy process, they seem to enjoy resurgent energy, a sense of joy and heightened self-esteem in this period in time.

5. *Resolution Stage: The Peaceful Self.* In this final stage, Korean immigrant women experience a sense of resolution. They now can internalize their new identity as Korean American women or Korean American Christian women while simultaneously re-identifying themselves with their Korean background. They engage their efforts in a self-renewal process through which they can make sense out of their feelings of lostness and confusion. They take time to withdraw periodically so that they can experience personal rebirth, enjoy a new perspective on life, and take satisfaction in an inner realignment.[71]

They seem to wish to work on past issues, such as a realignment of inner psychosocial aspects, re-programming of new images, self-integration and deepening of their spirituality. They try to affirm themselves with a sense of serenity, meditation, compassion and service for others. Thus they want to feel comfortable with their own integrated self, achieving the notion of a peaceful self within themselves. They want to engage in humanitarian activities, feel one with nature and the universe, and feel enthusiasm for life.

Although realizing that her true roots are still in old and dear Asian foundations, the Korean American woman ultimately reaches out to immerse herself psychologically in her new life. She develops new relationships, begins new projects, and enjoys a new image of herself, and owns and wears the identity of her own. Her disengagement consciousness fades and she begins to feel ownership of her new personhood and identity. The old social rules do not fit some facets of her new orientation so she must learn how to move beyond them. Yet she rejoices in the new discovery of herself, gives the credit to herself, and reaches out to be one with the universe. She feels power in forgiveness and wishes to name what she wants and claim it.

She is in the midst of a recovery process in which she enjoys a new consciousness and a new cognitive process. At times, she may experience the original pain, yet mainly she reprograms a new image for herself and launches in a corrective experience toward authentic self-love which she believes God wants for her. In this valuable recovery process, her authentic sense of wholeness emerges. Thus she is able to discover the peaceful being within herself, and is able to embrace the serenity that she wishes. She is able to have good self-control, unconditional love and acceptance of others, and she is able to grow consistently and unceasingly. Her self-esteem rises again.

Now, she is able to work with both men and women from any ethnic group; she can tolerate the old rules, but also launches herself into a new life of creativity, reaching toward the sense of wholeness which Rollo May calls "creative consciousness of self."[72] She particularly finds herself wanting to work for the alienated and the suffering, in all groups and societies, engaging in the praxis of Christian love, and generally desires to work for higher human causes on a broader scale.

4. Other Themes From the Interviews

In the writer's research, all the women interviewed reported that they had been conscientized on women's issues either in Korea or in the United States.

1. All the women who participated in the study had suffered periods of cultural and personal conflict. They had especially suffered discord with their children because of the widening culture gap between the generations.

2. Women experienced the conflict over the allocation of time, as to how much time should be devoted to the care and comfort of their

family and how much to their own process of self-renewal and self-actualization.

3. All the women had experienced sexism in the Korean church and community. They definitely felt that they had been dehumanized and oppressed just because they were born women.

4. The women had found that American society had a rigid stereotyped image of Asian women. The women felt that breaking such deeply held societal images was harder than just plainly asserting themselves in public.

5. Some of the women had experienced an acute identity conflict in relation to having two entirely different names. After marriage, a woman in Korea continues to use her maiden name. In America, one takes the husband's family name as her own. So, Jung-Sook Kim becomes Mary Lee for she has adopted her husband's surname, Lee, and a western-style first name for convenience. The women say that they do not know who they are.

6. The women interviewed were all seeking to get their own income and independent status so that they could be recognized as persons in their own right. Those who could support themselves financially felt more satisfied with their life than those who were dependent on their husbands for support.

7. All the women who participated in the study were struggling painfully with the patri-local system. The family normally located their home near the husband's job site. When a wife has her own business and the husband gets transferred to another city, she is faced with a critical decision of whether or not to move with the family or stay with her business. In many of the cases, wives who wished to maintain their career had to endure the stressful alternative of long-distance commuting.

8. Most of the research participants seemed to be in the late introspection stage of their search for personal identity as they struggled with self-development, affirmation, and assertiveness.

9. It was satisfying to learn that some of the women had resolved their personal conflicts satisfactorily. They knew exactly what they wanted out of life and knew how to attain it. All wanted to function as independent agents and at the same time have meaningful family relationships in which their humanity and dignity were supported and maintained. Furthermore, they were wise enough and persistent enough

to work out a concrete solution to these issues amidst their demanding lives.

10. All women affirmed their faith in Jesus Christ through which they were able to sustain their dignity, courage and sense of wholeness. They believed that Jesus supported the full humanity of women, respecting women as thinking and authentic entities.

Conclusion

After their cultural and ideological transition, Korean American women must embark on a special journey toward the achievement of cultural and personal definition in the larger society. Having been reared in a Confucian patriarchal culture and having been challenged by western humanitarian ideals, Korean women must seek new and more adequate identities that reconcile the two traditions on both cultural and personal levels.

The immigrant women seem to experience five phases in working out their cultural identity. They are; pre-encounter, dissociation consciousness, encounter, redirection to Asian roots, and incorporation. In their personal identity formation process, they also experience five stages which lead them to affirm and accept themselves as true Korean American women or Korean American Christian women. The stages were: conformity stage, conscientization stage, encounter stage, introspection stage, and resolution stage. Many times for many women the contents of each stage seem to overlap, and/or women seem to travel back and forth to different stages at different times with different issues.

After much struggle, she enjoys a new consciousness and a new cognitive process. She reprograms a new image for herself and an authentic sense of wholeness. She launches herself into a new life of creativity, being able to discover the peaceful being within herself, and is able to embrace the serenity, compassion and service she wishes.

Most of the women interviewed lived in a multi-ideological context. The degree and manner of their adaptation to western ideologies varied considerably from individual to individual. It is especially pleasing to note that in spite of an abundance of difficult issues and responsibilities, many Korean American women today are living with high self-esteem and respectable careers.

Based on firm Christian conviction and faith, the research participants were able to make significant contributions to both the dominant American community and the immigrant Asian community. They were able to affirm themselves as Korean American Christian women. The women were generally satisfied with the degree to which their expectations have been fulfilled, although their efforts toward self-development continue. They affirm themselves as women living in America with an Asian cultural background, and they have become excellent role models for future Asian American women.

Appendix A

Brief Biographical Sketches of Study Participants

The following is a brief biographical sketch on each study participant. The names have been altered to secure their privacy. All participants were born and raised in Korea, identified to be first-generation immigrants.

1. Marie: Age 53, married with two children. Youngest of six siblings, immigrated at 24. Works for family company, financially well off. Feels much stress in relation to company employees.
2. Heran: 30, married with one child. Immigrated at 23, a graduate student. Keenly aware of the oppressed status of women by her personal experience of being a daughter-in-law in a Christian, yet very Confucian, family.
3. Eui Sook: 49, married with a son in college. Raised by well educated Protestant parents. Immigrated at 23. Works in the field of education, administrative positions in east coast and mid-west. Active in church and women's organizations and in support of the second generation of Korean Americans.
4. Jung Eun: 46, married with three children. Youngest of four, immigrated at 29. Raised by middle-class parents. Runs a successful business in a metropolitan area. Active in church organizations.
5. Suzanna: 32, married with 2 children. Immigrated at 23, a late-entry graduate student. Feeling ambivalent about her future in the church setting because her husband will soon be ordained.
6. Jenny: 55, married with 2 sons. Immigrated at 45, lived on east coast for 10 years. Well conscientized on social, political and women's issues, active in church work.
7. Hyunja: 31, married without children. Younger of two, raised by well educated parents. Immigrated at 24, a doctoral student. Well conscientized on women's issues, still arrested in the midst of anger period.

8. Kyung Sook: 41, married without children. Oldest of six. Raised by poor but liberated parents. Immigrated at 26, obtained M.A., works part time. Talks as a liberated one, acts as a part of her husband in Korean community. Does not cook at all. Reveals much inner anger and conflict.
9. Jean: 30 and single. The youngest of four. Raised by jobless parents, influenced positively by grandparents who were in the field of Christian social work. Immigrated at 18, is a successful business woman. Struggles acutely psychologically for self-actualization.
10. Haejin: 51, married with three children. Raised by middle class parents. Immigrated at 25, moderately successful business woman in a metropolitan area. Active in church work and women's organizations Suffers deeply with issues of child rearing and generation gaps.
11. Sandra: 57, married with 2 children. Fourth child among six. Grew up under socially well- known parents. Immigrated at 18, presently working in a church setting. Comfortably self-actualized.
12. Hae Eun: 41, married with three children. Oldest of four. Raised by upper-class professional parents. Immigrated at 24, re-entry graduate student. Husband has strong earning power; she feels much constrained by his dominance and Confucian male attitude.

Appendix B

Demographic Profile of Research Participants

1. Number Used for Analysis	12
2. Gender: Female:	12
3. Age Cohorts:	
30s	4
40s	4
50s	4
4. Age at Immigration	
Upper Teens(18)	2
20s	9
30s	0
40s	1
5. Years in U.S.	
Under 10 years	3
10-20 years	5
20-30 years	3
30-40 years	1
6. Education:	
BA/BS	8
MA	4
7. Marital Status:	
Married	11
Single	1
Divorced	0
Separated	0
Widowed	0
8. Socio-economic Class:	
Low	2
Middle	4
Upper Middle	2
Upper	4
9. Religious Affiliation:	
Independent	1
Protestant	11
10. Occupation:	
Business (Sales)	4
Professional	2
Church Worker	2
Graduate Student	4
11. Place of Residence:	
California	2
New Jersey	6
New York	2
Washington D.C.	1
Pennsylvania	1

Chapter Nine

Shame and Asian American Experiences

Angella M. Pak

Introduction

"Naked we are, ashamed we are not." This statement would draw the attention of practically everyone. While some individuals feel, or claim to feel, perfectly at ease when they are naked in the presence of others, most of us do not feel this way. We are therefore greatly intrigued by the statement that we may at one and the same time, be naked and not ashamed. By this statement, I do not mean to promote any numbing of our feelings of shame in the most shameful experience of nakedness. On the contrary, I wish to stress the importance of revitalizing the feelings of shame in our lives.

The basic argument of this paper is that shame is a God-given gift to human beings, which has been denied from human experience because of our misuse of it. In other words, shame is an essential experience in our relationship with God and others; but unfortunately, misunderstanding of shame and its role in these relationships has prevented us from relating meaningfully to God and others. The purpose of this paper, then, is to free us from the misconceptions of shame for the betterment of our relationships with one another and with God. I have two objectives. One is to challenge the Christian community to expand its theology to address the experience of shame; the other is to identify implications of experiences of shame particularly on Asian American experiences.

To this end, I will examine selected verses from Genesis, explore the nature, manifestations, and defenses of shame, and consider the Christian response to shame in light of Christian doctrines. In addition, while the experiences of shame apply to all cultures, I will focus on the experiences of shame among Asian Americans. Because my major concern is to clarify the meaning of shame from the perspective of Christian doctrine and its implications in Asian American experiences, I will not deal with such issues as the comparison between shame and guilt, cultural and gender differences in the experience of shame, and the role of shame in addictions and abusive situations. Some comments on these topics will be made for illustrative purposes only. A survey of the use of the word "shame" throughout the Bible is also beyond the scope of this study. As noted, I will be focusing on the understanding of shame presented in the book of Genesis, specifically chapters two and three.

1. Shame in Genesis

The first experience of shame in the Christian tradition is recorded in the creation and the fall narratives in Genesis 2 and 3. Verse 2:25 makes a statement about the condition of the human race before the fall: *And the man and his wife were both naked and were not ashamed.* This passage raises the question: "Was shame a part of human experience when God created human beings *in the image of God* (Genesis 1:27) or was it a consequence of the Fall?" Closer examination of the nature of shame below will enable us to answer this question. Some, however, may argue that Adam and Eve, unlike most of us who would naturally experience the shame of our nakedness before others, were unusual or atypical. The human condition depicted before and after the fall is more evident when we examine verse 2:25 simultaneously with verse 3:7.

Verse 3:7 states that Adam and Eve became aware of each other's nakedness: *Then the eyes of both were opened, and they knew that they were naked; and they sewed fig leaves together and made themselves aprons.* The verse does not specifically mention the word "ashamed," but it indicates that they became aware of their exposed state and tried to cover up their exposed selves. Consequently, both before and after the fall, the two were naked. Before, their eyes were not opened, and after, their eyes were opened; before, they did not feel exposed in their nakedness, and after, they did feel exposed; before, they did not see the need for covering up, and after, they did see that need. The fall then separates human beings not in their physical condition but in their different attitudes toward their physical condition. Nakedness, which once was not considered as exposure impelling covering up, was later seen as such exposure.

This suggests two possible answers to the question raised above. One is that human beings already had shame as one of their active affects at the time of creation, and that it was only after the fall that nakedness became one of the causes or conditions of the experience of shame. The other is that human beings were incapable of feeling exposure before the Fall and therefore did not experience shame; only after the fall did they begin to feel exposed and thus to experience shame. The second answer seems to be the more viable option as the expression, *the eyes of both were opened* (3:7) denotes a change in the condition of awareness.

New awareness has come about, and this condition of new awareness makes human beings very uncomfortable. It creates a negative feeling from a sense of wrongness and makes them want to cover up and even hide from the presence of others. This hiding is evident in dialogue between God and Adam. When God calls to Adam, Adam responds by saying, *"I heard the sound of thee in the garden, and I was afraid, because I was naked; and I hid myself."* (Genesis 3:10) God's question to Adam in verse 3:11, *Who told you that you were naked?,* indicates that the awareness of nakedness -- hence, the experience of shame -- was a consequence of the fall. It was this awareness of their nakedness -- and not the fact of their nakedness -- which caused their experience of shame.

This consequence of the fall is what Christian tradition has called the consequence of original sin. In other words, the experience of shame resulted from original sin, or the first brokenness of relationships, i.e., the relationship between God and human beings and among God's creatures -- Adam, Eve, and the serpent. Consequently, shame acts as a signal for brokenness of a relationship. Does this then lead to the conclusion that since shame is a consequence of original sin, it is a punishment from God to human beings? Genesis 3:14-24 delineates God's punishment against the serpent and Adam and Eve. Is shame then an implied element of God's judgment? I would answer in the negative.

Verse 3:22 restates this new awareness as a part of the ability that the divine possesses, of *knowing good and evil.* Before the fall, Adam and Eve did not possess this divine ability of knowing good and evil. Before the fall, Adam and Eve lived in a state of innocence. After the fall, Adam and Eve came to possess the divine ability of knowing good and evil. After the fall, Adam and Eve no longer lived in a state of innocence. After the fall, Adam and Eve had an eye for judging their own wrongness.

After the fall, Adam and Eve acquired a sense of shame for their wrongness. This ability to know good and evil then can be partially described as an ability to look at oneself as a separate being, i.e., self-consciousness. While the word self-consciousness may carry a negative connotation of excessive awareness of oneself, its normal usage -- awareness of self from the self's ability to be both subject and object, i.e., both the observer and the observed -- should be stressed here.

While Adam and Eve had the experience of shame concurrently with the ability to know good and evil, I do not think that the experience of shame is automatically concurrent with the ability to know good and evil, or self-consciousness. In the case of Adam and Eve, they found themselves to be exposed in their eyes of knowing good and evil, and thus experienced shame. Although God holds this ability to know good and evil, God certainly would not experience shame, since God is perfect and would not find any wrongness with Godself. However, God may experience shame not because of God's own failures but because of our failures. It is because God intends to have a close relationship with us that our failures in becoming who God intends us to be create the sense of shame in God. It is only because we matter to God, and our status as God's children matters to God, that God would experience shame.

From the examination of Genesis 2 and 3, I thus conclude that after the fall, human beings come to possess the divine ability to know good and evil. This ability to know good and evil creates in one the experience of shame when one realizes that one is outside of the realm of good. This ability to know good and evil is a special kind of awareness and seems to denote, at least partially, the awareness of self or self-consciousness. The experience of shame, thus, can be considered an affect of conscience. Shame can therefore have a very positive role in Christian life for the people of God as a signal for the brokenness of a relationship, because shame is meant to occur when we find ourselves standing outside of God's will.

Now that I have examined the experience of shame in the creation and the fall narratives in Genesis, I now turn to the human sciences to see how human beings actually experience shame, and whether human experiences of shame are consistent with the conclusions made above based on the biblical account of the primordial experience of shame.

2. Nature of Shame in the Light of Human Sciences

The survey of human sciences with respect to the issue of shame supports the conclusions made above in the examination of Genesis 2 and 3. According to human sciences, shame is associated not with others' evaluations of oneself but with one's ability to discern what is appropriate and what is not. In addition, shame is perceived as a signal for brokenness in relationships and not as a cause for broken relationship. Lastly, human sciences point out the totality of the experiences of shame, i.e., the involvement of the total self instead of only certain aspects or actions of oneself. Andrew P. Morrison's definition of shame aptly addresses the fact that one's own eyes determine the causes of the experience of shame and defines shame as follows:

> Shame, then, reflects feelings about a defect of the self, a lowering of self-esteem, falling short of the values of the ego ideal, a flaw in one's identity representation.[1]

With this definition, Morrison emphasizes the nature of shame as that which involves one's own sense of damage to self or weakness of self. In other words, shame is experienced when one feels imperfect in one's own eyes or that one has not met a certain ideal. It, therefore, involves the failure of oneself and fear of abandonment or rejection. In addition, it is an indication of one's own inferiority and inadequacy.[2]

Helen Merrell Lynd, whose work on shame is very extensive also correctly asserts that shame is experienced when one experiences oneself to be inadequate. She holds that shame is experienced when one's own "peculiarly sensitive, intimate, vulnerable aspects of the self"[3] are exposed. Unlike the common understanding of shame as exposure to others, Lynd, just as Morrison claims above, holds that while exposure may happen in the presence of others, exposure to one's own eyes is that which causes the experience of shame.[4] Erik Erikson's description of shame as "self-consciousness" that makes one feel "completely exposed and conscious of being looked at"[5] echoes Lynd's assertion that shame is experienced because of exposure to one's own eyes and not to the eyes of others.

Shame as the exposure to one's own eyes can be demonstrated by one of the illustrations that Lynd uses. In Nathaniel Hawthorne's "tragic novel of shame and redemption," *The Scarlet Letter*, Dimmesdale longs for the exposure of his love affair with Hester Prynne to the public or even to one person so that he can be freed from his shame of having had a love affair in spite of his religious vow and the additional intensified shame of not having been honest about it. He is, therefore, in anguish as he increasingly hates himself. In order to free himself from anger and bitterness toward himself, he desires an exposure to the public that would make him available for public punishment, i.e., shaming by others and possibly opening up a possibility of acceptance or forgiveness of his love affair with Hester Prynne by others. Consequently, Dimmesdale sees Hester as happy since her shame is no longer her own struggle but is now owned by the public. Dimmesdale thus cries out to Hester:

> Of penance, I have had enough! Of penitence there has been none! Else, I should long ago have thrown off these garments of mock holiness and have shown myself to mankind as they will see me at the judgment seat. Happy are you, Hester, that wear the scarlet letter openly upon your bosom! Mine burns in secret! Thou little knowest what a relief it is, after the torment of a seven years' cheat, to look into an eye that recognizes me for what I am! Had I one friend -- or were it my worst enemy! -- to whom, when sickened with the praises of all other men, I could daily betake myself and be known as the vilest of all sinners, methinks my soul might keep itself alive thereby. Even thus much of truth would save me! But, now, it is all falsehood! -- all emptiness! -- all death![6]

The fact that the exposure to oneself instead of to others is that which causes the sense of shame in people is consistent with the examination of Genesis 2 and 3. It is the internal guideline, not the evaluations of others, by which one discerns what is or is not appropriate, that triggers the sense of shame in oneself. This internal value system is referred to as the ability to know good and evil in Genesis examined above. The attempt to hide is thus to cover from exposure to others that which has been exposed as inappropriate to oneself already.

Gershen Kaufman was correct in asserting that shame is a signal for a brokenness in relationship. Kaufman calls the meaningful relationship based on trust that is established between two or more people the "interpersonal bridge." He describes the way in which the interpersonal bridge is developed and writes:

> Relationships begin when one person actively reaches out to another and establishes emotional ties, much as we might go about the process of taming a strange animal. Such a process entails the establishing of a bond. In this way relationships gradually evolve out of reciprocal interest in one another along with shared experiences of trust. Trusting essentially means that we have come both to expect and to rely upon a certain mutuality of response. An emotional bond begins to grow between individuals as they communicate understanding, respect, and valuing for one another's personhood, needs and feelings included. That bond deepens along with trust and makes possible experiences of openness and vulnerability. The bond which ties two individuals together forms an **interpersonal bridge** between them. The bridge in turn becomes a vehicle to facilitate mutual understanding, growth, and change.[7]

Kaufman further maintains that shame is generated when there is a break in the interpersonal bridge and writes, "The critical step occurs when one significant person somehow breaks the interpersonal bridge with the other. This is the basic way in which shame is generated."[8] A more alarming aspect of shame is that according to Lynd, the more and more one experiences shame, the less and less one puts trust in oneself or one's environment. In other words, as one experiences unexpected exposure of one's incongruity with the situation or one's own inappropriate self-image, one loses trust in one's own confidence and in confidence in others and the security of environment. Since one faces situations that one does not know how to deal with and feels helpless about oneself or the environment, lack of trust is an inevitable result.[9] Shame, then, caused by the break in the interpersonal bridge gets whirled in a spiral where shame and lack of trust continuously feed each other.

This point particularly has implications for Christian community and Asian American community. In Christian community, which is encompassed by the compassion and grace that our Lord Jesus Christ has demonstrated to us, people can be free from the fear of experiencing shame and, as a result, they can build strong trust and confidence in Christian community. The opposite, however, can also be true. When Christian community cannot embrace the experiences of shame, people lose trust not only in themselves but also in Christian community, and ultimately in God. Moreover, the implication becomes intensified for Asian Americans. Asian Americans are people who share multiple cultures in their daily living regardless of their level of assimilation to American culture. When two or more different value systems exist, one is open to more situations in which they experience shame. For instance, a Korean American high school student, who received a score of 1600 on his SAT and admission to Harvard University, was having a graduation party. The guests included both European Americans and Korean Americans. His family was very much assimilated into the mainstream of American culture. During the party, one Korean American guest, a friend of his mother's, started cleaning a mess on the kitchen floor from the party by bending down on the floor with a rag in her hand. It was an unexpected scene that he did not want his Caucasian friends to see. He did not want his image to be associated with non-assimilated values or a non-assimilated cultural system. In America, people are supposed to use a broom or something else to clean so that one does not have to have to lower oneself close to the floor nor have one's hands touch rags. Even though he and his family were well assimilated into the mainstream of American culture, he was still subject to a portrayal of himself as more Korean than he would like because of his family's association with other Koreans and Korean culture. Consequently, trust started disappearing and doubt, the brother of shame as Erikson calls it[10], started creeping in.

Lastly, Lynd, along with Morrison, is perceptive and posits that unlike guilt, shame involves not just a specific act or non-act, but the whole self. In other words, when one experiences shame, one's whole self is at stake. It is not isolatable specific action or non-action or aspects about oneself but it is about the whole self. Consequently, Lynd makes a very important assertion that one's experience of shame is closely linked with one's own identity. It is difficult to deal with the experience of shame, not only because of its nature as the unexpected exposure of incongruity, but also because of its involvement of the whole self. Since it involves the whole self, it is very difficult to undo what is causing the experience of shame.[11] For instance, if one breaks a bowl that one had borrowed from another person, one only needs to buy the same bowl and return it to the owner with an apology. However, this buying and giving the same bowl to the owner cannot take away the feeling of shame about one's own carelessness. Shame can only be wiped away if a change in the whole self occurs and not just in certain aspects of one's own being, attitude, or behavior. Thus, for Lynd, the "transformation of self" is to shame as "expiation" is to guilt.[12]

The involvement of the total self with respect to the experience of shame has a particular implication for Asian Americans. For Asian Americans, one's point of view about one's Asian culture, as opposed to the mainstream culture, can create a shame-based identity. For instance, one can be in an eternal state of shame if one is either ashamed of one's Asian heritage, not being "American" enough, or ashamed of one's lack of Asian heritage, not being "Asian" enough. Christian community, especially Asian American Christian community, thus faces grave responsibility with regards to the implications of an inappropriate handling of shame. Specifically, in providing pastoral care or counseling, Asian American churches need to be sensitive to where each individual or each congregation as a whole stands with respect to how proudly or shamefully one perceives Asian culture. Asian American churches should try to provide a model culture as Asian American, which includes some aspects of both Asian and American cultures and is different from both Asian or American culture, so that Asian Americans can easily accept their identity based on neither Asian culture nor American culture. Asian Americans then can have less of a shame-association when they do not all possess Asian or American culture. In addition, variations in the degree of assimilation into American culture by Asian Americans must be respected and considered on an individual basis, taking into account their backgrounds such as the number of years in the United States, the place of stay, the number of years in American education, etc.

3. Manifestation of Shame: Discretion and Disgrace

The manifestations of shame in human experiences are "shame as discretion" and "shame as disgrace" and are often referred to as positive and negative sides respectively.[13] I hold that this differentiation of positive and negative sides of shame is inappropriate and this position will become evident in the discussion below.

Shame as Discretion

Shame as discretion is often called the positive side and seen as that which has a social and moral function in the society, since we use our discretion to avoid shame from creating disturbances in social life or from doing immoral acts. Shame as discretion provides unwritten contracts among people which prescribe that which is permissible or not permissible in order for a certain amount of stability to exist in society. Otherwise, we would start living in anxiety and fear of what may happen wherever we are and go. One would not feel safe with one's own life or property if people did not share the common understanding that one is entitled to one's own life and property, upon which others are not to impinge on. This is an adult ability corresponding to what Erikson calls a child's ability to "hold on and to let go with discretion."[14] Erikson holds that a child will not develop pathological shame if this ability is well developed in the second stage of his eight psychosocial developmental stages of human beings. When a child learns when it is appropriate to hold on and let go, a child will develop sound discretion. On the other hand, when a child lacks a safe environment to acquire the adequacy of holding on and letting go, a child develops a poor sense of discretion. In the latter case, the child would experience shame as a restrictive and not as a guiding force, since shame functions as judgment on one's actions or non-actions; in the former case, on the other hand, shame functions as a precaution to one's actions or non-actions. Consequently, the child in the latter case develops doubt in himself rather than pride in himself.

Shame, then, in its discretionary function is helpful in keeping us within boundaries in order for us to be social beings and is, by its nature, a relational experience. In other words, shame may not play any role at all if we all live separately in all aspects of our lives and not just in physical separation. If we never have to be concerned with others and our conscience is never bothered by others, we may never have to feel shame.

This is the reason why shame is often misunderstood as exposure in the presence of others while it is more of an exposure to oneself. A deeper understanding of shame, as noted by Kaufman's study on shame, draws out that shame is a feeling of damaged selfhood with respect to one's relating with others. This then resonates with our relationship to God. God has created human beings in order for God to relate to us and for us to relate among ourselves. Since God has made us and the world "relational," we can not help but experience shame. Shame as discretion, therefore, can be perceived as a part of our ability to *know good and evil* (Gen. 3:22) by drawing boundaries for good and evil. Unlike law, however, the boundaries that shame draws for us are very ambiguous. Law draws clearer boundaries for us, specifically noting what to do and what not to do, whereas shame draws an elusive boundary. Accordingly, Lynd is insightful when she points out how difficult it is for one to express the experience of shame in communication.

This elusive nature of shame seems to reflect the inexplicable nature of God's will in our lives. The will of God is itself certainly clear but appears ambiguous to human beings, not because God makes God's will difficult for people to discern, but because it is our sinfulness that blinds us from discerning God's will more clearly, even though God makes it clear. The mainline church's criticism of fundamentalism is pertinent, in that fundamentalists often list the will of God in black and white language and make the will of God as clear as black letters on paper. Mainline Christians tend to treat the will of God as mystery and as a challenge to Christians so that they make their life goal to be in line with the will of God. This is quite evident in Karl Barth's *Church Dogmatics* when he explains atonement as the receiving of freedom to experience divine freedom, i.e., naturally knowing and doing the will of God.[15] I, however, think that the mainline churches, with other churches, are not free from a similar mistake. In describing our sinful nature, Christians have accustomed themselves to the use of the language of guilt. Jesus describes evil manifested in us as *evil thoughts, fornication, theft, murder, adultery, coveting, wickedness, deceit, licentiousness, envy, slander, pride, and foolishness* (Mark 7:20-23). Moreover, Jesus said that these evils in us come from the heart of man. Unfortunately, the language of guilt is inadequate in encompassing the entire nature of sin in human beings. The language of guilt promotes the concept of sin as that which is external harm done to others. Moreover, the language of guilt promotes the concept of sin as that which is determined by external sources especially when the legal system of society bases itself on the foundational clause, "innocent until proven guilty." The concept of sin is no longer determined by God's Word written in our hearts but by the fact that one is caught in doing wrong and that one's culpability has been proven. In that respect, while sins such as fornication, theft, murder, adultery, deceit, licentiousness, and slander may very well be covered by the language of guilt, sins such as evil thoughts, coveting, wickedness, envy, pride, and foolishness may easily go unnoticed or even intentionally ignored as sins when we are used to using the language of guilt.

It is easier to deal with sins using guilt language for specific actions or non-actions to others, but is not adequate in encompassing all sins. Therefore, Christianity inadvertently has made a similar mistake as the Pharisees had made by making things clear with the list of do's and don'ts. Although Protestants have kept their pride in keeping the spirit of God's will instead of being legalistic about God's will, their effort has not come to a full realization. We still face the task of including the experience of shame, which is more effective in encompassing some sins. When we can name shame as part of the human experience, as well as a theologically significant experience, we can begin the task of sensitizing people to shame in our experiences. As Lynd accurately points out, ambiguous human nature should not be expressed in categorical language, such as guilt language, but ought to be expressed by holding its ambiguous nature through ambiguous language such as shame language:

> A language that is confined to labeling rather than defining to denotation at the expense of connotation, does not have the means of expressing experiences whose nature includes ambiguity and surplus meaning. It omits from its purview some of the most significant dimensions of human nature, and possibly distorts others that it may seem to express more fully.[16]

Certainly, we as Christians must raise the question as to whether or not the boundaries that shame as discretion draws for us correspond with God's will. In other words, if shame as discretion is to be used as the guideline for one to discern whether or not one has committed sin, then shame as disgrace must be informed by the Word of God. I see this as a theological task for Christians, i.e., determining which shame experiences involve sin and which do not. Consequently, shame as discretion, when appropriately sensitized, is one that helps us to discern God's will and move away from our sinful nature and closer to God's ways of acting.

Shame as Disgrace

Shame as disgrace is an excruciating experience, damaging to one's own selfhood after the exposure and, thus, often called the negative side of shame. Unlike the common understanding of shame as the cause of broken relationship, Lynd is correct in asserting that shame as disgrace can inform us of our human nature or identity if we allow ourselves to confront it.[17] There are many different situations that can trigger shame as disgrace. The different types of experiences of shame can range from something as simple as a blunder to something as serious as racism or other types of "isms."[18]

The first type of shame as disgrace is experienced as embarrassment from social blunders, mistakes, errors, or accidents. It is an unintentional exposure of one's inadequacy which does not hurt anyone but one's own perception of one's own image. Mistakes such as a woman's going into a man's restroom can create different ranges of experiences of shame in different people. In this case, it is probably better if one learns to treat it as an honest mistake and not take the mistake too seriously. It is often difficult to do this because of the presence of laughter by others. This type of experience of shame as disgrace manifests several aspects of human beings. One is that we have replaced the humorous part of life with all the seriousness of life. When others laugh at us, we also can laugh at ourselves and treat our mistakes as honest mistakes. Instead of trying to make ourselves a perfect machine, we need to reclaim a sense of humor in our life. Secondly, the implication of the first point is that we all make mistakes and not everything is within our control. It shows the imperfect nature of the world and of human beings such that shame as disgrace from social blunders or errors can be seen as God's gentle reminder that we do not live in a perfect world and that our pursuit of perfection is fruitless. In fact, our attempt to guard ourselves and create a perfect image of ourselves is not much different from Adam and Eve's eating the fruit from the tree of the knowledge of good and evil. I think that it is appropriate to consider these harmless mistakes as God's gentle and humorous way of reminding us of our humble status before God and of how grace is ingrained into our lives by God.

Another type of shame as disgrace is shame from exposure of a physical handicap or imperfection. Shame from exposure of a physical imperfection ranges from something as trivial as a crooked nose to as serious a condition as retardation. Logically speaking, no one should be ashamed of their physical handicap or imperfection since they are born with it and have nothing to do with it. These handicaps are given to them and they did not take any part in creating them. Their only participation is the fact that the handicap is part of their physical attributes. It is, however, a well-known fact that physical imperfection creates damage to one's own self-image or self-esteem. It is apparent from the huge sum of money spent on cosmetic maintenance and surgery by both men and women in society today. This type of experience of shame as disgrace is again a reminder that we do not live in a perfect world. It is, however, important to distinguish to whom the shame belongs. In this case, the experience of shame does not belong to those who possess physical handicaps or imperfections but it is the whole of human beings who should claim the experience of shame associated with physical handicaps of people. In other words, physical handicaps and imperfections should not be perceived as their own flaws but flaws of the human race. I think that the physical handicaps and imperfections should be perceived as the sign of shame just like the embroidered letter "A" that Hester Prynne wore on her bosom to let everyone in her town know her status as adulterer. From this perspective, we can not see the other's physical handicap or imperfection as his/her inadequacy but as our own inadequacy. We can not have a condescending attitude toward others' physical handicaps or imperfections but have a sorrowful and humble attitude for our inadequacy before God as a human race as a whole.

One important remark should be made with respect to shame and Asian American experiences. Asian Americans often consider the Asian-ness in their physical condition an inadequacy or a flaw. Asian Americans are often ashamed of their physical attributes such as small physical stature, genetic appearance of having black "stubborn hair" which is not as easily styled as that of European Americans, small eyes, black or brown eyes as opposed to blue or green eyes, etc. Asian American churches must take this into consideration in their strategy for pastoral care and counseling. Asian Americans should be affirmed in their beauty and uniqueness as God's creation just as Americans from other ethnic backgrounds should experience the same. It is the church which can provide pride in one's physical attributes, because physical attributes, however different they may be among different races, are themselves gifts from God. In providing care to a particular Asian American, the pastor must therefore assess the extent to which individual carries shame related to his or her Asian physical attributes, in addition to helping him or her to grasp pride in possessing what God has granted him or her.

A third type of shame as disgrace is shame attributed to victims. Victims of verbal abuse, physical abuse, emotional abuse, sexual abuse, and other types of abuse have developed a sense of self that incorporates a flaw. They consider that a defect exists in themselves such that they consider themselves to be inadequate. They typically manifest low self-esteem. Because they consider themselves to be a shameful, any remark of criticisms about them, however minor it may be, will trigger the experience of intense shame. While it is obvious on paper to see that shame does not belong to the victim but to the aggressor, people often think that the victim deserves the violations that happened to him or her. People treat victims like Hester Prynne carrying an embroidered red letter "A" in her bosom. I think that they should instead be the reminder to us of the real existence of evil in this world. This evil force is not a mythological or metaphorical reality but its very existence is alive among and close to us. With victims, it is our responsibility to open our arms to them and comfort them that these abuses should not have happened to them and that they are as precious as Jesus to God. They do not deserve to carry shame with them but our compassion with them because God first provides compassion to them. Our effort also should be gathered in trying to remove evil forces in our lives so that we see increasingly fewer victims of abuse in our society.

The fourth type of shame as disgrace is the shame assigned to inferior groups determined by different "isms." "Isms" such as sexism, racism, classism, ageism, and other "isms" are used by one group of people in society to make another group of people feel inferior. For instance, women are shamed because they are born as women, the wrong sex, and treated as second-class people. In Asian communities, it is a well known fact that the belief in the inferiority of women to men is a strong controlling factor in society.[19] Women then live with inferior feelings about themselves, and shame becomes a part of their identity. Shame then becomes more of a woman's attribute whereas guilt becomes more of a man's attribute. The experience of shame has been downplayed because of patriarchal influence in society. Instead of looking at both womanly and manly attributes as strengths,[20] women are shamed because their attributes are considered to be of second class. They are further shamed if they do not develop any of the womanly attributes. Consequently, women live in double or triple jeopardy because they are shamed because they have feminine characteristics and further shamed if they have not developed feminine characteristics.

The same kind of analogy can be used with racism as well. People of color are thought of as less than perfect by people of non-color who consider themselves to be perfect people.[21] The color of one's skin is a gift from God and not a criterion for classifying people into different grades. People of color -- blacks, Asians, Hispanics, etc. -- are taught explicitly and implicitly to consider the color of their skin as the color of shame. The same is also true with people who are less educated, less prosperous, and have less specialized occupations. Some people are treated blatantly lower than others and learn to regard themselves to be inferior to others. Elderly people today also experience themselves as those who are out-dated and have not much to contribute to the society. They are considered as an inconvenience to society and are considered as less than perfect human beings. People who are led to feel inferior about themselves by different "isms" become the victims of social attitudes. They are treated like Hester Prynne carrying an embroidered red letter "A" upon her bosom.

These experiences of shame inform us of our nature, that we prefer to differentiate rather than to integrate in the name of imperialism. Our nature is that we would rather relate to others with power than in equality. Just like the shame of victims, the shame associated with racism reminds us of the very real existence of evil in this world. The shame associated with different types of "isms" should be the fuel for grasping the reality of evil in the society and for motivating ourselves to do away with those "isms." Our responsibility is to eliminate undeserving shame. We need to open our arms in Christian freedom as noted in the letter sent by the Apostle Paul to the Galatians: *There is neither Jew nor Greek, there is neither slave nor free, there is neither male nor female; for you are all one in Christ Jesus.* (Galatians 3:28) We must claim our own self-esteem as children of God who have received the grace of Jesus Christ. We must be able to transcend differences of sex, race, class, and age, and move away from the concept of inferior or superior. Indeed, we are all free from the bondage of classification of superiority or inferiority; we are all acceptable, precious, and special in God's eyes.

The shame associated with racism has an important implication for pastoral care and counseling among Asian Americans. It is not an overstatement to say that Asian Americans live with racism everyday, whether one is aware of it or not. From a baby taken to a day care center because his or her parents are at work; to an old lady living in a nursing home; from a woman cleaning a school building to a man teaching at the school; from a woman cleaning vegetables in Chinatown to a man owning a huge incorporated computer company; from an Asian gangster to a valedictorian; from a woman just arrived in the United States to a man who is fourth generation; and from a child at a friend's birthday party to a man at a business or scholarly conference, no Asian American can escape from the racism that is deeply embedded in the organic structure of this society. Pastoral care and counseling with Asian Americans must be able to address the damage done by racism and restore counselee from such damage. Although one may argue that racism is a social issue that should be dealt with outside the church, I am not of this opinion. God would not be pleased if the church ignores the wounds of its congregation incurred from racism. Extensive study and education regarding racism should take place in Asian American churches, and pastoral care and counseling must be informed by the study.

The fifth type of shame as disgrace is the shame associated with counter-society behavior and personal failures and abuses. The types of shame experiences noted above are mainly shame that is wrongly attributed by aggressors. The shame as disgrace with counter-society behavior and personal failures and abuses includes both wrongly attributed shame and self-triggered shame. Counter- society behavior such as eccentric hairstyles or attire or personal failures should not be treated as a mark of inadequacy. Instead, it should be treated as an individual's creative expression. What they are trying to convey through the eccentricity should be the focus of our concerns. In addition, personal failures should not be an occasion of pointing to inadequacy, but an occasion for people to gather together in support of the person. Personal abuses such as alcohol or drug abuse, however, are more associated with self-triggered shame. The shame associated with substance abuse is an appropriate experience which can be a motivating fuel for people to desire to be otherwise. Our responsibility is to sensitize such shame in order for people to find the motivation to stay away and move away from such abuse.

A specific kind of addiction which is more common in Asian American communities is noteworthy, and that is religious addiction. Asian Americans often use religion as an escape from shame, and religion becomes an addiction. John Bradshaw cautions us of the problem of "religious addiction." According to him, people with shameful feelings often have addictive problems, and religious piety may serve as a "mood-altering experience." In other words, people can be addicted to "feelings of righteousness."[22] Shameful experiences then promote religious behaviors, but this outward religious behavior does not reflect the true state of their maturity in faith. Asian American churches thus need to be cautious in distinguishing between genuine religious fervor and religious addiction which is a way to escape shame. The writers of both the Old Testament and the New Testament emphasize the importance of the uprightness of heart, as well as the consistency of the outer appearance with that which is in the heart (Deut. 11:13; Josh. 22:5; I Sam. 12:20; Deut. 13:3, 30:6; Matt. 22:37; Mk. 12:30; Lk. 10:27; I Sam. 16:7; Ps. 44:21; Ezek. 18:31; Matt. 5:8; Rom. 10:10, etc.). God is not concerned with only the outer appearances but looks at both the heart and the outer appearance. In fact God is more concerned with the heart. Consequently, the religious behavior does not mean anything unless it is caused by a love for God and others and not by the need to feel righteous. Again, mistreatment of shame results in sin, and idolatry -- love of the outward appearance of righteousness -- which Christianity works hard to prevent.

The sixth type of shame as disgrace is the shame associated with one's own wrong-doings against others. This type of shame as disgrace needs no more detailed explanations. These are illustrated with the shame Adam and Eve experienced after their disobedience to God. One significant point, however, is that aggressors who caused the shame of different types noted above themselves belong in this group. For instance, shame can be triggered when I make somebody, intentionally or unintentionally, feel inadequate for his or her social blunder, physical handicap, eccentricity, etc. While it is normal for aggressors to experience shame, it is also true that a fair amount of shamelessness is at work. When aggressors cause the experience of undeserving shame in others they often push away the sense of shame and believe that what they are doing is right. People need to be sensitized to shame as disgrace associated with wrong-doings to others so that we do not repeat the same wrong-doing to others. Shame as disgrace in this case then works as a corrective force in helping us to discontinue the sin we have committed.

Finally, a special kind of shame is shame associated, not with one's own inadequacy, but with that of one's family members or close ones. We experience shame when our family members or close ones experience the different types of shame explained above. One can say that one should not feel shame because he or she is not his or her brother, sister, mother, father, uncle, aunt, grandparent, or friend. This certainly is an individualistic approach which ignores more important aspects of this experience of shame. However painful this experience of shame caused by the shame of one's family member or close ones is, it unfolds a very important aspect of human nature. It reveals the communal nature of human beings, i.e., we are accountable to one another. We do not stand on our own feet alone. We stand together with our neighbors, including our family members and close ones. This accountability is consistent with what God wants us to be in Jesus' Great Commandment, *You shall love your neighbor as yourself.* (Matthew 22:39) This then is consistent with the conclusion made above that God would experience shame over our failures because God intends to be in communal relationship with us.

This is theologically sound and yet seems to have an internal flaw. What do we do with others' experience of shame if we are going to applaud it as a sound signal for our communal nature? Especially for Asian American communities whose social value puts so much emphasis on filial piety, how can we alleviate the excruciating nature of the pain associated with shame? Do we merely emphasize accepting the excruciating feelings of shame because Christians on this earth are supposed to experience suffering before the Kingdom of God is finally fulfilled? My response to this question is both yes and no. Yes, we must expect and accept suffering associated with Christian responsibility, being accountable for one another. Moreover, we celebrate the intensity of pain from experiences of loved ones' shame because the intensity of pain measures the depth or closeness of the relationship. But no, we do not just hold on to the suffering, but find freedom in the grace of Jesus Christ. Just as God through Jesus Christ intends to forgive us and indeed does forgive us, we also need to forgive others who cause this painful feeling of shame. With shame, therefore, grace is even more highlighted in order for us to relate to one another in freedom and to appreciate the experience of shame.

The discussion on shame as discretion and disgrace exhibits the conclusion that shame as discretion and disgrace is a blessing and not a curse, and holds positive characteristics. Shame is a signal, not a cause, for broken relationships. Shame, when faced honestly, informs us of our sinful nature and helps us to stay humble before God. Shame also draws boundaries of right and wrong, and works both as prevention and correction of our sins. With these findings, in order to conscientize ourselves about shame, we must make a commitment to the theological quest of determining which forms of shame involve sin and which do not. Christianity, therefore must broaden itself to include not only guilt language but also shame language in accounting for human sins.

4. Defending Against Shame

Even though a deeper analysis of shame shows shame as being positive in nature, the pain associated with shame causes people to hide from their shame. The Adam and Eve account in Genesis reveals how the experience of shame creates the need to defend against further shaming, as evidenced when Adam and Eve trying to cover their nakedness by tree leaves. People accordingly develop "defending strategies against shame." Gershen Kaufman's list of defending strategies is helpful. They include rage, contempt, striving for power and perfection, and the transfer of blame.[23] It is interesting to note that Capps in his book *Deadly Sins and Saving Virtues* has assigned anger as the sin caused by shame in the second stage of Erikson's eight epigenetic stages of life.[24] People use anger as a defending strategy in order to protect themselves from more shame by disconnecting any more influence from others. Patton is insightful in seeing that "the degree of its [anger's] intensity is an indicator of the degree of injury to the self."[25] In other words, anger reflects the painful nature of injury to oneself. Protection here means a shield from further relationships with others. This is precisely the reason that Capps sees anger as a deadly sin. Anger basically isolates one from another person's effort to reach out. Anger that is intended to cut off any negative reaction from others ends up cutting off any reaching out by others out of love. Anger eventually turns against oneself, as is evidenced in Dimmesdale's case.

In order to feel secure about one's own shame, one starts developing misconstrued judgments about others. People start looking down on others and enjoy finding fault with others. As long as others are viewed as more inferior, one's own feeling of inferiority are allayed. Thus people develop contempt as a protection against shame. People with contempt end up isolating themselves from others and are unable to have open relationships. Because of their degrading remarks and their condescending attitude, they are perceived as aggressors. In light of this analysis, however, such people are indeed the ones who need our understanding and support. In essence, these people who need more support from others, but lose that support because their attitude of contempt makes other people stay away from them.

Another form of defense against shame -- one may say that it is a cousin to contempt -- is the transfer of blame. While contempt is more of an everyday attitude of looking down on others, the transfer of blame is more specific and associated with particular events. In order to avoid one's own shame, one habitually shifts the focus of shame to another person. One does not accept any accountability for any of his or her actions that may trigger the experience of shame. One's own inadequacy or wrong-doings are not faced honestly but blamed on others or on situations so that the person is free of any responsibility. This transfer of blame is quite evident in the account of Adam and Eve in Genesis. When God asked Adam why he had taken fruit from the tree of knowledge of good and evil, Adam blamed Eve and told God, *"The woman whom you gave to be with me, she gave me fruit from the tree, and I ate."* (Genesis

3:12). When God asked Eve, *"What is this that you have done?"* Eve blamed the serpent and said, *"The serpent tricked me, and I ate."* (Genesis 3:13).

People also try to have power over others or to perfect themselves in order to hide their experiences of shame. Having power over others gives a secure feeling of superiority over others. It is, however, unfortunate that one relies more on a hierarchical relationship than an open relationship with others. In essence, while one's power over others is perceived as a protection from the experience of shame, it also shields the person from any relationship of mutuality. Along the same lines, striving for perfection is a way of minimizing one's inadequacies and attempting to reveal the perfect self. This drive to achieve perfection in all that one does is a kind of suicidal attempt. Since shame is never intended but happens unexpectedly, one works very hard to prevent it from happening and can still fail at it. As it was noted, the attempt for perfection is a fruitless or futile effort. It is also the most basic of sins, i.e., trying to be God.

These defending strategies against shame illustrate again and again how mistreated shame can aggravate a broken relationship. Kaufman, as noted above, refers to this disconnection of the relationship as "breaking the interpersonal bridge."[26] Lynd is accurate in warning us of the most damaging effect of mistreated experiences of shame, i.e., impersonalization and dehumanization. Lynd notes that people with shameful experiences try to avoid relationships with others and seek isolation. They are also faced with the difficulty of communicating their experiences of shame because of its elusive nature. Because of this double bind, Lynd suggests the possibility of impersonalization and dehumanization among those who suffer due to experiences of shame . Lynd states: "If I cannot communicate with others, then I will at least not risk openness; I will deny the possibility of openness; I will protect myself against it."[27] Lynd's warning to the human race is a warning to Christianity. Christianity is relationship -- our relationship with God and relationship to one another. Mistreated shame then challenges the very core of Christianity. If no openness is practiced among people, a meaningful relationship can not find its place among people, not even among Christians. A superficial relationship would prevail. People would not accept the fact that we grow in pain, joy, and love, and not out of a vacuum. Mistreated shame thus jeopardizes our relationship with God, although everyone is already exposed, so that our efforts to hide ourselves from God are fruitless.

Conclusion

Difficulties still exist and challenges yet remain. Shame is not well known nor well studied. There is no good tool by which people can communicate their experiences of shame; there are no discernible patterns that can describe the experiences of shame; there is no clear way to respond to shame; shame is an isolating experience; and shame is not easily traceable to causes. The challenge for Christianity is that Christianity must be able to embrace those who have experiences of shame and at the same time to eliminate causes of undeserving shame that put people into a predicament as noted above. These difficulties must not stop Christianity from delving into shame issues and developing ways to deal with these challenges. Two practical suggestions in this paper, therefore, are to sensitize people to shame while emphasizing grace and a commitment to a theological endeavor to determine which shames involve sin and which do not. Christianity must face shame honestly and help people name their experiences of shame in order for people to learn about their human nature truthfully. At the same time, it needs to emphasize grace in order for people to have a sense of acceptance of their inadequacies and worthy identity as one accepted by Jesus Christ. In addition, as people name their experiences of shame, Christianity also needs to discern which experiences of shame concern sin and which do not, so that shame can effectively work both as a preventive and a corrective of sins.

We must remember that "our Lord Jesus also suffered the shame of the Cross because He was put on public display as the recipient of God's wrath (2 Cor. 5:21; Heb. 12:2)."[28] Each of us should try to find comfort in sharing the shame that Christ experienced on the cross and also try to comfort each other. Lynd is accurate when she notes that although shame is a very difficult experience to share with others, the sharing of shame experiences brings closeness.[29] This then is consistent with the Christian emphasis on compassion. Through compassion, we can show mutual love for each other and provide a secure place to share the experiences of shame. This unconditional acceptance of the person who has experienced shame is, in fact, the radical grace that is shown by our Lord Jesus Christ who calls and challenges us to show such radical grace to others. By developing a compassionate relationship, "exposure without shame" as Lynd describes it, can be achieved.[30]

I would like to end this paper with a metaphor we can use to bring comfort to ourselves within our own experiences of shame and to comfort others with their experiences of shame.

> *The Lord God made for Adam and for his wife garments of skins, and clothed them.* --Genesis 3:20.

Just as Adam and Eve were exposed to God, we are still exposed to God even though we may be able to hide ourselves from others. We are naked before God and God clothes us and we will never be ashamed again.

Chapter Ten

The Eclectic Therapy for Korean Batterers

Young Hoon Hwang

Introduction

Consider this case: K is a 32-year-old Korean wife batterer and child abuser (beating and throwing his children to the ground) who has become paranoid. He has been in America for five years. He married his wife, who was a 1.5 generation Korean American, through a blind date. That was the reason why he could come to America. He was a high school graduate and working as a jewelry cutter in L.A. His wife, who graduated from junior college, was a full-time clerical worker in an American company.

From his early childhood he regularly witnessed his mother beaten by his alcoholic father. "Whenever my father came home with low feelings as usual, he drank and we got away from that place with fear. And then beating began to happen. We heard the screams of mother, father's shouting, curses, and beating sounds. We [his brother and sister] cried together with tears without knowing what to do. After it was finished, we had a dinner together, and then I usually went to the bathroom for diarrhea." He was also abused by his father and mother. Neither parent paid enough attention to him enough during his childhood, either.

Because he could not enjoy his family life, he wandered outside the home. He became a street kid and struggled to be the top fighter in his slum area. Other kids became his admiring followers. One day a guy who moved in from another village attacked him on the way to school. That guy thrust a three-pronged spear to K's neck and forced him to give in, while making fun of him and mocking him. He was so afraid of being killed that he surrendered before his followers.

K said it was such a shameful experience for him that he was sick for a few days and had nightmares and sweats every night. He said it was the most humiliating experience in his early life. This incident happened when he was in 5th grade. Even to the present, he sometimes dreams of becoming a huge giant to beat that attacker.

He has no endurance of others' criticism because he has become too sensitive to slights. He does not get along with others well; as a result, he can not maintain a durable job. His wife complains about his selfishness and his spending too much money to take care of his body for his health. He bought all sorts of expensive exercising tools and bought the best quality food for his health. After changing many jobs, he has begun to show slight symptoms of paranoia, saying that his wife and the whole world are trying to do harm to him. He also declares that "nobody loves me." He is a Christian. To quit from his habitual beating, he fasted for 10 days asking God to help him, but he failed . . . and he resumed beating his family.

Have you ever seen the dreadful scene in which a man beats, kicks and pushes her head on the wall; while the woman just receives all the beatings without resistance with bleeding and the children crying out with fear and shaking their bodies in helplessness . . .

It is such inhumane and destructive behavior. However, why should such physical violence keep taking place in marriage and family relationships? Are there any solutions to root out or at least to lessen battering behaviors?

I worked at a Korean Marriage and Family Counseling Center in Los Angeles as a counselor and was shocked when I found out that the number of Korean batterers tops the list of the Los Angeles Police Department's "Battering Crime List". Why is the number of Korean batterers top in spite of a lesser density of population than Americans, Mexicans and other minority peoples? Why does a man beat his partner? How does one counsel batterers? These questions will be the main issues to be dealt with in this essay.

Why Do Men Batter?

The extent and nature of batterers' violence differ. The men are all the "everyday" type batterer. They come from a vast cross section of classes and occupations and display a diversity of personality temperaments and styles.

There are so many theories to explain for wife abuse, but three theoretical positions are generally acknowledged: "psycho-analytic", "social learning," and "sociopolitical theories." The psychoanalytic theories focus on stress, anxiety and anger instilled during child rearing. The social learning theories consider the abuse to be an outgrowth of learned patterns of aggressive communication. The sociopolitical theories hold the patriarchal power plays of men oppressing women to be at the heart of wife abuse.[1]

1. Psychoanalytic Approaches

This approach is the "insight model." This model is the traditional approach to understanding violence. In K's case psychoanalytic theorists will search for psychological causal factors associated with K's wife abuse. They will focus on K's psychopathology to deal with K's battering behavior.

The theme of this approach is that certain intrapsychic problems give rise to violent behavior. The list of intrapsychic problems is long: poor impulse control, low frustration tolerance, fear of intimacy, fear of abandonment, dependency, underlying depression, and impaired ego functioning resulting from developmental trauma.[2] These symptoms are believed to be the result of earlier developmental problems such as rejection by one or both parents, overdependency on the mother, fear of the father, failure to relate well with peers, and so on. This approach seeks to help the abusive man become more aware of how he has been affected by past experiences so that he can learn to respond more appropriately and consciously to present relationship.

Many theorists claim that parent-child dynamics play an important role in wife-battering. Shults suggests in his research on men who tried to kill their wives that "abusive men transfer their dependency needs from their mothers to their wives and then lash out when their wives cannot or will not meet these needs."[3] From this viewpoint I will illuminate the relation between "narcissistic rage" and "battering" in terms of object relations theory and Kohut's view of self psychology.

Psychopathology of the Self

Major psychologists agree that self psychology is the result of the personality of the parents and not of specific events in the life of the child.

Kohut's view is that parental self pathology generates self pathology in the child through insufficient mirroring and inadequate response by the self-object to idealization. When the emerging, fragile self of a child experiences traumatic, sudden, unempathetic failures or rejections by a self-object, the healthy grandiosity and idealizing functions of the nuclear self will be damaged by psychic splitting or repression. They are not internalized as accessible parts of the self. Then the person is left feeling enfeebled, weak, defective at his core, and highly vulnerable to attack or violation, for one of the constructive elements of a cohesive self has been lost or damaged.[4] The child, then, evolves without adequate response to his ambitions and ideals, and frequently develops with impoverishment, depletion of his nuclear self. Such persons present with a grandiosity which defensively covers an emptiness of self, an absence of attainable ambitions, sustaining ideals, or meaningful affirming personal relations.[5] Due to unrealistic goals, they repeat failures and they feel empty and worthless.

Narcissistic Disorder

Kohut basically divides narcissistic disorders into two categories: narcissistic behavior disorders and narcissistic personality disorders. Referring to Mr. X's behavior (Kohut, 1977, pp. 199-219), Kohut explains narcissistic behavior disorders. Mr. X's insistent claims for attention and praise, his arrogant superiority are not manifestations of the specific personality structure -- characterized by simple deficiencies due to insufficient mirroring attention in childhood -- but the manifestation of a sector of his personality that was isolated from his nuclear self by a "vertical split" -- a split that had come about not because of a lack of mirroring attention in childhood but because of a specific fault in his mother's responses to him.[6]

The root cause of Mr. X's behavior disorder was his mother's excessive approval of her son. Her mirroring had not been selected to develop an independent self. She manipulated her son to retain him within her own personality organization and to satisfy her own defects of the self.

This process is very similar to the overindulgence of a caretaker in object relations theory. A developmental object relations theory provides a framework for this process. It says that in normal development the separation-individuation stage is immediately preceded by the symbiotic stage. Symbiosis can be defined as an interdependent relationship in which the combined energies of both partners are necessary for the existence of each.[7] This stage is very similar to Kohut's primary narcissism. This stage will support the fertile soil in which ego development takes place.

After completing this symbiotic stage, the caretaker (usually mother) has to help the child with a positive attitude to get through the separation-individuation stage. During this phase (usually 18 to 36 months) the child experiences his separateness in many ways and the child's sense of individual entity and identity -- the image of the self as an object -- develops.[8] However, if the mother clings to the child to prevent separation, discouraging moves toward individuation by manipulating her child, then the child will fail to develop the essential characteristics of individuation. When the child is continuously threatened with the withdrawal of mother's support, he/she will form defects in personality structure. There is a consensus among clinicians about the observed phenomena referred to as difficulties with the self: poor self-regulation, low self-esteem, and inhibition of self-expression.[9]

One of the distinctive characteristics of the Korean family structure is the closeness of the relationships among family members, especially between mother and child. Korean families emphasize a continuous relationship between parents and children, whereas American families encourage children to develop independence and autonomy. The Korean mother-child relationship can be described as an "enmeshed relationship" in which the processes of separation-individuation are blocked.[10] I think this enmeshed relationship is due not only to social tradition, but also the lack of women's real self.

Korean women have experienced long dehumanizing suffering and have been afflicted under the systems of patriarchy and sexism. Korean women have had to live under self-negating and self-destructive cultural rules and customs. Because there has been no ground on which Korean women could unfold their dreams, as a result, they derive their pride from their children's accomplishments. They totally devote themselves to their children's development and well-being.

Various studies show how deeply the enmeshed relationship between parents and children is rooted in the Korean mentality. For example, according to a study of 561 Korean mothers from both rural and urban areas who were under thirty-nine years of age, *89.5% of them answered that they would die for their children; 97. 2% answered that their children's success meant their own success; and 94% believed in their own sacrifice for their children.*[11]

We have learned that a mother's acknowledgment of the child's emerging self is necessary and indispensable for the development of the child's self. Through appropriate response and optimal frustration, the child's self needs to be differentiated from the symbiotic matrix of the mother-infant relationship. However, Korean mothers over-accept and encourage their children's narcissistic-exhibitionistic grandiosity for a longer period of time. Korean child-rearing is highly child centered. Korean mothers continue to accept children's self-centeredness beyond the appropriate period and this self-centeredness later becomes "selfishness." Korean mothers frustrate the development of children's emerging selves under the mask of protection through overindulgence and over-acceptance. As a result, Korean children usually fail to develop autonomy and independence. And then the self becomes a weakened self.

I believe the mother is not the only one to blame. When we remember that most batterers have been abused and deprived as children, we can easily guess that there must be traumatic damage in the battered child's self. We have learned that the real healthy self emerges and develops under the appropriate acceptance and optimal frustration. When this process fails to work, there is a split between the healthy self, which is impaired, and the false defensive selves. In addition, "the false defensive selves are based on fantasy, not reality, and their principal function is not to cope with reality as such but to defend against painful effects at the cost of reality."[12]

The separation-individuation phase is the stage in which the child begins to exercise aggressive impulses as a sign of the child's trials for differentiation. The chronic child battering which is beyond his ability to cope with will damage the child's weak self and will bring out a narcissistic personality disorder. When the child is battered by the father, the principal psychic mechanisms at work are those of resentment and hostility against frustrations inflicted by the parents, which are the psychological results caused by the caretaker's punishment.

This chronic and unexpected response might cause the processes of narcissism to begin in the child's psyche. In an embarrassing and humiliating situation the child is caught off guard. The child does not have any firm ego boundaries to protect him/herself; the self is easily damaged by a shameful experience. The sudden and unexpected exposure of vulnerable aspects of a child's self will create a lack of self-esteem in a child, especially in the period of "autonomy vs. shame and doubt." When the positive side of this stage is shrunk, the negative side of "shame and doubt" will grow.

For the narcissistic personality all others exist to fill his needs. Narcissistic patients are characterized by a specific vulnerability: their self-esteem is unusually labile and, in particular, they are extremely sensitive to failures, disappointments and slights.[13] In their later lives, refusal of a demand is likely to be categorized as evidence of the partner (wife)'s indifference, insensitivity, incompetence, and sadism.[14] When they are frustrated, the patient is likely to react with narcissistic rage. Narcissistic rage, which is intense aggression encountered in narcissistic disorders, can be recognized as the response of the vulnerable self to a variety of injuries. Kohut explains narcissistic rage:

> *In every infant there is* nondestructive aggressiveness which is a part of the assertiveness of the demands of the rudimentary self, and it becomes mobilized whenever optimal frustrations are experienced. Under normal circumstances it develops to mature forms of assertiveness in which aggression is subordinated to the performance of tasks. If, however, the infantile basic needs for omnipotent control over the self-object had been chronically and traumatically frustrated in childhood, then chronic narcissistic rage will be established.[15]

Rage is reaction to failures of traumatic degree in the empathic responsiveness of the self-object vis-a-vis a self the child is beginning to experience. All narcissistic personality types are capable of flying into rages. They have this capability in common and it may represent a regression to a diffuse infantile rage in the face of severe feelings of narcissistic injury. His feelings of helplessness which he had experienced as a child often turned to rage. Though he is careful not to release his narcissistic rage toward others, he can blow out his rage when he meets an appropriate partner such as wife or children.

Burnstein classifies four types of narcissistic personalities: the craving, the paranoid, the manipulative and the phallic narcissistic personalities.[16] The craving personality includes many people who have been called "dependent" or "passive aggressive". Indeed, their interpersonal relationships are characterized by the need to have others support them. They are clinging, demanding, often pouting and whining.[17]

Bursten says the essential features of their personalities can often be seen in their marriages. They seem to function well outside, but they collapse at home unless their wives give them a great deal of attention. I believe that narcissistic rage can be turned into aggressive violence.

2. The Social Learning Approaches

Social learning theory sees problem behaviors such as violence as socially learned. In this case social learning theorists will pay attention to the presence of violence in K's family of origin. K learned to be violent by being a participant in his violent family.

Learning about violence starts with physical punishment in the family. In Korea physical punishments such as spanking and beating typically begin in infancy to correct and teach. There is an old Korean saying, "Give one more piece of cake to a dumb boy, give one more whip to a good boy." That plus "Spare the rod and spoil the child" are very popular sayings. By being hit, they will unconsciously learn that it is morally right to hit others, when something is really important. And using violence will become a fundamental part of their individuals's personality.

These experiences with physical punishment lay the groundwork for the normative legitimacy of all types of violence in the later life. Family is not the only place to learn violent behaviors. Students are whipped for "better education" at school, because traditionally beating and whipping has been regarded as a way of education. Physical punishment is a mechanism which is believed to help reinforce societal expectations and proper behavior in Korea. We often hear news that

Korean immigrant parents are arrested as child abusers for behavior which is common in Korea.

Social learning of violence does not stop at high school. We reach the climax of violence in the army. Every Korean man must join the army for nearly three years. It is mandatory in Korea. During that period Korean men fully learn how to be tough, strong and courageous, how to endure ordeals and how not to feel feeble emotions nor vulnerability. In the army they learn that human beings are nothing but animals, because they realize that by being beaten up we can be made to obey and listen to our superiors. They learn how to control inferiors and how to make them obey easily through violence. They learn that violence is the best means of control in order to make something happen.

How about the Korean political situation? After the liberation from Japan in 1945, Korea has hardly had a non-military government except for few years. The military government has been controlling politics, economics, education and everything for nearly 40 years. Military slogans such as, "If it is impossible, then make it be possible!", "There is no reason, just obedience!", "Knock it dead with one chop!", "Just obedience unto death!", operate in public society. The working theories of a military culture have been applied to the all corners of our daily life. When something does not work via communication, people usually resort to physical violence. It is not uncommon to see a free fight during the session of the National Assembly, and this year's Assembly was adjourned by blood fighting between assembly men. It is a shameful story to share, but this is the reality in which Koreans have been brought up.

They learn from a young age that violence is a successful means of ending disputes in our daily life. Men are systematically socialized into violence as a problem-solving technique in order to maintain their privilege in a society. The examples of governmental violence (police toughness, brutality of soldiers while dealing with demonstrating students, the widespread practice of physical punishment in the schools, etc.) provide powerful models for the behavior of individual citizens. They implicitly deliver the message that violence can and should be used to attain socially desirable ends. Korean cultural norms legitimize the use of violence in every situation.

This approach claims that socially learned violence can be dealt with by a cognitive-behavioral model. In this approach violence is the primary focus of treatment. Since violence is a learned behavior, nonviolence can similarly be learned, according to the cognitive-behavioral model. This approach tends to view battering generally as a skills deficit or a stress management problem. Their emphasis on skills deficits is reflected by their use of "anger management," "conflict containment," "stress control," or "men and anger" to publicize their counseling groups.[18] The majority of interventions are aimed at helping abusers better manage their anger, cope with stress, and to improve communication skills. Systematic relaxation training or assertion training are emphasized in this approach.

3. Sociopolitical Approaches

This approach claims that violence grows out of the nature of social structure. In this approach it is important to understand how society works and how social life affects our relationships. This approach links wife abuse to social norms and cultural values that "legitimize the sexist structure of male/female power relations and men's prerogative to use force against their wives."[19]

If we examine the Korean situation with this viewpoint, then, we will see that the seeds of Korean men's battering lie in the subordination of females and in their subjection to male authority and control.[20] I believe the systems of *patriarchy, hierarchy* and *sexism* are major social factors which have contributed to producing battering of women in Korea.

Patriarchy

If we say that patriarchy is any system that runs on a hierarchical principle, with the "Top man" invested with absolute power over those under him[21], then the Korean family structure is nearly a perfect hierarchical structure of the patriarchal family. Under the influence of more than 600 years of Confucianism, which emphasizes hierarchical order and obedience to higher authority, the Korean father as head of a family exercises total authority and power in his family. Naturally, absolute obedience to the family head is required from the family members. For example, Confucianism teaches three basic important human relations: In the relationship between sovereign and subject, a subject should *obey* his sovereign because the sovereign is the standard of the subject. Secondly, in the relationship between father and son, a son should *obey* his father because the father is the standard of the son. Finally in the relationship between husband and wife, a wife should *obey* her husband because the husband is the standard of the wife.

We see that Confucianist teachings emphasize *obedience* in human relationships, which concept could be easily distorted into domination, control and manipulation -- particularly in that of husband and wife. In this hierarchical pattern, authority comes from the top down and man as the head of the family has the right to dominate and control women. Women are considered to be by their nature obedient to men. We find out, predictably, that the Korean marriage relationship is hardly mutual or equal.

Sexism

Sexism, the belief that men are superior to women, is bias, prejudice or discrimination based on gender.[22] But Koreans think men's superiority is given to them from heaven, and that it is natural. There is an old saying, "Namjonyobi", which means that man is higher and noble, and woman is lower and ignoble. There are many reasons for this belief, but one major reason is the Korean family system based upon genealogical succession through the son. The most important family concern is perpetuity of the line through the birth of a male successor. This concern is still so pervasive in Korean society that the birth of a female infant may cause some degree of dismay. Because of the preference for boys over girls, after discerning the fetus's gender became a widespread medical practice, a disproportionate number of boys were born within the next generation. That tendency becomes problematic in elementary school. It is right now becoming a social issue in Korea.

Equality does not exist in marriage in Korea. For hundreds of years vicious ethical codes were established for women and put into practice. The woman's life was totally in the hands of a man. The traditional Korean society demanded too much endurance of difficult situations and self-sacrifice to sustain their false view of womanly virtue. As the old saying goes, to lead a successful marriage life in the husband's household, women should be "dead for three years, dumb for three years, and blind for three years."

A woman without feelings, without a mouth, and without her own will was the ideal image of woman in Korea. Until now, these kinds of womanly images have been pervasive and strongly demanded in Korean society. In every aspect of social life sexism is working without notice, because it is deeply entrenched into Korean concepts and ways of thinking. In this kind of culture Korean men are brainwashed into believing it is their right to lead and to exercise power over women.

With the change in the times, there has been some extension of women's rights; however, there is still a long way to go. One Korean doctor, after examining patients diagnosed with *Hwa-byung* (anger syndrome = depression), surveyed the underlying conditions of traumatic shock and anger. Some findings include the followings.

> 1) Women outnumbered men by a ratio of 49 to 12, and the majority were in their late 30's.
> 2) The causes of anger were identified as follows: All the women but one felt anger and shock due to domestic problems, the most frequent being husband's battering and extramarital affairs; whereas, all the men but one were angry due to disappointment in social life.[23]

As this report indicates, Korean women still suffer from physical abuse. It is reported that 51% of Korean husbands have the experience of beating up their wives.[24] I think the real percentage is higher than this one. Working with Korean couples has disclosed that many wives of urban middle-class and upper-class families conceal physical abuses by their husbands because of a sense of shame or fear of possible harm to their husbands' social position. It can be inferred that physical abuses take place among middle and upper class couples to a larger extent than reported.

These kinds of mal-structures of society force domestic violence to bloom in a hothouse.

What is the Major Factor in Wife Beating?

Psychological approaches suggest that wife abuse results from abnormal behavior. However, the widespread prevalence of physical abuse indicates that it may be more a function of the normal psychological patterns of most men than of abnormal personalities.[25] This approach explains that loss of control, poor impulse control, low frustration tolerance and low self-esteem are used to explain the violence. Then one may ask a question: does increasing self-esteem really get rid of battering problems? I do not think so. Especially this approach might give batterers a chance to find excuses to blame their parents or wives instead of taking responsibility for what they have done to wives. There should be a challenge to violence. In this sense, purely psychological explanations of battering are not enough.

How about the cognitive-behavioral approach? The merit of this model is that it directly deals with the battering itself. However, many men who have been victims of physical violence do not become batterers. The major weakness is that this approach does not see the larger picture of the problem. As feminists claim, this approach ignores the important power and control dimensions of wife abuse.

Men do not exercise violence every time they get angry. It depends upon with whom they are interacting. The status and gender of the persons will decide their release of anger by violence. Some research has shown that men are better listeners when interacting with male coworkers and other male peers than when with female coworkers or their spouses.[26] Abusive men's attitudes with bosses will be different from those toward battered women. The violent husband's selectivity for abusive behavior supports the theory that men's violence is deeply involved with power issues.[27] The sociopolitical theory asserts that wife abuse must be addressed as an ingrained social problem. The notions of patriarchy and sexism are enacted most strongly and unconsciously in wife abuse. The major issue is dominant-submissive power relationships which are easily turned into violence. It seems that violence is built into the very structure of the society and the family system.

How does the child's self become a defective and damaged self? It is when the weak self experiences the critical damage of power abuse by parents or others. How do they learn to exercise violence? They learn it when they see the powerful beats the powerless. Just dealing with assaulting husbands is not enough. These hazardous social structures should be challenged and changed into healthy social structures. This is the only way to root out the tragedy of our society thoroughly.

New Model to Counsel Batterers

Psychoanalytic and cognitive-behavioral therapies have been popular approaches to deal with batterers. However, feminist therapists' claim that wife abuse has to be viewed as a result of the dominant-submissive power relationships in patriarchal and sexist society challenges us. Changing the vicious social systems will be a more fundamental solution to the problem of wife-beating.

Women are victims of current sociopolitical systems. I fully agree with this claim. However, I believe that Korean men are also victims of sociopolitical systems in a sense. The degree of women's suffering is far severer than that of men. My question is, however, how many men are enjoying wielding their power in patriarchal and hierarchical society? I believe men suffer and should be liberated from the bondage of hazardous social systems.

There are well-developed theories of feminist therapy for battered women, but not many for batterers. We will borrow some concepts of feminist therapy to develop theories of therapy for batterers. For this model, psychoanalytic and behavioral therapies will be used together for a better counseling. We will seek to connect our psychological analysis and behavioral insights with understanding of the sociopolitical theories. Men's liberation's therapeutic technique here will be one of education: batterers could learn to live with a new, more rewarding set of social values.

Korean Men's Harmful Adaptation

Is it too much saying that Korean men are also the victims of a patriarchal, hierarchical, and sexist society? Korea is becoming a modern technical-industrial society. Korean fathers hardly have a time to spend with their children. It is perplexing that there is no appropriate model of manhood to follow. In this environment boys cannot achieve a masculine sexual identity. Boys rarely experience fathers as sources of warm, soft nurturance. The most salient adult available for the boy is his mother. What does it mean to be male in this environment? In this sense the overly idealized sex roles have been imposed on Korean children. This process of "masculinization" must be abrupt, and the boy's male sexuality becomes a compulsive masculinity.

Korean men also becomes the victims of sexism. In every stage of man's socialization process, they have to kill "the tenderness and loving-kindness and take on aggressiveness as the symbol of our male identity."[28] Traditionally men have been expected to be physically strong, instrumental, lacking in emotions and relating to women in a dominant manner.[29] If a man shows that kind of tenderness, he is called "sissy." From childhood men hear, "Boys should never cry!", "Do not show your tears!", "Boys are not sissies!". Men tend to disassociate themselves from femininity and despise it in others. The accusation of "sissy" while growing up teaches boys to deny "feminine" feelings early on and engenders a rejection of open relationships. Korean men are taught that real men are not allowed to express or to reveal one's feelings. Especially in the army, men learn that manhood means bravery, and man should suffer in silence without complaint. Men learn to destroy the feminine characteristics of feelings.[30]

William S. Coffin says that men who repress in themselves the feminine side of their nature, will generally, in more or less subtle ways, be anti-feminine.[31] As we are not allowed to express our feelings freely, we have lost touch with our real emotions. Since there has been no proper outlet to express our emotions, our emotions and feelings are not only oppressed but also distorted.

During five thousand years of Korean history, the Korean people have suffered severe oppression and exploitation under the tyranny of various rulers, both foreign and domestic. Korean men have been seeking power for a long time. After the Korean war Korea accomplished a rapid economic development within a few decades, creating many side effects. A human being's value is evaluated by his/her wealth and status. The Korean man as the head of a family has the heavy responsibility of supporting his family. The man's role is just work and success. Work is seen as the primary criterion of a man's worth and self-esteem. While growing up, we often heard that a man who cannot feed his wife and children is not a man. Korean men always have been chased by the compulsively imposed sex role of a man. If he fails to meet the ideological aspect of this socially imposed sex role, he is humiliated. When a man feels threatened and devalued at work or when he loses his job, it is devastating and extremely shameful for him. Traditionally, Koreans show extraordinary concern for "*Chemyon*," which refers to "face", "prestige", or "honor". As a man, he never asks for help to save his "*Chemyon*" even though he might starve to death. Korean men feel tremendous shame when they lose face. After retiring, Korean men die sooner than Korean women because they think they are worthless as a man if they are not working. In America the immigrant husband who once was a strong leader in Korea is not a head of the family anymore. Because of language and cultural problems, a significant proportion of Korean immigrant husbands experience a downward occupational mobility after arriving in the U.S., and usually it is very difficult to get a stable job in the beginning of immigrants' residency in their new home. Therefore, these kinds of downward mobility and unstable job situations damage their self-esteem, in addition to inferiority complexes due to language problems and racial inferiority as a marginal people. If we consider that employment and financial problems (stresses) are contributors to family violence, I think it is very easy for a Korean man to get hurt and exercise physical force under the influences of the overly imposed patriarchal role and their mal-adaptation to American society.

In the hierarchical business world, one's ability as a family provider is minimal; it is beating another competitor that lifts one higher in the poor structure. Only a few manage to win big at this game. Consequently, men are left to exercise their courage in the one domain left to them: their home.

I wondered why Korean culture became a "drinking culture." Come to think of it, men do not learn to express their emotions and to share what we feel to others. When men are sane, they hide most of their emotions and feelings. Korean men hardly express their heart because they are taught that real men do not show their real heart to others. Only women show their hearts to others. But while drinking, men pour out what is inside of them freely. Most of the time the suppressed emotions explode in somewhat distorted ways, and it becomes misconduct affected by alcohol. The Korean society generously accepts the drunken rowdiness because that is the way of solving and expressing the oppressed feelings. The problem is that when those feelings come out, they are displayed in distorted ways. Nelson says that the emotional damage done to men through the deprivation of feelings is enormous, and it takes its toll in violence.[32] Korean men are totally deprived of expressing their emotions and feelings, and they therefore have emotional damage. When the damaged emotions -- especially the anger -- come out, the frozen and distorted anger is displayed by violence. Joy M. K. Bussert says, "When threatened or hurt, they should learn to "stand up and fight like a man." Being deprived of human tears (I think tears could be emotions), they, in turn, victimize women as a means to live out this impossible cultural assignment to control the feminine within themselves."

From these aspects Korean men are double-bonded and heavy burdened under the compulsively imposed roles of the larger systems. In this sense Korean batterers are also the victims of a patriarchal and sexist society.

Theological Implications of Battering, the Abuse of Power

What can be theological implications for the issue of battering? We learned that violence is the result of power imbalances and controlling. In this sense Genesis 1:26-27 and the story of the Fall will help us to reshape men's distorted views on power and dominion. Genesis 1:26-27 says, "Then God said, 'let us make human being in our image, after our likeness, and let them have dominion over the fish of the sea. . . ' and so God created human being in his/her image, in the image of God created he him male and female, created he them."

Our basic terms here are the Hebrew "tselem," which translates into the Greek "eikon" and English "image," and the Hebrew "damuth," which in Greek is rendered as "homoioma," "likeness." Theologians agree that there is no essential difference between "image" and "likeness."

There are many meanings of the concept of image of God. Traditionally, it has referred to the very meaning of our humanity. It points to all the characteristics whereby the human being surpasses the animals. One characteristic of the image of God could be that human beings are speaking creatures. God never speaks to the creatures except the human creatures. "This is the one to whom God has made a peculiarly intense commitment (by speaking) and to whom marvelous freedom has been granted (in responding)."[33]

Another meaning of the concept is human beings' powers of self-transcendence and freedom. This means that the human being is a rational, moral, and religious agent. We are free agents to shape our own destiny within the limits of creaturehood. We can say that the concept of the image of God means, in essence, women and men's freedom of transcendence under God. This freedom is manifested in his power of reasoning and the power to analyze one's experience and learn from it. Ultimately this power of freedom, or transcendence, especially manifests itself in human beings' awareness of God as the Other. In all these matters, man remains free to shape one's own destiny within the limits of creaturehood. Of course, the freedom of human being is not absolute as that of God. There is nothing here of coercive or tyrannical power for humankind.[34]

However, the story of Fall says that Adam abused this power of self-transcendence wrongly. Adam did not recognize the limits of creaturehood. The first human beings wanted to exercise power as God does. As sinners, human beings cannot exercise power appropriately. They begin to abuse the power which God gives.

Human beings are like his/her God in that there is a dignity in every human being which is an engraved image of God. Violence could be the worst sin, because it consists of not recognizing the true worth and dignity of our neighbor. "Imago dei" implies the worth, the dignity, and therefore all kinds of rights and freedom which should not be violated by one's fellow human beings. In domestic violence, the male abuses power between himself and the female to dominate and to control the female. The problem is that men do not see and do not want to see that all human beings are created in the divine image, and they abuse perversely the power which God has given us. Batterers should realize that they are destroying not only their partners but also God, who is with them in the form of the image of God. "Imago dei" implies that we should seek to love all for their intrinsic worth, to give their rights for which we are created. This involves striving for justice.

Dominion

The dominion of human beings is the exercise of those powers with which human beings were endowed by God when God created them in God's image. Human beings were endowed in creation with the responsibility to exercise dominion over nature, not over human beings. The "dominion" here mandated is with reference to the animals. The dominance is that of a shepherd who cares for, tends, and feeds the animals. In this sense dominion accompanies responsibility. Thus the task of "dominion" has nothing to do with exploitation, control and abuse.

It has to do with the well-being of every other creature. The problem is that men exercise their dominion perversely. By exercising violence they demolish the structure of human relationships ordered by God.

A Christian understanding of dominion must be discerned in the way of Jesus Christ. The one who rules is the one who serves. Lordship means servanthood. It is the task of the shepherd not to control but to lay down his life for the sheep (John 10:11). In verse 27 we should note that human being is spoken of as "singular"(he created him) and "plural"("he created them"). This peculiar formula makes an important affirmation. On the one hand, humankind is a single entity. All human persons stand in solidarity before God. But on the other hand, humankind is a community, male and female. Only in community of humankind God is reflected. God is not mirrored as an individual but as a community.[35]

From this viewpoint, Bernard Loomer's two conceptions of powers are very helpful to understand what kinds of power human creatures are supposed to exercise in human community.

Traditionally, power has been defined as "the ability to produce an effect."[36] In actual human level power means the capacity to actualize one's potentialities for good or evil. The heart of this traditional view is the conception of power as "the strength to exert a shaping and determining influence on the other, whatever and whoever the other might be."[37] Although this definition is just one aspect of power, we cannot deny that the status or worth of individuals or groups has been measured by how much power they can wield. The practice of this kind of power has caused inequalities of life and led to life-denying injustices. Loomer defines this kind of power as "unilateral power," which is the ability to produce intended or desired effects in our relationships to nature or other people." More specifically, it is "the capacity to influence, guide, adjust, manipulate, shape, control, or transform the human or natural environment in order to advance one's own purposes."[38] As we see, this is one-sided, non-relational and non-mutual. The main problem of this kind of power is to produce a desired effect on the other for one's own purpose. It is destructive and "its ideal is control."[39] The oppressor exercises all the powers in the systems of patriarchy, sexism, racism, and classism. Its end results are the demolition of relationships and self-alienation within the oneself.

The alternative conception of power is relational power. This is the ability both to produce and to undergo effect.[40] Under unilateral power the worth of an individual is measured by the range of that individual's ability to influence others.[41] An active openness for a creative transformation of ourselves and world is the other component of relational power, and that point is a genuine meaning of power. When we accept this aspect of power, there comes true and mutual relationship.

God gave us freedom. The individual's self-creativity is an expression of the strength of this freedom. When we exercise one-sided power, it blocks freedom of the other, and its result is non-mutuality. "Relational power is the capacity to sustain an internal relationship. The sustaining does not include management, control, or domination. Rather, it involves the persistent effort to create and maintain relationship as internal."[42] Domestic violence is the worst form of unilateral power, and we must work for batterers to be ones who will exercise relational power.

The Song of Paul, from Saul to Paul

From a persecutor to a liberator = From a batterer to a liberator"

Prior to his conversion, Paul was the persecutor of Christians. He was devoted to the Law as a student of Judaism, following the direction of the Pharisees. By his own account, he was a zealous legalist, a "Hebrew of Hebrews." He must have begun to hear about the new "sect" that was filling Jerusalem. Due to his zeal and natural ability he soon became a leader in persecuting the church. His blindness led him to persecute the community of the crucified God. He "began ravaging the church, entering house after house; and dragging off men and women, he would put them in prison" (Acts 8:3).

However, on the way to Damascus, he met Jesus Christ: "he was approaching Damascus, . . . suddenly a light from heaven flashed around him; and he fell to the ground, and heard a voice saying to him, 'Saul, Saul, why are you persecuting Me? . . . It is hard for you to kick against the goads'" (Acts 9:3-4; 26:14). Paul had not known that the people whom he was persecuting were children of God. Paul had not known that his persecution of Christians was tantamount to opposing God. Paul had not known the fact that persecuting people was hurting himself like kicking against goads. Through this event he came to know the truth, and Saul was marvelously and eternally transformed. His job had been changed from a persecutor to a proclaimer of the good news. He finally became a liberator.

Because Korean batterers are so deeply entrenched in the thoughts of patriarchal and sexist systems, they do not know what they are doing. "Men's therapy for batterers" will play the role of the light of the truth, which Saul received from God on the way to Damascus. Batterers will experience a kind of "conversion." Similar to a religious conversion, the "converts" will see themselves saved from the bondage of vicious social systems. They eventually become "true believers" and will become "witness" to the world. The counselor will play the role of Ananias, who helped Paul to regain his sights and strength.

This therapy and the counselor will not satisfy only to help Saul stop persecuting God's people. The goal of this therapy is not only to help batterers to quit battering, but also to change batterers to be proclaimers of the good news. That will be the end result of this therapy.

Counseling for Batterers

While the focus of early treatment is on the identification and elimination of violent behaviors, later interventions will focus more on personal transformation. Here, I will use Mr Kim's case whereby I will unfold the "The Eclectic Therapy for Batterers." (The Batterer = Mr. Kim)

1. Challenging the Denial

Korean batterers are reluctant to admit that they have a problem and hardly accept responsibility for their behaviors, because wife-beating is not a big deal in Korea. They are excused for their abusive behavior.

When the counselor questions about the violence, the counselor will assume that excuses will arise. Just listening dispassionately might give the impression to the batterer that it is all right to beat one's wife. The counselor will not keep on confronting the batterer, but, if it is needed, the counselor can take a more assertive approach toward the batterer. That attitude will challenge the batterer that violence is a serious matter. Therefore, the first step is to help the batterer take responsibility for his behavior.

Domestic Abuse Project of Minnesota invented a "Violent Behavior Inventory" questionnaire.[43] While answering that questionnaire, the batterer begins to accept that he has a problem. If the batterer is a Christian, the counselor can share the theological implications of battering with him. The counselor should clearly deliver definitions of violence. The feminist model defines violence more broadly as any act that causes the victim to do something she does not want to do. Intimidating acts such as punching walls, and psychological abuse such as yelling, swearing, sulking, and angry accusation, are regarded as violence.[44] Throughout this session, the batterer must be reminded that he is responsible for his behavior.

2. Building a Trusting Relationship.

It is a little bit difficult to have a trusting relationship in the beginning session. As we mentioned above, the counselor's confrontative attitude might result in defensive and superficial responses from the batterer. Sometimes the batterer will quit counseling.

Baker Fleming explains:

> "Critical to working with abusive men is finding a basis for identification with them, their goals, aspirations, frustrations and being empathetic with their plight. In general, men are conditioned to believe that the need for counseling or therapy is a sign of weakness or inadequacy, so that it is vital to establish a basis for trust."[45]

More empathy for the man's position may also be a prerequisite for a counseling for batterers. The more experience the counselor grasps the experience of men who batter, the more likely the batterer will be to accept treatment and to develop the desire to change.

3. Behavioral Change to avoid Violent Behavior

The batterer needs to be taught early in the program just how to avoid being violent. The counselor will help the batterer to learn to control his anger or frustration in order to stop the violent behavior. As we know, the source of violence is related to a matrix of social factors.[46] An accumulation of negative emotions leads to a feeling of displeasure, pain, and eventually indignation that is likely to be expressed into violent actions at home.

Behavioral techniques are helpful only if the men are sufficiently motivated to use the techniques and aware enough of their anger to respond to it.[47] Here is one of the techniques, the "Time-Out" technique, that most programs recommend.

"Time-Out" Technique

1. Recognize physical or behavioral "cues" that signal you are intensely angry.
2. Assert immediately "I need to take a time-out" or make a "T" sign with your hands without speaking.
3. Leave the house for a full hour to cool off and collect your thoughts.
4. Take a brisk walk and call a crisis phone line, good friend, or "buddy" from the program. (Do not drink, drive, or go to a bar!)
5. Return to the house in one hour no sooner or later.
6. Check in with your wife and talk about how you feel and why. (Don't try to change her behavior; simply start by airing your gripes.)
7. Report and discuss the close call at the next meeting.

* Source: Daniel Sonkin and Michael Durphy, *Learning To Live Without Violence* (San Francisco: Volcano Press, 1982), 14.

In this session the counselor will instruct the batterer how to use various kinds of techniques such as guided imagery exercises, relaxation exercises, assertive communication exercises, rules for fair fighting, problem solving exercises, and so on. These exercises can be taught in group sessions.

4. Exploring one's life history

We could divide batterers into largely two groups. As Bussert says, one group belongs to the "compulsive masculinity syndrome"[48] group. They have the notion that a man has the power to correct or chastise an erring wife. If she does not live up to his expectations or perform her role properly, he believes himself to have the right to "punish" her. The other group is a pathological one. In addition to the compulsive masculinity syndrome, they have usually had hurtful personal histories. They were abused or were the witnesses of their parents' physical abuse. They usually have feelings of helplessness, fear, inadequacy, and insecurity. Their violence is more severe and happens more often than that of the compulsive masculinity syndrome group.

After listening one's life history, if the counselor thinks, the batterer has psychological problems, then the counselor will deal with psychopathology of the batterer.

K's case: From his story we can guess that he was not well taken care of as a child. There must not have been enough acceptance and care from his parents. His self could not become a healthy and strong one. In addition, his weakened self received further damage by his father's battering not only to his mother but also him. His self structure was damaged and became a vulnerable one. For him, the only way to satisfy his exhibitionistic wishes and to get approval from others was to become a top fighter in his town. However, his last hope was cut off when he was humiliated by an attacker in front of his followers. I think his self-esteem was damaged again by this shaming incident. From this moment he became obsessed with taking care of his own physical body.

K's constant striving for physical power can be seen in conjunction with a sense of low self-esteem and his dissatisfaction with himself. He was selfish because his narcissistic needs had never been satisfied. He might think there was no one who would love him except himself. He was licking his wounds and obsessed with himself because he thought nobody else loved him.

K's selfishness prevented him from having good fellowship with others. This led him to his isolation in the social field and becoming paranoid. His vulnerable self could not endure others' criticism, and he exploded into narcissistic rage, which is a response of a vulnerable self to injuries. His self was too sensitive to slights. These narcissistic rages were blown off by beating his wife and children, which was an internalized pattern learned in his childhood from his father.

The pastoral counselor will make an empathic and accepting matrix so that his weakened self may be restored in that counseling environment. Each counselor will use his/her own method of psychotherapy to deal with psychological problems of batterers. During the counseling sessions the counselor will help him to release his oppressed emotions such as anger, bitterness, sadness and so on. The counselor will let him know that it is all right to cry or weep if one's heart wants to do so. The counselor will explain how he has been affected by his hurtful and shameful past experiences.

Forgiving One's Father

Many men do begin to relate their violence to the violence they experienced in their family of origin. Many batterers carry around within themselves an angry or judgmental father as a battered child. The "angry father" theme reflects the tension between fathers and sons growing up, the way that they are rivals to each other, with little opportunity to heal their connection.[49] One way of healing the wounded father is to plunge into the history of a battering father. A man needs to find ways to empathize with his father's pain. The counselor will help the batterer (K) to understand what kind of life his father had to live as a poor father in the world where human beings' dignity was judged by one's status and financial success.

He can recognize his father's actual wounds, the way his father had been wounded by his life. As the poet Robert Bly writes of his father, "I began to think of him not as someone who had deprived me of love or attention or companionship, but as someone who himself had been deprived, by his parents or by the culture. I've begun to see him more as a man in a complete situation."[50] Healing the wounded father means accepting that there is no perfect father as we wish we had. The batterer (K) will realize that K's father also had a hurtful story and then K will have empathy toward the father as a man.

So the process of exploration may lead to acceptance of father and finally to forgiving his father. Then the counselor will encourage K to take care of his family instead of being taken care of. In his life he must not have experienced taking care of his family members' needs and feelings. He will learn how to be a father: a father to his kids, a husband to his wife; an empathic figure who attends to the emotional needs of others, not just through a paycheck.[51]

Instead of getting angry and yelling, after the stressful day, the counselor will recommend him to say, "Hi, how are things going?" to his family members and then picking up his children for hugging. This action will heal the rage and sadness which he had experienced from his own childhood. By having a close involvement and physical contact with his wife and children, he begins to realize that he is an adult who can give love to others. This kind of experience will be reinforcement to heal his wounded self and will give him conviction that he can be a mature father. The counselor will help the batterer become more sensitive and expressive. Slowly, the batterer will change his self-image. He will see himself not as compulsive masculine creature prone toward anger and violence, but as a man capable of empathy and gentleness.[52] Robert Bly and a number of thinkers and activists are urging men to substitute empathy for efficiency, stewardship for exploitation, generosity for the competitiveness of the market place.[53] The batterer begin to realize that he can effect a change in his surroundings.

Undoing sex roles and challenging social structure by taking actions

We can have these sessions in the mode of a group seminar. An essential objective of group counseling is to educate men to the sex role dynamics that sanction and perpetuate violence against women. The men who batter must be helped to see how they are socialized by society to dominate women. They will also recognize how social structures and institutions systematically exclude women and elevate men.[54] They will see how wife abuse is a consequence of patriarchal and sexist society. Men are socialized to be in charge of women, treat them as sex objects, and subject them to abuse and violence. The counselor will let them trace back that how their own mothers and grand-mothers had gone through *Han*-ful lives as women in Korean culture. And let them imagine what kind of life their daughters will live out as a woman in Korean society. They will realize that Korean men have had a privileged position within social culture.

Various kinds of aids will be employed for men's consciousness-raising. Women speakers, films on abuse, battered women, rape victims, women lawyers, woman economists, charts on household duties and the situation in the job market for women, and so on can help challenge a group of men with realities of sexism. Another possibility is that the batterer can be a speaker in men's meetings or can take a further step to serve as a public speaker on abuse at churches or other meetings. These aids will be more powerful than the lecture of a counselor.

In this stage, as we examined in the chapter on "Harmful Adaptation of Men", the batterers will see how they were socialized and suffered as men under the pseudo-male stereotypes propagated by the male mystique. Counselors will let them realize that "we are not, after all, what we are told we are."[55] These kind of activities will evoke reactions from men. They will get some empathy for the woman's situation. Men will also realize the women's vast support and hopefully develop a greater appreciation for their wives' contributions. The counselor will help them not only transform their old paradigms but also encourage them carry out what they realize.

It is at this point that men become more self-motivated to confront their own controlling behavior. "Acceptance that he should not and cannot control the ways others act is the final stage of change for the batterer."[56] The men also need to unlearn their overbearing sense of rigidity, domination, and control that they associate with manhood. They should realize that patriarchal power is inappropriate and self-destructive. As the batterers become "feminized," their relationships improve and their violence will subside. As they begin to share responsibility and authority and nurture their own individuality, they in fact changed and were able to change.

Mark Gerzon outlines the implications of this diversification on family relationship:

> "As these emerging masculinities gain strength, men will no longer feel compelled to keep masculine and feminine roles separate. We can allow them to be shared. The lines of responsibility, such as his for making money or hers for taking care of the children, can soften. Men will be more balanced breadwinners if that responsibility is shared. Women will be more balanced caretakers if that responsibility, too, is shared. And as couples may wish to reverse roles completely; others may retain clearly divided roles. But if the freedom to choose is increased that outcome, whatever its form, will be liberating for both men and women."[57]

I believe these kinds of activities and experiences can change one's surroundings. Especially man-to-man discussion can be a key experience in self-discovery and personal empowerment. But these personal experiences are not enough to reverse the victimization of men and women. As the men's movement gathers strength, it is critical that this increasing sense of personal liberation be channeled into political action which will leads to social changes.

Conclusion

To meet the needs of the times, Korean laws have been changed to give women substantially equal rights as husbands in respect to inheritance, divorce, property ownership, and adultery. However, the thick door of "Battering" is still firmly closed in the name of "family privacy" like a sacred place. As a result, too many Korean women and children suffer and groan in pain and fear behind that door. They are in a totally defenseless state.

Strengthened social and legal sanctions against domestic violence are indispensable to prevent men from battering. Above all, to make this "Men's therapy for Batterers" to work, there should be a law which will force batterers to take a mandatory counseling for a period of time. Those batterers who fail to comply with treatment should be brought under the law. Without carrying a law into effect, no batterer will come for counseling in a Korean context.

As we examined, enacting a law against physical abuse is not the fundamental solution to get rid of battering. Changing the vicious social systems is the only way to eradicate the root cause of battering. Without significant changes in our society there will be continued hopelessness and frustration both for women and men.

In this paper I could not specifically explain the process of challenging and changing the social structures by organizing a pressure group. That is because I do not have experience with or ideas about the procedure. I will research more about this area.

How long will it take to finish this program? I do not have an exact period in my mind. However, it will be a long-term counseling program because it offers a more complete picture of becoming nonabusive, rather than focusing on simply extinguishing battering. Is it really possible for batterers to participate in social actions and changes?

Will they really give up their vested rights and interests in patriarchal and sexist systems? Can batterers really be protectors of feminism? Feminists might look upon this trial with suspicion.

Feminist theory sees that male-centered social and psychical structures place biological men as enforcing agents for those structures.[58] Feminist theory has its exclusive mechanisms. Men must be an alien to women's experience in the male-centered society. That is why feminists doubt about men's participation in changing systems.

Like traditionally oriented women, men are conditioned by their culture. If men perceive only the prerogatives and advantages of the traditional male role, it will be very difficult for them to become reformers. However, if they see its destructiveness, burdens, restraints, and disadvantages, they will participate in reforming. Men's liberators will work with feminists because feminists' discourses are instructive in relation to issues which are simultaneously men's problems and feminism's cause.

We will not look to the system to solve the problems of the system because the system maintains itself and is entirely non- normative in character. We can look to the exercises of human rationality in and through free discourse in counseling sessions or men's groups in which they could discern the good from the evil. After seeing the truth, they will fight back against human beings' loss of control over the system. In this sense 'The eclectic therapy for Korean batterers' is a difficult but promising and necessary task.

Chapter Eleven

Uncovering Past Despair, Giving Present Hope:
Clinical Analysis of the Relationship Pattern of "T" Family from India

Kurien George

Brief History of Immigration of Indians to USA, Focusing on Christians.

According to a study by Susan Gordon (1990) (as referred to in the doctoral dissertation by Dr. Kondoor Varghese Abraham) there were several waves of Indian immigration to the USA.

1st wave 1900-1946:
Most of these immigrants came from Punjab via Vancouver on the West Coast of Canada. They found jobs in the forests, farms, and railroads of California.

2nd wave 1946-1965:
In 1946, the US Government passed laws and gave rights to Asian Indians to become naturalized citizens. Only about 6000 Asian Indians came to the US.

3rd wave 1965-1975:
The number of immigrants increased during this period. Subsequent to this period the immigration was mainly of professional people like doctors, engineers, nurses, etc. resulting in the 'brain drain' from India. In the last few years the immigrants have been computer engineers, and the wave is still continuing.

Immigration from Kerala:
Kerala is one of the smallest states in India, with a Christian population of 21%. The job opportunities in the US resulted in the arrival of a large

number of nurses in the late 1960's and early 1970's. The immigration was dominated by persons professing the Christian religion, as most persons who took up nursing were Christians. At the moment the immigrants from Kerala are either those for whom relatives have filed earlier, persons coming through marriage, or computer professionals.

Brief History of Indian Christian Churches in the USA:

Christians from most states in India other than Kerala have joined the local churches in the area they live in. They also have joined the same churches they came from back home in India. This is generally the case of people belonging to the following denominations:

1. Roman Catholic
2. Methodist
3. Church of North India (joining the Episcopal Church)
4. Baptist
5. Presbyterian

There seems to be no published material on the Asian Indian Christians. However, there are two books on people from Kerala.

1. Kerala Immigrants in America (Annamma Thomas and T. M. Thomas), 1984
2. Keralites in America (K. P. Andrews (ed)), Literacy Market Review, 1983

The Kerala Christians (St. Thomas Christians) belong to the following denominations:

1. Roman Catholic
2. Syrian Orthodox
3. Orthodox Syrian
4. Mar Thoma Syrians
5. Church of South India
6. Pentecostals

An exact distribution is not available. The Mar Thoma Syrian church has about 5000 families distributed over the USA. This denomination has 65 worshipping centers and 35 clergy. The diocese is under the guidance of a Bishop.

Introduction

Mr. "M" is 22 years old and is a college sophomore expecting to major in finance and business. He was introduced by the Diocesan Secretary to the counselor, who is the Youth Chaplain for the Diocese of North America of the Mar Thoma Syrian Church of Malabar (India). This is a church of the Eastern Orthodox rite. "M" is doing his studies and at the time the counseling began was working part-time at valet parking. He has one younger brother, "B," and his parents, Mr. and Mrs. "T," are very sincere and family-oriented people.

I. Pre-History

Mr. and Mrs. "T" are from Kerala in India. Kerala is one of the smallest states of India, having 100% literacy. The population demography is as follows: Hindus: 60%, Christians: 21%, Muslims: 19%. The overall Indian Christian population is 2. 5%.

They both belong to the Syrian Christian community (also called St. Thomas Christians) in Kerala. This community is deeply rooted in history, going back to AD 52. The community is clannish, and family and community centered. People in the community, in general belong to the middle class and are very industrious. They strive to maintain their faith and cultural roots. Mr. "T" is from Tiruvalla and Mrs. "T" from Pathanamthitta. Both villages are in Central Kerala with a high population density of Syrian Christians. Mrs. "T"'s family is closely knit, large and extremely clannish. Mr. "T"'s family is back in Kerala, preventing a close-knit relationship.

Both Mr. "T" and Mrs. "T" are self-made people. Mrs. "T" studied one year in college. She did not follow through. However, both studied typing, shorthand, and have good knowledge of the use of computers. They met in Bombay where Mr. "T" and Mrs. "T" were working. Mr. "T" had left his house at the age of 16. He came to Bombay and worked hard to sustain himself. Mrs. "T" grew up in a family where all her siblings were female. Her father worked in Bombay and she grew up with her mother. The father used to come home for vacations or take the family to Bombay. Finally, Mrs. "T" and all her sisters came to Bombay to find jobs. Mrs. "T" and Mr. "T" met at this stage where they attended the same church and prayer meetings. They married young. Mr. "T" was 24 and Mrs. "T" was 18. Through hard work, Mr. "T" rose financially. They went to Dubai and Mr. "T" got a very good job in which he rose to the level of administrative assistant to the managing director. Mrs. "T"'s sisters and family had migrated to USA in 1972. They filed for the "T" family, who visited them in 1988. Mr. "T" returned to Dubai, and Mrs. "T" along with the children remained behind. Mr. "T" finally came here in 1990.

Initially, when "M" and his brother, "B," along with their mother came to the US, they stayed with their relatives (Mrs. "T"'s sister). The initial years created a lot of tension for "M," as he found the mother's sister domineering and fussy. His maternal grandparents also lived with them. They were hypercritical of "M" and "B." All of this combined with the absence of the father alienated "M." "M" was in his adolescent years. The process of alienation continued for him into college. He started drinking, smoking, and hanging out with friends late into the night. His father, who joined them in 1990, was unable to provide emotional nurture. "M" had a lot of suppressed anger that was surfacing at home. He had become violent with his younger brother and also a friend.

II. Counsellee Profile

"M" is 22 years old. When the counselor initially met him, the first impression was that of a young adult who had been emotionally hurt, but who had a desire to change. It was apparent that if the situation was not resolved, he could become violent with himself or with a family member. He seemed angry with his father and was unable to communicate with him.

An initial meeting (2nd interview) was fixed to evaluate the situation. The initial meeting with the parents and "B" paid off, since a subsequent request for an interview with "M" was accepted.

"B," the younger son, seemed very indifferent to the family situation. He has shown indifference after the first interview, though he conveyed a positive opinion about the counselor to the older brother "M." However, at the moment he is relating better with the counselor.

Mr. "T," "M"'s father, seems depressive in his behavior. He is critical and tends to be a complainer. He is 47 years old and regrets having come to the US. He has a feeling of insecurity and feels unhappy about his dependence on his wife's family (especially for coming to the US). At the same time, he is a loving person. Mr. "T" has a problem keeping jobs. His job turnover is too frequent and affects his credibility as a consistent person.

Mrs. "T" seems very evasive and excessively conscious about public image. At the same time, she tries to understand the family dynamics better than her husband does. She also loves her husband deeply and is committed to the children.

Family Profile

The intimacy levels in the family, especially between the father and the children, were very poor. There was no point of negotiation in the sense that the discussion would always lead to quarrels. Communication was need-based, and the children did not think it necessary that the parents should be obeyed. Basic trust between the parents and the children was missing and was not even considered necessary, since the children did what they wanted anyway. The parents are very active in the church and maintain a good spiritual discipline.

Community Profile

One of the problems associated with the community, which is highly educated, is that of being excessively self-conscious. This prevents them from having an open attitude to counseling. They have to be approached very cautiously. The methodology can only be interventional. Excessive questions put off the counsellee and at times even make them suspicious of motives. Therefore, the process is slow and tedious. The following write-up is a result of a slow and time consuming process of interaction with the counsellees.

III. Verbatims

1st Interview

At first introduction:

The introduction is done by a conference call on the telephone by the Diocesan Secretary, Rev. Oommen Philip.

Rev. Oommen Philip: Rev. George, I would like to introduce to you Mr. "M," a promising young person from our church. "M," have you met Rev. George?'

"M": No, I have not (sounds polite).

Rev. Philip : You should meet Rev. George. He is our new youth chaplain. At the moment he does not have a car, so you can help him in his work by taking him around.

"M": Sure, Rev. Philip.

Rev. George : "M," what are you studying?

"M": I am a sophomore in college, majoring in finance and business.

Rev. George : I hope to meet you sometime soon.

"M": I hope so too.

Rev. Philip : OK, "M," I will talk to you later. Keep in touch with Rev. George. Bye.

(The line with "M" is cut off. Rev. Philip and Rev. George continue the conversation.)

Rev. Philip: Achen (another term for Reverend, also meaning Father in the Malayalam language) "M" is going through a crisis. He will need your help. I will tell his parents to contact you. Is it okay with you?

Rev. George: Okay Achen. Bye

2nd Interview

"M"'s mother calls up. She wants to meet with the counselor. A date and time are fixed. They expect "M" to come along. However, "M" does not come. "M"'s younger brother comes. After they are seated.

Mr. "T": Achen, the children do not have any respect for us. They do not obey us.

Rev. George: Tell me about yourselves.

Mr. "T": We regret coming to this country. I had a good job in Dubai and we were doing well. We gave up everything and came here. Now we have lost everything. Our children do not understand. Instead of understanding our sufferings, they are going their way.

Mrs. "T": Achen, the children were both very well balanced till recently. It is only in the last one year that "M" has become like this. This one (i. e. "M"'s younger brother) also has now started in the same direction. He also comes back at midnight.

(The younger "B" looks very uncomfortable.)

Rev. George: Generally young people go through such a period of crisis in their lives. We have to give them time to settle down. This is the process of identity development and expression. As long as they do not break the law or violate moral values, we have to be patient.

At the counselor's response, "B" smiles and says, "Yes, Achen, they are very strict." "M"'s father is not very happy about the whole process. He feels that I should shout at "B" and "M." Rev. George tells them that doing so would only alienate them further and increase the frustration of the parents. Rev. George explains why he believes that there should be greater space for the young persons. He explains the whole process of Erikson's identity development and identity confusion. He says that the parents have a right to object to undisciplined behavior. Yet, at the same time, dignity should be maintained. Repeated haranguing of the children would hurt their sense of dignity and subsequently they could lose respect for the parents. "M"'s mother interjected that she always tells this to her husband but he never seems to be able to accept it. The interview is terminated.

3rd Interview

The counselor visited the house of the counsellee. "M" came down to sit at the table. The father and mother were also present. As a means of empathy to break the ice, the counselor became vulnerable.

Mr. "T": "M" does not obey us. He has no concern or respect for us. He is continuously violating the norms of behavior in this house. This cannot continue.

"M": Dad, there you go again. (Appearing very sulky).

Mr. "T": Tell me what time you came in yesterday night. If the car gets into another accident, we cannot afford the increased insurance

"M": If this is the way that we are going to be discussing the issue, I think I better go.

Here the counselor intervened.

Rev. George: Just a minute "M." Wait for awhile. Let me share some thoughts with you. As an adolescent and subsequently as a young adult I was a very aggravated person. I had a tendency to do things that were not agreeable to my parents. It was only when I reached my 27th birthday that I finally realized my conflicts and found resolutions.

Mr. "T": Achen, (i. e. the term used for Church priest), I do not agree with you. We work so hard and these children do not realize that unless they obey us they will not make good in life.

Rev. George: Mr. "T," give your son time, he will change. He needs to understand himself and his surroundings. This will help him to come back on track.

Mr. "T": The way you are saying things we do not need any church or moral laws. In time people will change.

Rev. George: Please do not misunderstand me. My purpose is not to belittle your efforts. The hard work you and your wife are putting will lead to nowhere if you do not give your children emotional space to grow.

Mrs. "T": I keep telling him to wait, but he cannot. He gets very disturbed when he sees the son behaving like this.

The counselor guides the discussion back to his own life situation. He explains how he was conflicted with his parents and how he drifted away from them. He explained how his lifestyle impacted on the life of his younger brother. He gave "M" the choice of trying to understand his life situation. On the way back to the counselor's home ("M" dropped him off), "M" explained that he loved his father and he had not realized the damage that his behavior would have done to his brother. "M" promised to change and the counselor told him that he would talk to the parents to give him space to change.

Paraphrase of Interview with Mother

The mother felt that Mr. "T" was excessively demanding on the children and had a tendency to be hypercritical. She also felt that he took a negative view about everything. Initially her attitude was that this issue had to be resolved between them without the counselor. She also suggested to the counselor that resolution was only possible through God, and human intervention was superfluous. She thought her husband was excessively depressed and this had resulted in the crisis of the family. She was also worried that the counselor may provoke the son unknowingly to precipitate a serious crisis in the family.

Paraphrase of Interview with Father

The father kept on repeating the same complaints again and again. The counselor asked the father why he portrayed such a depressive picture to the family in general. This made him feel that Mrs. "T" had revealed family secrets to the counselor and this was why the counselor asked him a question of this nature. The counselor explained to him that this was not true and his evaluation was based on the conversations the counselor had with the whole family. He also reiterated that the father should give the sons space to change.

Evaluation

It was apparent from the beginning that the father was not very keen on the process. His attitude was depressive and negative, possibly out of helplessness. The mother seemed to understand the process. However, she had reservations on revealing too many details about the family, probably out of fear that people would look down on them. The counselor had two initial purposes.

1. Establish a rapport with the younger brother so that he would share with "M" (who was hesitant to come) that the counselor understands. This would help the counselor in the future to meet "M."
2. Provoke the parents to think and understand that:
   a. As young persons grow they will develop their own self-identity, and this involves a process of 'going away' (not literally) and 're-approachment'.
   b. They have to journey with the children without being repressive, but at the same time stand by moral and spiritual values.

The above purposes were met, even though on the surface the father did not agree with the counselor. The stage was set for future interaction and change.

As the counseling proceeded, it seemed that the father was not in a position to understand the dynamics of the counseling process. However, "M" had started responding to the counseling and had taken a positive attitude to the process. He therefore became a key person for bringing about change in the family. A key factor in the whole process became the depressive tendency of the father. It became necessary to find out the family patterns whereby he developed such an attitude. This case study primarily focuses on the key factor. This is to enable "M" to understand the family dynamics better. It is hoped that through this process there will be an unblocking of the family system. Other areas relating to the maternal relational patterns have to be studied separately.

IV. Relationship Analysis

As the parents were not in a position to cooperate in the process, it was initially thought fit to empower "M" to enable healing of the family.

Paternal

A discussion with "M" elicited hardly any information regarding the paternal family structure beyond the third generation. Even what was available was sparse and conveyed little information on relatives. However, "M" was certain that Mr. "T" had a very fused and conflicted relationship with his father. In fact, Mr. "T"'s father had fused and conflicted relations with Mr. "T"'s mother and Mr. "T"'s sister, but a close relationship with the younger son. Mr. "T"'s father hardly ever spoke to Mrs. "T." Mr. "T"'s father became an alcoholic who lived off the family property and did not take responsibility for the family. This was what forced Mr. "T" to leave home at the early age of 16 to seek employment. Mr. "T" also had a fused and conflicted relationship with his younger brother whom he had educated and who had now turned to alcohol. This conflict has subsequently healed and at present they relate well. Mr. "T" has a very close relationship with his sister.

Maternal

Mrs. "T" has very good relations with all her siblings. Mrs. "T"'s parents though have a fused and conflicted relationship. Mrs. "T" also has an open relationship with her children. She had a distant relationship with her father-in-law but a close relationship with her mother-in-law. Her sons had a problem with her parents as they felt that the grandparents had not treated them well when they first came to USA. Mr. "T" has a very good relationship with Mrs. "T"'s family.

Siblings

"M" and "B" have a very close relationship at the moment. Earlier there was a fused and conflicted relationship. "M" has been trying to resolve his conflicts with his father through the counseling process. Both brothers have a conflicted relationship with the paternal uncle and a fused and conflicted relationship with the maternal grandmother.

Subsequent developments

The process of building confidence through "M" has worked. Over a period of time it became possible to interact more freely with the parents. Details regarding the family structure that were not available earlier became clearer. The key factor remains the same for this case study; to help "M" to understand the behavioral pattern in his family and if possible to help his brother and parents to redefine their relationships based on the same.

V. Chronology of Key Factors and Events as Elicited through Interventional Processes

1. "M"'s grandfather had one brother and three sisters. The girls were married off with dowry and settled in the neighborhood.
2. The marriage of the girls and their settlement in the neighborhood increased their influence in the family and continued into the time of "M"'s father's childhood.
3. "M"'s grandfather had a fused and conflicted relationship with his brother. This brother sold off all his property and migrated to North Kerala. This migration had an emotional impact on the family as there were two sons in the family after a long time, and when they did have two sons, the brothers fought and parted.
4. "M"'s father also had a conflicted relationship with his brother and for a time they did not communicate. Subsequently this healed.
5. "M"'s father grew up in a family where the aunts (by virtue of their proximity) always interfered.
6. One of "M"'s grandfather's sisters had to be married off thrice. The first two husbands died. In all of this the marriage was by giving off land, thus reducing the landed property. "M"'s father grew up witnessing these deaths in the family.

7. "M"'s grandfather was very attached to his mother. After her death, he started drinking.
8. "M"'s father lived in his mother's house when he was very young. Mr. "T"'s mother belonged to a very large and well-established family.
9. "M"'s grandfather had a fused and conflicted relationship with his son Mr. "T." He used to self-torture himself by not taking his medicines. Mr. "T" has a tendency of hurting himself physically when upset.
10. "M"'s grandfather was opposed to the marriage between Mr. "T" and Mrs. "T." He went to Mrs. "T"'s house and verbally abused Mrs. "T"'s family.
11. Mrs. "T" grew up in a family of girls. In addition, her father was away working in Bombay. Therefore, her relationship with the male gender was very limited.
12. Mrs. "T"'s mother has a tendency to be dominant in the relationship with her husband. This relationship is fused and conflicted.
13. Mrs. "T"'s father has one brother who has two daughters and one son settled in India.

VI. Interpretation of Relationships

The interpretations of relationships are based on the concept that the family is a dynamic organism and a system.

A. Family Structure

The culture of the community to which the family belongs is patriarchal and clannish. However, in the case of "M"'s family there has been a dilution of the patriarchal structure, as can be seen from the parent/child relationship. Mr. "T"'s father was patriarchal. He had a tendency to abuse Mr. "T" emotionally. He did not take responsibility for the family and subsequently became alcoholic. When Mr. "T" was young his father and his uncle (father's brother) fought with each other and broke the cohesion of the family unit.

1. Household Composition

The household composition of Mr. "T"'s family was initially multi-generational as can be seen from the genogram. The multi-generational nature of Mr. "T"'s family created tensions at home. Mr. "T"'s mother had to face the constant interference from Mr. "T"'s aunts and mother-in-law. This resulted in a conflicted relationship between Mr. "T"'s father and mother. All of this created an atmosphere of insecurity in the family, a loneliness which Mr. "T" took on and carried into adult life. Subsequently, Mr. "T" started his own family which was nuclear.

Mrs. "T"'s family was in a way mostly a 'single parent' family (though not literally) as the father was away working in Bombay. The father would either come for leave during summer or take his family to Bombay. After the "T" family migrated to US, the sisters of Mrs. "T" were always living in the neighborhood. All four sisters and Mrs. "T"'s parents lived in the near vicinity of Mrs. "T," whereas Mr. "T" did not have any close relatives in the US.

These help us to understand the following:

Mrs. "T" is able to handle varied situations without getting traumatized. However, Mr. "T" gets disturbed very easily. He lives in a constant fear of being unloved, deserted, and even killed. He is not able to handle the complex growing-up process that his sons are going through. He relives his childhood insecurities. These insecurities were compounded by the adolescent aggressiveness of the sons, as they became autonomous.

2. Birth Order

Mr. "T" is the eldest in the family and was forced to take on adult responsibilities at the age of sixteen. This prevented him from having a proper transition from adolescence to young adulthood and finally adulthood. Another effect of Mr. "T"'s being the eldest was that he was always under pressure, especially because of his father not taking an active role in the family responsibilities. This put demands on him, resulting in his being filled with self-doubt and anxiety. His depressive moods can also be attributed to this background. This also resulted in his having great expectations of his elder son, "M." He transferred all his attitudinal conflicts on to "M," in the process alienating him.

Mrs. "T" is the second daughter and has learned to be accommodating in her relationships. Mrs. "T" took on all the burdens of

Mr. "T"'s inner conflicts as they surfaced. The complementary sibling position of Mr. "T" being the elder son and Mrs. "T" being the 2nd born in her family of four daughters has its positive effect on the relationship. Mr. "T" is emotionally dependent on Mrs. "T," though he is very parental and responsible. Mrs. "T" has grown up in an "all female" environment. She is therefore probably not enabling her husband to get over his feelings of insecurity. Though she is accommodating and perseverant, yet the resolution has not yet occurred.

B. Life Cycle Fit

1. Mr. "T" left home for employment at a very early age. Every time he came home he had a very conflicting relationship with his father. This also resulted in further alienating him from the parent and increased his hurt vis-à-vis the relationship patterns he had with his immediate family This also resulted in "M" taking the brunt of the pain of his father.
2. The life cycle transition in the family is very indicative. Mr. "T" left home at the age of 16. Mrs. "T" left home at the age of 17. They met at a prayer meeting and got married in a year when Mr. "T" was 24 and Mrs. "T" was 18. The marriage age for a person from the Syrian Christian community at that time would be 27 for a male and 21 for a female. They married 3 years too soon as per the standard for the community. This was also because their marriage was not arranged by the parents. The decision to marry was made by them, and then the parents arranged it. As stated earlier, Mr. "T"'s father had objections to the marriage.

The following became clear from the above:

a. The transitions for Mr. "T" and Mrs. "T" from adolescence to young adulthood and adulthood did not proceed smoothly, and they carried their personal unresolved conflicts into the marriage.

b. Their commitment to each other as they understood it prior to the marriage took on a different understanding after the marriage. The 'real' persons started becoming revealed to each other as they lived together after marriage. This necessitated a redefining of their understandings of each other. This process is still continuing. In the process of this redefinition over the last 23 years, the children have received confusing signals regarding the personalities and positions of the respective parents. Thus the father got considered to be a boor and every thing/person related to him got sidelined. The mother's position became that of an intervener who always seemed to be accommodating the father and so she was seen as more approachable. Communication channels with the father became badly distorted resulting in "M" and "B" moving away from Mr. "T."

C. Patterns of Functioning

Repetitions

1. Mr. "T" had a conflicted and fused relationship with his father. A similar pattern exists between "M" and Mr. "T." Mr. "T"'s father and his mother had a conflicted relationship. Mr. "T" sees the same pattern in his relationship with Mrs. "T." Mr. "T" had a conflicted and fused relationship with his brother. This has now healed. "M" and "B" had a conflicted and fused relationship with each other. Mr. "T" is very close to his mother; "M" is very close to his mother (Mr. "T"'s wife). Mr. "T" is excessively conscious of the conflicts that existed between his father and uncle; he is also conscious of the conflict between him and his brother. His conflicted relationship with his father and brother worries him, as he sees the same pattern between him and his sons. This worry tends to express itself in his behavior, which is why he complains so much about his sons' responses to him. Thus he is unable to be objective for helping with resolution.
2. Mr. "T" left home when he was 16. "M" had been on edge to leave home since he was 18 and the younger brother "B," who is 17, is leaving home shortly to join the Army. This probably is a reaction to the continuous drumming at home that Mr. "T" had to take up responsibility as a young person and he expected his sons to behave responsibly. This may have impacted on them the desire to leave home. (In the Syrian Christian community the sons are not expected to leave home.)

D. Family Functioning

Impact of Life Changes

1. The transfer from Dubai, a closed country in terms of cultural permissiveness, to this permissive country had an impact on the index person who was in his adolescence at the time of the immigration.
2. "M" came here when he was in the early stages of adolescence. This is a key factor in determining his behavior, especially due to the culture shock he has undergone.
3. The behavior of the maternal grandparents, especially the grandmother in critically reprimanding "M," affected the attitude of "M" in the home environment.
4. Mr. "T" came later to the country, after the wife and children had already been here two years. The new situation disturbed Mr. "T," as he left a good job and came to a place where he had to start life all over again. This affected him, triggering off old insecurities that became projected on to the family.

E. Relational Patterns

Dyadic relationships and triangles

Mr. "T" has a close relationship with his mother and had a conflicted and fused relationship with his father. Mr. "T"'s father and mother had a conflicted and fused relationship. Relatively, the relationship conflict patterns in Mr. "T"'s immediate family is scaled down. Yet, Mr. "T" has a feeling that his children have a conflicted relationship with him, whereas they have a close relationship with their mother. He also feels that the mother and sons are ganging up against him. Mrs. "T" does try "differentiation," i.e. relating to Mr. "T" and the sons in an individualized manner. However, the patterns will take time to settle.

F. Family Balance and Imbalance

1. The irresponsible behavior of the paternal grandfather put a lot of pressure on the father, who could not cope with the situation. This had impact on his relationship with the family, especially the children.

2. The absence of paternal relatives in the country has created a vacuum in the case of Mr. "T." There is an imbalance as all his wife's immediate relatives are in this country.

3. Mr. "T" grew up in a family where the father dominated the environment, whereas Mrs. "T" grew up in a situation where the mother had to look after immediate the needs of the family as the father was away working.

4. Mr. "T" had female influences in the home (the aunts who interfered) that he saw as negative. He therefore grew up with a conflicted understanding regarding the role of women except for the 'suffering mother' figure (which his mother was). Mrs. "T" on the other hand grew up with women who had to be assertive, taking an active role in the family.

5. Another factor of imbalance to be considered is that Mrs. "T" never worked after the marriage prior to her coming to the US, though she worked before marriage. She came to US, settled here before her husband, and started working. By the time her husband joined her in the US, leaving a good job in the Gulf, she was already settled in the American work culture. Mr. "T" came to the US and was not able to get a job as good as he had in the Gulf. He comes from a community that is patriarchal (though now in the US this is confused). This factor, combined with the lower job he had to take and the 'working wife' situation of Mrs. "T," triggered off insecurities in him. This insecurity was reinforced when he saw/heard about the assertive independence of the American woman. These factors provoked negative reactions in the family, all of which created an insecure family environment for "M" and "B."

Conclusion

The key factor in the family is the conflicts that the father has undergone as a result of emotional deprivation. This has four dimensions:

Insecurities:

a.. One of the essential elements in the stable development of the family is the 'continuity factor'. In the cultural situation of any community, stability and continuity of history give a sense of security. Looking backwards and being able to relate to the history of the past positively is a confidence booster for stability into the future. This holds good for nations as well as families. A rootless generation can be very insecure. This applies to the St. Thomas community as well. This community takes pride in the history of its families as going back to AD 52. In this cultural environment Mr. "T"'s great grandfather migrated into a St. Thomas Christian area and settled there. Originally he was a Roman Catholic. At the time there was tension between the Roman Catholic and St. Thomas Christian communities because of the Portuguese invasion of the sixteenth century. There would have been an ostracization of the forefathers in that community. Only economic strength and political clout could have prevented greater harm. The marriage alliances in the local community would also have helped. The family thus slowly got assimilated into the Mar Thoma Church. In the process, roots with the past were lost and the structure of a larger family that is common among the St. Thomas community was not available. New family structures were to be necessary as the continuity with the old was lost. In the process of growth the insecurities of isolationism took root in the family culture. Added to this, in the first two generations after the migration there was only one son in the family. This would have generated insecurity, as having more girls in those days would have meant the need for more wealth.

b. Mr. "T"'s uncle and father broke up with each other, and the subsequent migration of the uncle to North Kerala would have furthered the pattern of isolation and insecurity. The budding cultural affinities of the family as a cohesive unit again got disturbed.

c. The consecutive deaths of the husbands of Mr. "T"'s aunt in the family when he was young and then the death of his grandmother followed by the alcohol abuse of his father would have had a great negative impact on the life of Mr. "T."

d. Transferred guilt as Mr. "T" identifies with his father, especially in the pattern of hurting himself, feeling neglected by his wife and children, getting disturbed by new situations, feeling that he has no one in this country, and wilting under normal stress, are all indicative of inner insecurities.

Fears

Mr. "T" is fearful that ultimately, as his wife works and earns money he may get sidelined. He also fears that the sons may not be there for each other or for him. In this country he has none of his close kin, whereas his wife has a number of relatives. He fears that he will have no one in his time of need. The fear of loneliness is distracting for him.

Improper Transitions

a. In the cultural setting of the community the children are cared for by the parents unconditionally. Mr. "T" had to start life early at the age of sixteen. He had to strive hard for his livelihood. At adolescence itself he had to work like an adult. He therefore went through a premature adulthood. The mother figure is very important in the transitory period. The mother was away from the rough and tough situations of life in Bombay. The only option was to fill the gap by having a mate. This he found in Mrs. "T." He probably still seeks the mother in the mate as can be seen by the emotional dependence on her. This also puts him in competition with his sons.

b. This has also resulted in the functional role crisis in his understanding of the wife/mother figure. Seeing his wife work in a job outside the family makes him uneasy. As far as he is concerned the wife is the mother figure who 'looks after' the family. He likes to see his wife in a passive role, rather than as an active bread-winner.

Unresolved Conflicts

Mr. "T" wants his children to be with him, as he fears losing them, being deserted and, most important of all, he wants to feel loved. All of these are needed, but his problem lies with the fact that he has not got over his own pain from the past. He keeps on reminding the family of how he started to work hard at an early age. He still carries the pain in his interaction with his family.

VII. Clinical Analysis & Clinical Process for Change

A. Clinical Analysis

The crisis that "M" has gone through as a person is primarily because of the family cultural setting not being conducive. A hurt father, whose transitions from infancy to adolescence and young adulthood were traumatized by the father's father being emotionally abusive, could not provide proper emotional nurture and sustenance to "M." Therefore, "M" himself could not have a proper transition in the eight psychological stages as described by Erikson.

Table of Experiences based on Erikson's Eight Psychological Stages

	Stages	**Father, Mr. "T"'s experiences**	**"M"'s experiences**	**Remarks**
Infancy 0-11/12	Basic Trust v/s Mistrust	Mistrust	Basic Trust	"M" remembers that his father was very loving till the birth of the second son. After the second son was born he started becoming emotionally abusive.
Early Childhood	Autonomy v/s Shame and Doubt	Shame and Doubt	Autonomy	
Play Age 3-5	Initiative v/s Guilt	Guilt	Initiative	
School Age 5-12	Industry v/s inferiority	Inferiority	Partial Inferiority	The emotional abusive situation prevented proper transitions even though "M" did not become anti-social
Adolescence 12-18	Identity v/s Identity Confusion	Identity Confusion	Partial Identity Confusion	
Young Adulthood 19-30	Intimacy v/s Isolation	Isolation	Partial Isolation	
Adulthood 30-65	Generativity v/s Stagnation	Stagnation	Not Applicable	

The reason why "M" did not become anti-social is because the mother was nurturing and kept communication channels open. More important was the fact that despite the problems the father really loved the children and the children knew this. In the conflict between the real self (as "M" wanted to be an authentic person) and the co-dependent self (as "M" did not receive nurture from his father) resulted in a lot of suppressed anger. It is also interesting to note that "M"'s father did not become emotionally abusive till the birth of the second son. This probably is a repetitive process as Mr. "T"'s father also was close to the second son but emotionally abusive to the first. The same pattern was probably repeating itself in "M"'s case.

B. Clinical Process for Change

The whole family is traumatized. As a system, the whole family has been affected. The following processes have been done to heal the problem. The family is now engaged in the therapeutic process. The process of interaction with the family is continuing, and the various issues raised above are being discussed.

1. Unblocking the System

Through the genogram interview "M" was made aware of his own feelings towards his father, viz.:

i. He had felt that his father was an unreasonable and quarrelsome person, with whom communication was not possible.

ii. He had considered his father's side of the family as not so good and had hardly any information regarding them.

"M" was also made aware of the various factors in his father's life. He could see from the above the tremendous hurts his father had absorbed because of:

i. The abusive role of Mr. "T"'s father

ii. The improper transitions from adolescence to young adulthood, as Mr. "T" undertook family responsibilities at the young age of 16.

iii. The imbalance created by the migration from Dubai to the USA and the absence of any of Mr. "T"'s relatives in this country.

"M" is also able to see how his mother has tried to help, but how the same has resulted in the father image becoming contaminated in the process, resulting in the sons becoming further alienated from the father.

"B," who is joining the army, is now deeply concerned about his father, and one of the reasons he is going away is to rediscover the goodness of his family.

Mrs. "T" has been explained the need for a balanced approach as she handles the intra-relationships in the family.

Mr. "T" has been encouraged to feel more secure in his relationship with his children. It has been explained to him that children go away (not as he had to go away), to attain autonomy. He has also for the first time admitted his loneliness. The process of enabling him to find sublimation is continuing. The analysis has still to focus on the maternal side also for complete healing. It is presumed that as the system becomes more unclogged more maternal information will be revealed.

The above process enabled "M" to view the situation more empathetically. He worked towards building a better understanding of his father and mother to relate better with them. On his doing so, the system has become unblocked, and now there is the possibility of better communication between father and son.

B. Clarifying Family Patterns

The migration of Mr. "T"'s great-grandfather brought in a cut-off with the continuity from the past. This is now repeating itself in the case of the "T" family, with the resultant loneliness due to the cut-off of the paternal side expressing itself in the life of Mr. "T." This will also impact on the future of "M" and "B."

There are repetitive tendencies in the family patterns:

i. The emotional dependence of "M" on his girlfriend compares with the emotional dependence of Mr. "T" on his wife.

ii. "M" is not able to make the transition properly from adolescence into adulthood, as he faces pressure to fulfill his father's expectations of him, just as Mr. "T" had to. "M" continues to expect financial (especially) and emotional help from his parents despite the change into a cultural environment which promotes self-reliance, showing the improper transition.

iii. Mr. "T"'s father feared losing his son through marriage, which is probably why he objected to the marriage of Mr. and Mrs. "T." Mr. "T" fears losing his son to a traumatized world. "M" sees this fear as control.

iv. Mr. "T" was unknowingly passing on the pattern of emotional trauma as experienced by him from his father, on to his family.

C. Detoxifying Family Issues

Instead of seeing the family as depressive and dysfunctional, now "M" is able to view the family from a new framework. He sees the family as a system which became emotionally clogged up and which needed release. "M" and "B" have both tried to understand the father better. Instead of seeing him as controlling, they now try to see his anxieties as concern and an expression of his love. "M" tries to be more independent emotionally and is in the process of becoming a contributor to the family finances rather than only a receiver of funds.

IX. Future Plans

The process is continuing. An approach can now be made to Mr. "T" for enabling him to understand the processes involved. The rage levels in the family have been brought down. It is proposed to approach the family for processing internal healing. "M" has already found healing and has initiated the process at home. In addition, he has a new slogan, "Keep things in prayer." He finds sublimation in prayer.

"B" has to go through the same process of catharsis. The counselor has a good working relationship with "B" and has initiated a discussion with him.

Mrs. "T" is now very amenable to the counseling process. The relationship patterns in her family require study and evaluation. As the above is used to improve the emotional environment at home, more work can be done in that direction.

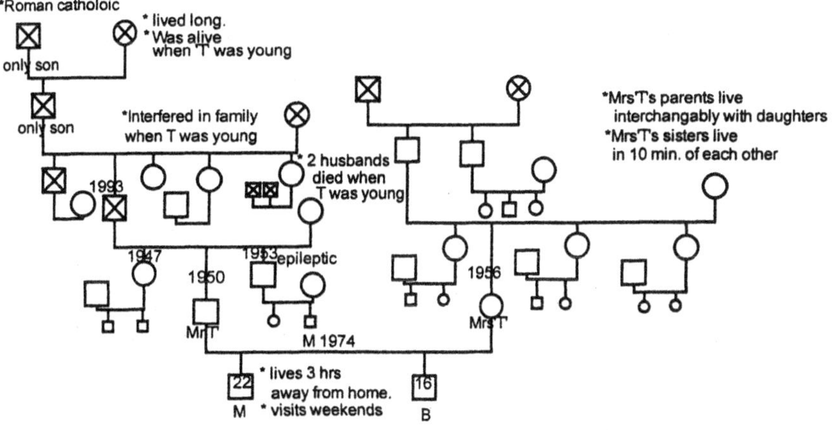

Genogram for 'T' family

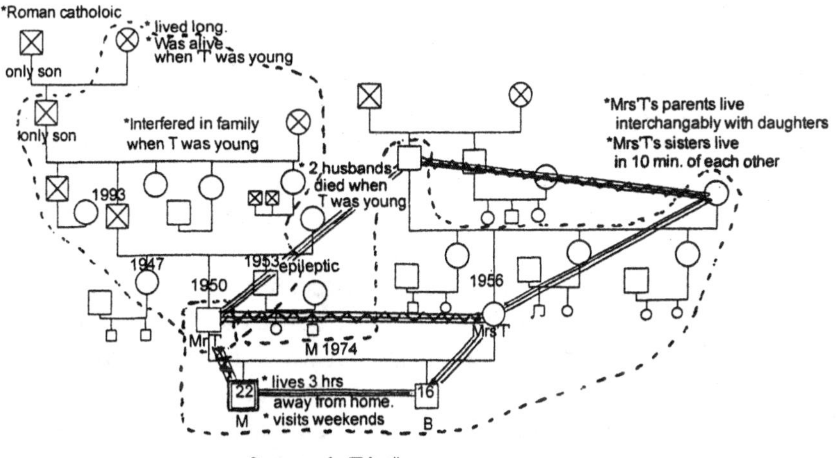

Genogram for 'T' family

Chapter Twelve

Religious Participation of Korean Immigrants:
Relationship between Motivation Factor Theories and Religious Participation

Douil Kim

Introduction

Many American church leaders look almost enviously at the spectacular growth of Korean American congregations. They seem amazed by Korean Americans' high participation level in their religious activities, including religious education. As a matter of fact, in about thirty years of immigration history since 1965, Korean Americans have established almost three thousand churches in North America alone. What made them so enthusiastically participate in religious activities? Why are Korean American adults so actively involved in various religious programs? Through study of their motivation, can we possibly learn something valuable for the American church's adult education?

There seems to be no doubt that almost all adults are busy. Whether they work full time in their office or at home, adults are busy because they carry a certain amount of responsibility for themselves or for others in their family. Then why do they participate in adult education classes outside of their work? Merriam and Caffarella report that there are 23 million adults who enroll in adult education classes in America.[1]

For the sake of our discussion, it is necessary to define who adults are, what adult education is, and to find out why adults are involved in adult education. The U.S. Department of Education defined adult education in relation to the definition of adult as ". . . any course or educational activity taken part-time and reported as adult education by respondents seventeen years old and over."[2] Then, what is the chief motivation of adults? The U.S. Department of Education survey reveals that most adults are involved in adult education for practical reasons: 64%

of the participants were involved in adult education to get a new job or for advancement in their present job.[3] In other words, most adults are involved in adult education for a better living. Simply put, for more money.

How about religious participation of adults? Why do adults go to church? What motivates them to spend their precious time to participate in religious education? In this study, the time spent in worship and Sunday School classes is considered religious education, because in these two places religious education formally take place for the most of time. To meet the basic requirement of participation in religious education, an adult should at least go to church for worship or for Bible study once a week on a regular basis. The qualification for being an adult is the same as above for non-religious education (17 years old or over). In this study the religious participation of the Korean immigrant church will be considered. The factors that motivate Korean immigrants to participate in religious education might or might not have some correlation with the factors that motivate adults to be involved in non-religious adult education.

The specific aims of this study are: (1) to review studies of the factors that motivate adults to be involved in non-religious educational activities, (2) to analyze the motivating factors that affect Korean immigrants to participate in religious education, and (3) to explore whether or not there is any correlation between the motivating factors of 1 and 2. Then through this comparison, we might be able to draw a conclusion about whether or not the Korean American adult participation model can be applied to American religious education.

1. An Overview on Theories of Motivating Factors in Non-Religious Adult Education

Johnstone and Rivera conducted a national survey to find out why adults participated in adult education. Their findings show that the top three important reasons adults participated in adult education classes were: to become a better-informed person (37%), to prepare for a new job or occupation (36%), and to keep the job held at that time (32%).[4] All three of them are related to their job, although the meaning of "to be a better-informed person" is not clear as Johnstone and Rivera evaluated.[5] The later surveys seem even more convincing. The surveys conducted by the National Center for Education Statistics confirmed the fact that the job-related reasons were the most frequently cited for all six surveys (1969, 1972, 1975, 1978, 1981). As mentioned earlier, 64% of 1984 participants indicated that getting a new job, advancing in the job, and other job-related reasons accounted for their participation in adult education. Merriam and Caffarella comment on this phenomenon as "not surprising," since they thought that most adult learners are employed and derive much of their identity from their work.[6]

Houle conducted in-depth interviews in which he found three types of learners: goal-oriented, activity-oriented, and learning-oriented learners. Goal-oriented adult learners are the ones who learn to meet their needs through education, while learning-oriented learners have intrinsic motivations to learn apart from any given need; they learn for the sake of learning itself. Activity-oriented adult learners are motivated by social contact or just the idea of doing something.[7]

Morstain and Smart's six-factor theory was derived from their observation and survey of 611 adults in evening credit courses at a college in New Jersey. The reason I use their theory is because their factors are broad and inclusive. Their six factors are as follows:

1. *Social Relationships:* This factor reflects participation in order to make new friends or meet members of the opposite sex.
2. *External Expectations:* These participants are complying with the wishes or directives of someone else with authority.
3. *Social Welfare:* This factor reflects an altruistic orientation; learners are involved because they want to serve others or their community.
4. *Professional Advancement:* This factor is strongly associated with participation for job enhancement or professional advancement.
5. *Escape/Stimulation:* This factor is indicative of learners who are involved as a way of alleviating boredom or escaping home or work routine.
6. *Cognitive Interest:* These participants, identical to Houle's learning oriented adults, are engaged for the sake of learning itself.[8]

This six-factor theory of Morstain and Smart is important for our study, since we are going to compare the motivating factors between non-religious adult education activities and religious adult education activities. Morstain and Smart's cluster theory is crucial because it provides us much room to categorize the underlying motivations of adult participants.

2. Religious Participation Of Korean Immigrants in the United States

We shall now turn our attention to religious adult education, especially in Korean ethnic churches in the States. According to the 1980 census, the Korean population in the States numbered 354,529; this number reached about 814,000 in 1990 and is expected to be about 1.3 million by 2000.[9] 90% of all Korean immigrants have come to the States after the Kennedy Immigration Act opened the door for legal immigration in 1965. The number of Korean immigrant churches has also grown from about 75 churches in 1970 to about 2000 today--an unprecedented increase of about 27 times.[10] Korean immigrants have become known as "churchgoers." Citing from Illsoo Kim[11], Hurh and Kim said Koreans are know as churchgoers and compared with other Asians by saying: "When two Japanese meet, they set up a business firm; when two Chinese meet, they open a Chinese restaurant; and when two Koreans meet, they establish a church."[12] According to Hurh and Kim's recent studies in Los Angeles, 69.9 percent of the Los Angeles sample is affiliated with Korean ethnic churches, 84% of the church affiliates attend church at least once a week, and one-third of them hold leadership positions in the church.[13]

According to Hurh and Kim, involvement in religious education, especially in Christian church education, is a way of life for the majority of Koreans in the United States, as contrasted with that in Korea where only 21 percent of the national population is affiliated with Christian churches.[14] Hurh and Kim continue their research by raising following questions:

> Why such an unusually high degree of church participation among the Korean immigrants? Is it due to the Christian background of the Korean immigrants (the pre-immigration factor)? Or is it attributable to some

> socio-cultural and psychological factors closely associated with the migration process (uprooting and adjustment)? In other words, would the immigrants become more involved in the ethnic church's activities because of their heightened need for a communal bond or *social belonging* and *psychological comfort* in a strange land, and/or would they become more religious because of their intensified search for the *existential meaning* of uprooting from Korea and rerooting in America?[15]

According to Choy, for Korean immigrants, the church functioned as a social center and a means of cultural identification (specifically for language and traditional values); it serves an educational function by teaching American-born Koreans the Korean language, history and culture; and it keeps Korean nationalism alive. Choy continues to explains how the Korean churches began to function as educational and social service centers:

> Most of the early immigrants had no opportunities for education in Korea and about 5% were illiterate. Therefore the church leaders felt that the first order of Korean community projects was the establishment of evening schools. Immigrants [adults] and their children were encouraged to learn how to read and speak Korean . . . As a result, within a ten-year period, illiteracy among Korean immigrants was wiped out, while Korean children were able to read and speak their ancestral language and to have some background of Korean history and culture.[16]

Hurh and Kim found out that religious motives predominated over social or psychological motives. Social or psychological motives were found to be the second most important reason for participating the worship service in the church.[17]

Are there then some other theories in relation to motivating factors? Of course, there are other several motivating factor theories. Peter Berger's concepts of "cultural, political, social, and psychological religions" are helpful.[18] Also, the concept of "civil religion," formulated by the famous sociologist, Robert Bellah, is one of religion's functions.[19] Sullivan's theory of "personal world" and "cultural forms" can be a great tool to look at the motivation of Korean immigrants from a psychological point of view. Sullivan's view is particularly valuable to see why Korean immigrants have a tendency to cling together. Sullivan rejects the notion of the individual as an autonomous social unit[20], and Sullivan's concept of humans as social beings is very similar to the one of George Albert Coe which is found in his famous *A Social Theory of Religious Education.*[21] Hence, these immigrants seem to have composite reasons for their pervasive participation in church education: to pray and to be saved (the religious), to meet friends (the social), and to seek peace of mind (the psychological). Thus the religious (Christian) fellowship and the ethnic (Korean) fellowship influence each other to provide the individual church members with psychological comfort or personal solace.[22] Therefore, four crucial motivating factors can be delineated for Korean immigrants to participate in churches: cultural motivating factor, social motivating factor, psychological motivating factor, and religious motivating factor.

3. Relationship between Motivation Factor Theories for Non-Religious Adult Education and Religious Participation of Korean Immigrants in the U.S.

As mentioned earlier, Morstain and Smart's six-factor theory will be used as one model of motivation factor theory--which includes social relationships, external expectations, social welfare, professional advancement, escape/stimulation, and cognitive interest, for non-religious adult education; while four integrated factors, which are cultural, social, psychological, and religious (basically an assessment of Hurh and Kim's theory), will be used to understand religious participation of Korean immigrants in the United States. The task of comparing the two is to find out the relation between the two models and to find some practical implications after comparison.

Among the six motivation factors from Morstain and Smart's theory at least four of them have ingredients and characteristics similar to the factors motivating Korean Americans. The factors are as follows: social relationships, external expectations, social welfare, and escape/stimulation. The factor of social relationships certainly matches with one of the religious factors, the social factor (i.e., to make friends). In immigrant churches, new immigrants are always reminded that they should come to the church if they want to make friends. In addition, many couples are formed in the churches. In fact, even many non-church goers often ask the minister to conduct their marriage in the church. Surely the church is a center for social gathering.

Since Morstain and Smart's notion of external expectations means that participants come because of the wishes of someone else with authority, this factor matches with the religious motivation factor, under which people come to church to be ruled by the authority of the Scriptures and God. Many Koreans have been accustomed to being submissive, throughout their cultural and religious history, to the authority which was once the king of the nation and is now God.

As far as the social welfare factor is concerned, the cultural or nationalistic motivation factor can be related. Korean immigrants tend to cling together because they know that if they do not support each other they can hardly survive. So they come to church and encourage others to come to church and join them. Such a sense of bond creates a lot of human power (mentally and materially) in the society. Korean immigrants gather together and establish a church, so that they have a center to work together and feel the oneness (or sameness) together. Moreover, they teach their children Korean language in the church in order to transmit their religious and cultural heritage to their descendants.

The last factor, the escape/stimulation motivation factor, can be matched with the factor of psychological motivation. Although it may sound unreasonable to say that people come to church to escape their routine, it is true that people do come to church to escape from the bondage of their life's on-going routine. Ethnic people come to their church to have the sense of security in their lives. As marginal people in the society, they often find themselves living in a strange land. Due to cultural and language barriers, it is impossible to communicate with the people of other culture/language in the society. These people, however, come to church to be stimulated by a higher standard in life through worship as well as Bible studies. Therefore, these two factors, escape/stimulation and psychological motivation, do have a lot in common. It seems apparent that Korean immigrants do not come to their ethnic church in relation to their jobs. In other words, there is no relationship between non-religious motivating factors and the participation of Korean immigrants in the church as far as money or professional advancement is concerned. As a matter of fact, Korean immigrants give a large amount of offerings to their churches. However, other than purely religious reasons such as prayer and almsgiving, there seems to be some correlation, in terms of social welfare factors and escape/stimulation factors, between the secular theories and religious theories on motivating factors that elicit adult to participate in adult education.

Conclusion and Implications

Through careful observation of the relationship between the theory of Korean American religious education participation, Morstain and Smart's study of nonreligious education participation, and Morstain and Smart's non-religious motivating factor theory, we can find some correlation between the two. It is, however, still unbelievable to see such a growth of Korean immigrant churches. To provide some answers to our surprise, Hurh and Kim explains this way: "The Christian legacy left by the early Korean immigrants was further reinforced by the influx of the new Korean immigrants who were largely drawn from an urban middle-class background, and most of them have a Protestant background in Korea."[23] With this human power, the church provides not only meaning but also belonging and comfort. The search for the meaning in life goes on not only in an individual context, but also in a corporate context as a church.

The Korean ethnic church has, nonetheless, provided many motivating factors as we discussed earlier, such as a well-established social, cultural, and educational center for Koreans in the United States. Korean ethnic churches have also provided a lot of opportunities for group interactions, by which the church contributed to form a communal bond and solidarity among people. In addition, the fact that Koreans are an ethnic minority group in the States has also accelerated the growth of their ethnic church.

We should note, however, there is an obvious point of departure in the Korean immigrant church case from Morstain and Smart's non-religious motivation factor theory. What is the point of departure? It is "money."

Korean Americans do not come to church for more money. Rather, they are known as good tithe/offering givers. Hence, when it comes to the issue of betterment of living conditions or financial matters, we cannot relate the nonreligious motivating factors to the participation level in the Korean church. (It is true, however, that these immigrants help each other in terms of getting jobs through the network in the church). Their reasons for coming to church are dominantly psychological, social, and religious ones. In sum, while non-religious participants come to adult education classes for a better life condition or more money, Korean Americans come to church education to build relationship with others and God. As a result, they find their identity in a group and solace by interacting with others and by seeking other-worldly hope together.

So, what can be concluded through this study? We can conclude that although it seems that the two theories have much in common, the Korean American participation theory can only work within their uniquely distinctive context in this time of history. We are to be satisfied only to know the fact that non-religious factor theories are a sure help but only aids (tools) in acquiring better understanding of Korean Americans' enormous participation in their religious education. Thus, the principles that worked for the participation of Korean American churches cannot be applied to promote the motivation level in American churches.

Chapter Thirteen

Encountering the Other:
My Baptism into a Korean American Youth Group - Toward a Culturally and Socially Informed Ministry[1]

Frank M. Yamada

I. Introduction

I must open with a confession. When I first envisioned this paper, I imagined that it would resemble, in some way, an ethnography (admittedly a novice's attempt at an ethnography, yet anethnography all the same). In the process of my research, ethnographic models and anthropological theories began to give way to periodicals and books that were essentially grounded in Asian American social activism. I found that these materials were much more relevant and engaging in light of the context for my study. Along side of my academic pursuits, I was ministering as a part-time "*Jundosanim*" (youth pastor) at the Korean Presbyterian church where I had intended to carry out my ethnographic experiment. I soon found, however, that being a minister and an ethnographer simultaneously is an extremely difficult task. In my role as ethnographer I felt the need to distance myself from the youth in order to interpret the data that I was collecting. This put me at odds with my role as a minister where I was required to be thoroughly involved in these young peoples' lives. Another tension was the trust issue. I couldn't collect the data that I needed (anthropologically speaking) without putting the pastor/parishioner relationship in jeopardy. These kids, who have few adult role models, would have had a hard time trusting me as their minister if they thought that I was simply there to get information out of them. As I began to research this paper, I ran across articles and books that pointed out social and political structures that created the framework for these Korean kids' struggle. Thus my paper, which originally began as an academic venture in ethnography, has ended up looking more like an attempt to raise awareness about the issues that confront Asian

Americans, and is a call for Asian American social justice and activism. This shift is representative of my ever-changing stance within and with regard to the Asian American community. The present essay will take the reader on a small portion of my journey -- encountering the "other," embodied in the members of this group. It will suggest my interpretation of the situation that confronts the youth at this particular church. With such a goal in mind, I have decided to open my paper with a prayer presented at the National Convocation of Asian American United Methodist Churches. I find it to be an appropriate starting point. It is entitled, "Remembering the Past":

> From many different communities we gather as one.
> We are one in the Spirit of the Lord, Jesus Christ!
> Our beginnings as Asian Americans were not always happy,
> gilt realizations of hopes and dreams.
> We came searching for a Promised Land,
> a land of opportunity,
> a land of equality, a land of freedom for all.
> We came to this land laden NOT with material wealth,
> But rather, laden with a wealth of beauty
> within the richness of our culture
> and the love felt within our family circles.
> Once here, we found many of our hopes and dreams
> dashed to pieces amidst ravages of evil,
> of hatred, of prejudice.
> Ours is a history of pain and suffering.
> Ours is a history of tears and toil.
> Ours is a history of struggling to cope,
> of being forced to assimilate
> of bowing in submission as a slave to his master.
> From many different communities we gather as one.
> We are one in the Spirit of Israel in bondage.
> May God draw near to us as we turn to him in prayer.[2]

II. Born Again: My Baptism into the Group

When I was first introduced to "the youth group," I came as a visitor -- an outsider. A friend of mine, Kevin Park, had invited me to do some guest speaking during the summer of 1993. I willingly accepted and made the 45-minute journey to a small old church building of some denomination that eludes me at the present. I really enjoyed my first encounter with the kids, and they apparently were very fond of me as well. I think this had something to do with the fact that I gave fifteen-minute sermons, while Kevin's were rarely shorter than forty-five. Either way, I found the kids very attentive and receptive. They considered me to be some kind of novelty. A few sermons and a couple of guitar performances later, I found myself working with this same group of high schoolers during the summer of 1994. It proved to be a summer that would permanently change the way that I see myself as an Asian American.

Our first official service together was held at a beach park in Delaware. I'll never forget how strongly they responded to my inaugural sermon -- my first real attempt at being a *Jundosanim*. My text was Joshua chapter one, and I preached on being "strong and courageous" through inevitable transitions. For some reason, this idea of transition and a life characterized by change struck many chords in my young audience. Later I would find out that their lives were characterized by transition: transition when they went to school in the morning, and transition when they came back home to their Korean speaking parents. This was my first encounter and extended relationship with any ethnic group outside of my own family. Though I recognized many similarities with my own relatives, I perceived many cultural characteristics that differed as well. This difference was highlighted by the fact that I am a third generation Asian American (very assimilated to western culture). More significantly, I am a third generation *Japanese* American. Most of the kids in the youth group had immigrated from Korea with their parents, and though they had good English skills, they seemed to maintain many elements which they acknowledged as being traditionally Korean.

As I continued to work with these youth, I began to notice shifts in my way of thinking. I found myself wanting to pronounce Korean words correctly and desiring to eat Korean food (which is very spicy, or perhaps American food is very bland). I began to feel the need to be accepted by this group, and in a very real way they did take me in. Yet there was always something that kept distance between us. The issue wasn't just language (I don't speak Korean), though this seemed to play a big part. There were and are aspects of their culture that I simply will never share with them, no matter how hard both parties strive to understand each other. My experience, while similar in many respects to theirs, is still inherently different. Nevertheless, I recognized that my weekly encounters with this youth group began to have a profound affect on the way that I perceived myself as an Asian American. Somehow as I struggled to get to know them, I was simultaneously wrestling with my own Asian identity long dormant by the years of assimilation and growing up in American schools. I found myself beginning to identify with their struggles as immigrant Americans, and I resonated, despite our differences, with their pains and sufferings. I had been baptized into the experience of the first and second generation (what is now called the 1.5 generation) Korean American youth. It was, in a sense for me, a conversion experience. Peacock's words describing field work are fitting:

> The analogy of conversion is perhaps too dramatic, but the field-worker does undergo some kind of inner transformation. He experiences "culture shock" when he enters the field and a reverse shock when he comes home. During the work, he has eye-opening encounters, which shatter assumptions held all his life. Gradually he becomes, as we say, "acculturated," which means that he develops some degree of identity with the new culture and group, more often than not coming to think of them as "his people . . ."[3]

I began to realize that in spite of our cultural differences, their struggles were in a very real way my struggles. As I began to embrace aspects of their lives as Korean Americans, I began to embrace areas of my own Japanese-ness. As I began to hear their stories one by one, so I began to hear my own story in a different light. Little did I know that this was just the beginning of a growing struggle and awareness concerning the issues that face Asian Americans -- struggles that were a part of my latent past, and which are the existence that characterizes the youth of the Korean American church. Before elaborating more on this topic, it will prove helpful to provide a brief socio-cultural sketch of the Korean immigrant to help us to understand the history and experience that lies behind our present inquiry.

III. The Story of the Korean Immigrant in America

The earliest Korean immigrants came predominantly as laborers for the sugar plantations in Hawaii at the turn of the century (early 1900's). During and after the Japanese occupation of Korea (1910-1945) waves of Korean immigrants moved to America, with the majority coming after 1965. In 1988, officials estimated anywhere between 700,000 and one million Koreans living in the United States, with most settling in large metropolitan areas such as New York and Los Angeles.[4]

The American public since the late 1950's has continually portrayed Asian Americans as the "ideal immigrants." This issue will be looked at more extensively later. Here I wish to emphasize that the Korean immigrant's existence in America is far from ideal. Sang Lee has identified the experience of Korean Americans as being characterized by "marginality." He says,

> Marginality, first of all, means that Korean immigrants experience a social and cultural displacement or uprootedness. They are no longer in Korea, nor are they really part of America. They are very much "in between," feeling a sense of ambivalence and the cultural conflicts that naturally result.[5]

This marginality is due, in large part, to the lack of acceptance by the "host society." Thus, Korean immigrants are very much on the "outside." While a large degree of cultural assimilation is possible for Koreans, based on models constructed in light of Japanese and Chinese Americans, full social integration and participation in American society is tenuous at best. Hurh suggests,

> Non-white immigrants may attain a high degree of cultural assimilation (adoption of American life-style), but structural assimilation (equal life-chances) is virtually impossible unless the immutable independent variable, "race," becomes mutable through miscegenation or

> cognitive mutation of the WASP. Koreans are no exception to this *Lebensschicksal*.[6]

This "life-destiny" leaves the Korean American in an isolated situation. The double-bind of Korean immigrant life (not being a part of either Korean or American culture) helps explain to sociologists the importance of the church to the Korean community. The Korean American church not only provides the immigrant with religious stimulation, but it also serves the socio-cultural function of providing a semi-familiar atmosphere with people who share a common plight and culture. These "socio-cultural needs" are amplified in the Korean immigrant in that he/she suffers from social dislocation and marginality as suggested above. This would help explain, as well, why Korean Americans take official church positions with grave seriousness. Hurh and Kim state,

> The involuntary ethnic containment and voluntary ethnic attachment of the Korean immigrants' life in the United States explain why they are so extensively and intensively involved in their ethnic church, which provides a focal point of social belonging, recognition, and emotional comfort, recreation, and of maintaining a vital linkage to their old country -- ethnic fellowship and solidarity.[7]

Thus Korean immigrants, because of their experiences of dislocation, create for themselves worlds of social and cultural meaning by association with and participation in Korean American churches. This information helps explain an apparent enigma that surrounded the church of my youth group: "What keeps these people coming back to this place?"

IV. Why Is Your Church So Far?

When I originally found out how far my friend Kevin travelled to his church (two times a week), I was shocked. The church, which is forty-five minutes to an hour south and west of Princeton, is located in a suburb near the New Jersey/Pennsylvania border. Most of the kids and adults who make up the congregation, however, come from the Philadelphia area (about forty-five minutes north and west). It was surprising for me to know how far each member of the church drove to attend bi-weekly meetings. On top of this, Kevin would leave his apartment two hours before each meeting to pick up the Philadelphia kids in the church van. This added another two hours to the ride back as well, when he returned the kids to their respective homes. Besides Kevin's personal commitment to the church, the kids, themselves, also show strong attachments to the group. Despite their peers' desires to play the weekend away, these youth religiously attend church meetings on Friday night and Sunday morning/afternoon. This group mentality is hard to describe to people outside of the church. A couple examples will prove helpful.

During the first summer that I worked at this church, we had a week long retreat in the Poconos. On the last night of the retreat, we had a candlelight service that started around 10:30 p.m. We gathered in a circle and lit our candles. After we had turned off the lights, Kevin invited members of the circle to share what was on their heart. There was a long period of silence as I played the guitar softly. The first to speak was Bill. Billy, who is normally a very shy person, began relating how he used to be a social misfit and a disappointment to his mom. He told of how hard it was to watch his single mother work her fingers to the bone ten to twelve hours a day, six to seven days a week. Billy tried to do well in school, but the pressure eventually got to him. His grades were falling, which made his mom worry more. Watching his mom suffer became too much for him. Billy paused to fight back the tears that had already begun to stream down his face. He found his composure and spoke of how this youth group had saved him from turning to the streets. "There's just so much love and support, and Kevin is like a big brother that I never had." By now, the whole group was crying out loud. One by one each began to share his/her story, all very similar to Billy's. Each had recognized the group's salvific power. There were, however, a few girls who could not lift their heads. For now, their stories go untold. Throughout the sharing, a common theme arose: "Where would I be without this group." As our candles began to burn down my eye caught the fluorescent numbers of my watch. Our meeting had lasted till 4:30 a.m.

In the early fall, while the leaves were still changing, I had the youth group over to my house one particular Friday night. It was a brisk night, and we decided that it would be a good night for an evening flashlight stroll along the Raritan Canal path. The youth meeting was exceptionally large that evening (about 25 kids). There were about five or six new kids who came from the Cherry Hill area (a couple blocks from the church). As we were walking that night I noticed that some of the new people were smoking. This was given a very negative reception from the youth group regulars. The next day I talked to some of the Philadelphia kids, in attempts to find out how they felt about the incident from the night before. Their response surprised me. I knew from past conversations that smoking was nothing new to most of these kids (they attend inner-city schools), but the behavior of the new people from Cherry Hill bothered them all the same. When I pushed them on this, their response was, "Smoking is disrespectful to the group, especially at church." What stuck out to me about their reaction was that their concern was for the group. The new kids by smoking -- breaking a collective norm -- were not showing respect for the group. This had very little to do with personal preferences or grievances, but was centered on a group mentality. In the minds of the regulars, loyalty to others should over-ride individual habits.

These two illustrations point to how the group reinforces and protects itself through its members. As the candlelight service suggested above, the member solidarity with each other was based on their experience of isolation, not only from their homeland, but also from their host country as well. Their association with the group is both voluntary and necessary. It is voluntary in that the individual members have chosen to associate with others of like experience. It is necessary in that they are driven to find support among each other since they are not allowed full participation in US culture. The smoking incident illustrates how the group exercises control over behaviors that it deems "out of line." This emphasizes the group's priority over the desires of the individual. Cultural anthropologists have suggested that such behavior is indicative of the dyadic personality, characteristic among eastern cultures. Within such a perspective, the individual views him or herself in light of a larger social group (e.g., the family). Thus, Billy does not think of his occupational success or failure in light of his own personal aspirations, but in view of his family's economic condition.

Billy's situation is typical for children of Korean immigrants in that he was drawn to this particular church based on his similar life experience. His own life is dictated by elements that are out of his control (i.e., his mother's difficult situation and his own inability to thrive in the American education system). The group has become his salvation. It is a place where he can be nurtured and find social belonging in a society that continues to leave him dislocated. This problem of marginalization, evident in the lives of the Korean American youth, is built on discrimination and racism that pervades American society. It is to this issue, with its systemic ramifications, that we now turn our attention.

V. Discrimination in the Asian American and Korean American Context

> There is a widespread belief that Asian and Pacific Americans do not suffer discrimination and disadvantages associated with other minority groups. The fact is that in spite of recent efforts to promote civil rights and equal opportunities for ethnic minorities in the United States, Asian and Pacific Americans have been largely neglected and ignored . . .[8]

The Korean Americans, and Asian Americans in general, suffer from discrimination that is both promoted and perpetuated by the dominant American culture. This discrimination is fueled by one particularly common stereotype, i.e., the Asian American as a "model minority." The US Commission on Civil Rights puts it this way:

> According to this stereotype, which is based partly on uncritical reliance on statistics revealing the high average family incomes, educational attainment, and occupational status of Asian Americans, Asian Americans are hardworking, intelligent, and successful.[9]

This stereotype, as flattering as it may sound, does have "damaging consequences." First of all it causes people to ignore the real social and economic problems that many Asian Americans face. This is especially relevant to the Korean Americans of my church, along with other Asian American groups that are economically and socially underprivileged. Second, this "model minority" stereo-type may distract people from the discrimination that *does* exist in modern American society (e.g., glass ceilings in employment for Asians and Asian Americans). Third, as is the case for the members of my church's youth group, the "model minority" image may create undue stress upon the younger generations of Asian Americans to succeed -- live up to the stereo-type. Finally, the "model minority" depiction of Asian Americans creates inter-racial stress between Asian Americans and other ethnic groups.[10] This was especially felt by the Korean American community during and after the L.A. riots of April, 1992. In times where there is an inordinate amount of racial tension, as was the case during and after the Rodney King trials, Asian American small businesses can easily become the symbolic targets of racially motivated anger directed against the "corporate devastation" of the inner city neighborhoods. Omatsu states that,

> (t)he Asian immigrant becomes a symbol of wealth -- and also greed; a symbol of hard work -- and also materialism; a symbol of intelligence -- and also arrogance; a symbol of self-reliance -- and also selfishness and lack of community concern.[11]

Thus, what on the surface appears to be a compliment to Asian Americans actually provides a stereo-type that fosters inter-ethnic hostility and competition. Simply put, this image of Asian Americans created by sociologists, politicians, and the media is a systemic way of keeping the "model minority" within the bounds of a discriminating system.

The discriminating stereotype, Asian Americans as the "model minority," has an adverse effect upon the children of Asian American immigrants. Lee characterizes the experience of the second generation Korean American as a double bind:

> The second-generation youth, by virtue of their particular situation, face a more difficult predicament than do their elders. For one thing, they are far more deeply involved in the white American world than is the first generation. This means that they are self-consciously aware of their marginalization much more acutely than are their parents . . . They never belonged deeply to the Korean culture or

> social world and, therefore, cannot return to it. They are truly in a wilderness, in the world of in-betweenness and homelessness.[12]

This is the dilemma for the youth of the Korean American church. They find themselves walking in two worlds simultaneously, neither one fully accepting them and their awkward situation. This can be seen in the life of Lisa, one of the newer members of our youth group. The first thing that I noticed about Lisa, when she first started showing up last summer, was that she dressed to impress. She always came to church in full make-up, usually wearing a skirt that was short enough to make the elders of the church nervous. Last December, as I was diligently finishing up my end of the year assignments, I received a call from Kevin on a Saturday afternoon. Apparently Lisa never came home from church on Friday night, and her mother was very worried. After talking through some well-intentioned coverups, one of Lisa's new found friends (a boy, of course), called me to let me know where the two of them were hiding out. I drove out to Cherry Hill where they were staying at another local church. Lisa, who is normally cold and aloof, related to me that her mother and she had gotten into another fight. Apparently this was happening with such frequency that it became too much for Lisa and she decided to run away for a few days. When I began to get to the heart of the problem I realized that Lisa was struggling with her life not only inside, but outside the home as well. She was on the brink of being expelled from school. She was having trouble fitting in with others. As well, she was presently in a romantic relationship in which she wasn't comfortable. She had started coming to our church so that she could meet other Asians, but had found that the members in the group did not think too highly of her because of her reputation. As she began to paint her own verbal self-portrait, I began to see an afraid and lonely teenager who wanted desperately to belong to something or someone. When I asked Lisa, however, if she had told her mom of her situation, she replied, "I could never tell my mom those kind of things, she would never understand." The truth is, Lisa was right. Her mom, who speaks very little English, has a hard time relating to many aspects of western culture, and therefore has a difficult time understanding the situations that her daughter is going through. Her mother's frustrations in the work place, coupled with her daughter's progressive distancing, often ended with Lisa's mom exploding irrationally over some trivial matter. Thus, Lisa feels trapped -- caught in the webs of two worlds. On the one hand she is not fully able to participate in the dominant culture, and on the other she is isolated at home by a mother who doesn't understand her. Her decision to run away from home wasn't too dramatic of a step for Lisa in that she never really had a home to run away from. The more she tried to accommodate herself to her peers, the more she alienated herself from her mother -- from her only source of Korean family. The more she tried to fit in, through dress and lifestyle, the more her life at home became unbearable. This two-sided dilemma is portrayed in another Korean American's story -- that of Bong Hwan Kim:

> I wanted to be as American as possible -- playing football, dating cheerleaders. I drank a lot and tried to be cool. I had convinced myself that I was "American," whatever that meant, all the while knowing underneath that I'd have to reconcile myself, to try to figure out where I would fit in a society that never sanctioned that identity as a public possibility. Part of growing up in America meant denying my cultural and ethnic identity, and part of that meant negating my parents.[13]

The problems that Bong Hwan and Lisa encounter as Korean Americans is based on their double marginality. They do not fit in as Americans, but they also can't relate to the first generation Korean immigrants -- their parents. Thus, double marginality characterizes the experience of second generation (and 1. 5 generation) Korean Americans.

Another way that Korean American youth are affected by discrimination can be seen in prevailing attitudes among Asian Americans toward education and success. In many ways, Asian Americans have bought into the lie of American capitalism: if one gets a solid education and works hard enough, life will be all right. Yoshiwara states,

> For the Asian Americans, as it was for many other peoples, the road to success was defined as being through education. Those who emigrated to this country from

> Asia soon resigned themselves to nonsuccess. They turned instead to dedicating their lives to the success of their American-born children. Education was defined as the key to social mobility and financial success early in our history, and the Asian Americans took up the cry and poured forth their every effort to pave the road to success for their children.[14]

During our summer retreat candle vigil, another young man by the name of Kyoung shared his situation. Apparently his sister was soon going away to college. This would leave Kyoung alone with his parents -- a thought that frightened him. Kyoung is very bright and gets good grades. In fact, recently he had scored a 1400 on the SATs. As he shared with the group about his struggles and about the stress put upon him to succeed by his parents, he began to weep uncontrollably. Though we tried to comfort him, and reassure him of his abilities, he kept on repeating over and over again, "But what if I fail, but what if I fail?" In his sobbing question I heard a plea -- an appeal to not have to be perfect. One wonders if Kyoung will have the strength to overcome his personal agony, which is rooted and perpetuated by the "model immigrant" stereotype. Apparently this ideal runs deep in him and deep in his family as well.

What often fuels this obsession for success in Korean American children is the guilt that they face in light of their parents' economic and social struggle in a society that does not accommodate immigrant Americans. Elaine Kim says,

> Immigrant Korean parents often view themselves as sacrificial lambs, believing that even though they go to their graves deaf, dumb, and blind, they are doing it so that their children can achieve the so-called American dream. Their kids work incredibly hard, knowing that only they can vindicate their parents for their sacrifice.[15]

Another recurrent theme in our candlelight service was the kids' confession of how difficult it is to see their parents work so hard. This causes them to feel all the more ashamed if they are not able to live up to occupational expectations of their parents. There is a sad irony in this picture. The harder that the Korean American kids work to please their parents, the more they (the children) are required to accommodate themselves to the American way of life -- to buy into the American dream. The more they desire to fulfill the wishes of their Korean parents, the less they look like Koreans. To satisfy and respect the desires of their parents, Korean children must ultimately denounce their parents. The reality is disturbingly apparent. In order for the Korean youth to succeed, thus fulfilling their parents wishes and living up to the "model immigrant" ideal, he/she must become a true blooded American and thus a non-Korean. Ichishita says,

> The truth of the matter is that the problem is not inherent in the Asian American place in this society. The problem is inherent in prevailing American concepts of national and racial identity. This nation is perceived as a nation of white, western European immigrants and their descendants. It is not sufficient, it is perceived, to be a child of God. It is necessary to be a white child of God.[16]

The reality of American society, however, "like the reality of the global society, is that it is not uniformly white."[17] The imposition, therefore, should not lie on the Korean American community (or the Asian American community, in general) to eke out an acceptable living at the expense of our families and culture, but the burden should fall upon the white American society "to relinquish its concept of dominance, and to become part and parcel of the rest of the human family . . ."[18] This does not advocate an oppression of the white male, so to speak, but encourages the dominant white American culture to become one among equals in the ever growing quest for true ethnic diversity.

VI. The Unheard Story: Women of Abuse in Asian American Families

Before some concluding remarks, a story must be heard that till now has been born in silence by the "other" who is often without voice. The story belongs to those women and girls who have been kept silent for many years on account of racial, sexual and patriarchal oppression. Sonia Shah accurately describes the plight of Asian American women:

> . . . we not only suffer cultural discrimination as men also do, but our own form of cultural schizophrenia, from the mixed and often contradictory signals about priorities, values, duty, and meaning our families and greater communities convey. We encounter sexist Asian tradition, racist and sexist white culture, anti-racist non-feminist women heroes, racist feminist heroes, strong proud Asian women who told us not to make waves, strong proud non-Asian women who told us to make waves, and on, and on.[19]

Thus, Korean American women encounter discrimination and its hazardous effects, but in a different way from their male counterparts. In a culture that stresses family maintenance, and where identity is wrapped up in one's family unit, Korean American women often find their hands tied in situations of domestic violence. As well, Asian American women, "because of linguistic and cultural barriers rely more heavily on the family structure than they would in their home countries."[20] Thus, Korean American women, and Asian American women in general, also face a double bind on account of discrimination. They are more isolated from mainstream society because of the language barrier. Thus, they have a strong need for family. This, however, puts Korean American women in a quandary when domestic violence is present. How can they turn against their only means ofsupport? Often their loyalty to the family will outweigh their ownpersonal misery.

One of my closest relationships in the youth group is with a girl named Jane. Jane is a vivacious and humorous thirteen-year-old who came over from Korea when she was about six. I had a conversation with Jane recently that shook up both of our worlds. In the course of our talk she suggested to me that she had a problem. As she began to describe her symptoms, it became apparent to me that she had all the characteristics of someone who had suffered from sexual abuse. When I hinted that this might be the case, she began to weep with her head in her hands, too ashamed to look into my eyes. As we began to talk through this incident, I became aware that she was in need of help that I was not trained to give. When I suggested that she consider psychological counseling, however, she was very resistant -- not because she herself was ashamed to go to counseling, but because she knew that her mother and the rest of her family would see such a decision as bringing shame on the family. This has a lot to do with Asian Americans' beliefs about mental illness -- it is shameful, and therefore you keep it within the family. While I think that therapy would ultimately help Jane, I know that the idea of going to a therapist could very well produce further psychic trauma due to family pressure and social stigmatization. This is the double bind described above. The very group that defines Jane's identity is at the same time destroying her identity. Those members who in a very real way sustain her life are also causing her silent death. May God grant her a voice to speak against the over-powering evil that has become a part of her existence.[21]

VII. Where Do We Go From Here?

Asian American studies have made significant advances toward bettering the situation for Asian Americans. This study, as well, has taken an initial step toward dealing with some of the problems that surround Korean American youth. By identifying systemic forces such as racism and discrimination that plague the intricate details of Asian American life, we have started down a promising path toward social change. This, however, is only the first step. For as I finish up this paper, and proceed to turn off my word processor, the lives of the Korean American children continue to move forward. In beginning to bring an awareness of the Asian American problem back to my context, I can start by educating those members in my church and youth group with these issues while seeking agencies for affirmative action (i.e., making members aware of the social services available to them). At the macro level, we should encourage participation in groups that advocate Asian American rights in the political arena. This move to the larger issues is crucial, otherwise all effort is spent on coping with the "symptoms" of systemic discrimination, without dealing with the social illnesses of racism and sexism. There must be a balance between dealing with the macro issues of racism, and helping the individual people who suffer from its effects. Within this balance is the beginnings of a socially and culturally informed ministry. I close this paper in the same way that I began it, with a prayer:

From any oppression and enslavement
because of race or color
Deliver us, O Lord.
When we cry to you out of our pain and suffering,
Choo yo, koo hae choo so suh! (Korean)
When even in this day, our sisters and brothers suffer injustices and despair,
Iligtas Mo Kami, O Panginnoon (Filipino)
From any guilt or depression of the past
Tsu-ah tsen-ch'iu wo-men (Chinese)
From every effort to prolong or increase the domination of one race over another,
of one people over any other,
Shu yo, tokihanachi tamae (Japanese)
Deliver us, O God of liberation, we pray,
Amen![22]

Chapter Fourteen

Spiritual Enrichment for Chinese Professionals:
Princeton Christian Church

Noel Y. Lin

The Chinese in America

Chinese first began to arrive in America in significant numbers in the middle of the nineteenth century. Most of these early immigrants were men from the southern Chinese province of Kwangtung who were drawn to California by the gold rush. Thousands of these so-called "sojourners" landed in America throughout the decade of the 1850s, and by 1860 there were over 30,000 Chinese in the U.S.[1] It was in the developing American West that the vast majority of these Chinese first settled. In addition to gold mining, they were also employed in agriculture, factory work, clothing manufacture, and construction. Perhaps the greatest example of the early Chinese contribution to America was the involvement of over 10,000 Chinese workers in the building of the western portion of the first transcontinental railroad from 1865 to 1869.

Initially, the Chinese were welcomed, or at least tolerated, by the resident American population. However, by the late 1850s, significant anti-Chinese sentiment had arisen. In California, a number of laws were passed that severely marginalized the Chinese population. Chinese were prohibited from giving testimony in the courts and were subjected to special taxes designed to harass and intimidate them. As popular resentment toward the Chinese grew, so did the level of violence directed against them. Throughout the western U.S., incidences of Chinese being beaten or killed became more and more common. Driven by antipathy towards foreigners in general and by fear of cheap Chinese labor in particular, a number of anti-Chinese groups appeared, all dedicated to saving the nation from the dreaded "Yellow Peril." In 1882, these groups got their wish when Congress passed the Chinese Exclusion Act barring the immigration of Chinese laborers for ten years. This act was renewed in 1892 for another ten years and then prolonged indefinitely in 1902.

The first few decades of the 20th century continued to witness both official and unofficial acts of discrimination against Chinese living in America. Indeed, it would not be until World War II that American attitudes toward Chinese would start to change. With the U.S. and China fighting as allies, a new, more favorable perspective began to emerge. In 1943, Congress repealed the Exclusion Acts and, three years later, passed a law allowing all Chinese wives of American citizens to enter the U.S. The next major step came in 1952 when the McCarran-Walter Act granted the right of naturalization to immigrants of all races. However, discriminatory immigration policies were not completely abolished until the passage of the Immigration Act of 1965, which established an annual allowance of 20,000 immigrants from each country. For the Chinese already in America, this meant first and foremost that their dreams of bringing family members to the States could finally be realized.

Since the 1960s, the Chinese American population has grown rapidly, from about 230,000 in 1960 to well over one million by 1985.[2] While many Chinese continue to congregate in urban Chinatowns, large numbers have also settled in suburban America. This latter group is typically more affluent, better educated, and more acculturated to the broader American society than the former. In particular, the second and third generations of immigrant Chinese have achieved significant cultural assimilation in this society and have found much success educationally and professionally.

Still, the present Chinese American population remains quite heterogeneous both in terms of socio-economic background and cultural orientation. The fact that new arrivals come to America from so many different points of origin (Mainland China, Taiwan, Hong Kong, the Philippines, Southeast Asia, etc.) means that differences in custom, language, and even diet are ever present. Of course, American born and American raised Chinese add still more diversity to the mix. Such differences in the Chinese American community give it a marvelous richness and dynamism, but it also produces tensions and prejudices that threaten to divide the community at large and individual families and associations in particular. The great challenge to this community at all levels now is to deal with these differences constructively.

Throughout its history, the Chinese American community has fostered numerous small groups and organizations that have served to assist their members in meeting the challenges of life in the U.S. Early on, Chinese immigrants banded together in mutual aid societies and benevolent associations. These groups continue to play an important role in the community today, along with Chinese American professional organizations and heritage preservation societies. In recent years, Chinese Christian churches have also become a key center of activity for new immigrants and older groups alike.

Chinese Americans and Christianity

The first Christian ministries in the Chinese American community were established by Caucasian missionaries who had returned from serving in Asia. In 1852, William Speer opened a Presbyterian mission for Chinese in San Francisco, and in subsequent years several other missions and small churches were founded on the West Coast and in Hawaii. Eventually, Chinese Christians themselves took up the leadership of these ministries. Nevertheless, development was generally slow throughout the rest of the 19th century and the early decades of the 20th, due primarily to the restrictions on the further immigration of Chinese.

Since the Second World War, however, and especially after the loosening of U.S. immigration policy in the 1950s and 60s, expansion in Chinese American ministry has been tremendous. A 1955 study reported a respectable number of 66 Chinese churches in the U.S., but by 1982 that number had mushroomed to 468.[3] In 1995, there were 695 Chinese churches in America.[4] In addition, a growing number of Chinese Christian organizations, including campus fellowships, publishing houses, resource centers, media companies, outreach groups, and even a handful of seminaries and schools of theology, have been established.

Most of these Chinese American ministries are evangelical in outlook and conservative in theology. The great majority of the churches are independent. Of those which are denominational, most are Southern Baptist or Christian and Missionary Alliance.[5] Relatively few are members of the so-called mainline denominations.

Although the percentage of church attendees among Chinese Americans is lower than that of the American population as a whole, it is significantly higher than the figures for church attendance in the Chinese speaking areas of Asia.[6] This is due primarily to the emphasis in Chinese American churches on evangelism and outreach. Chinese Christians typically are very strongly encouraged to share the gospel with unsaved family members and friends, many of whom are new immigrants. Many Chinese congregations and organizations now are language-specific, that is, they focus their ministries specifically on Mandarin, Cantonese, Taiwanese, or English speaking groups. In the view of many Chinese Christians, these separations are unavoidable and in fact necessary if the churches are to achieve greater success in reaching the diverse Chinese American community.

Apparently just as unavoidable, however, are the conflicts that arise because of such divisions. As Chinese American ministries continue to grow and expand, preserving a spirit of unity and cooperation among the churches and organizations will be a significant challenge. Another challenge is the training and equipping of more ministers, especially those who are bilingual or trilingual. The success of Chinese churches in the next century will likely depend on the emergence of younger, American born or raised pastors and leaders.

In many ways, Chinese American ministries as a whole are still in their youth, so to speak. A large number of churches and organizations were established in the 1970s or 80s and have only now begun to hit their stride. While certain segments of American Christianity have suffered from declining membership and dwindling programs, Chinese American churches are still experiencing growth in both numbers and resources. Most of the ministers in these churches would agree that greater opportunities are still on the horizon. The Princeton Christian Church (PCC) in Princeton, New Jersey, serves as a good example of a growing Chinese congregation that is now coming into its own and is poised for fresh ministry opportunities in the near future.[7]

Princeton Christian Church

***The Early Years*:** Like many Chinese churches in the U.S., the Princeton Christian Church began as a Bible study and fellowship group. The original small gathering consisted of Chinese and Chinese Americans studying at Princeton University. Although some of these students attended various churches in the local area, they nonetheless desired to join together for their own informal fellowship. The first meetings began in 1972 and were held on the University campus. With the help of Wing H. Lam, a doctoral candidate at Princeton Theological Seminary, the fledgling group achieved a certain amount of stability, meeting weekly for Scripture study and prayer. This Princeton Chinese Christian Fellowship, as it was called, soon attracted through word of mouth not only a growing number of students but also Chinese families and single professionals residing in the area. These new members of the group were drawn by the desire both for religious fellowship and for social interaction with others sharing similar cultural and linguistic ties.

This growth in attendance eventually necessitated a move to larger facilities, so in 1974 the fellowship began meeting at the Princeton Baptist Church on U.S. Route 1. The increase in numbers also led to a couple of other important changes. First, it was decided that the word "Chinese" should be dropped from the official name of the fellowship, reflecting a desire on the part of the members to have the group become more multicultural. In fact, the fellowship already included several members from different ethnic backgrounds, particularly Southeast Asians and non-Asian spouses. Second, the fellowship drew up a basic constitution and formulated a statement of faith. In the early days of the group, this had not been seen as necessary but as the fellowship grew questions and concerns about proper organization and faithful teaching arose. This compelled the members to compose a firmer structure for the fellowship both administratively and doctrinally.

By the time Princeton Christian Fellowship (PCF) moved to facilities at the Baptist church, therefore, it had clearly started to develop from a loosely organized, student-led Bible study to something more like a congregation. Indeed, the group was no longer meeting just once a week for fellowship but had begun to hold actual Sunday worship services. Membership was still relatively small, averaging only about thirty, but the brothers and sisters were committed to seeing PCF's ministry expand.

In the mid-1970s, the core group of members consisted mainly of professional people who had come originally from Taiwan or Hong Kong. This of course included some of the students from the early days of the fellowship who had graduated and taken jobs in the Princeton area. However, many others, including brother Lam, eventually moved out of New Jersey at the completion of their programs and thus the relative number of students in PCF decreased. Indeed, ever since the move off campus, PCF has struggled, even up to today as the Princeton Christian Church, to establish stronger connections with the population of Chinese students at Princeton University and other area campuses.

From Fellowship to Church: As PCF started to hold its own Sunday services, a search was begun for a full-time pastor to come in and assume leadership over the nascent congregation. This decision to look for a pastor, however, was not made without dissent. A vocal portion of the membership, influenced by the teachings of the well-known Chinese minister Watchman Nee and the so-called "local church" tradition, felt that there was no need for a full-time minister. They believed that the fellowship members themselves could and should exercise all the preaching and teaching duties of a pastor, which in fact had been the case for some time. Although this group's views did not prevail in this decision, their particular perspective would continue to exercise a strong influence throughout PCF, and later PCC's, development.

Early on in the fellowship's pastoral search, the American Baptist Churches in the U.S.A., of which the Princeton Baptist Church was a member, offered to make PCF an affiliate of their denomination. This offer included a promise of considerable financial assistance as well as help in finding a qualified Chinese American minister to become pastor. Debate among PCF's membership over this issue was vigorous. One side pointed to the obvious benefits of aligning with the American Baptist Church and argued that the surest way to secure and expand PCF's ministry would be to accept the offer. The other side held to the view that PCF's purpose and mission, what many members believed was its special calling to reach out to a certain segment of the Princeton area's population, would be better realized if it remained independent. The latter group prevailed and the search for a pastor continued.

In 1979, that search ended when Paul Chang was invited to become PCF's first full-time minister.[8] Pastor Chang, a former engineer, had served at a church in Los Angeles for some time, but then decided to begin studies in the Master of Divinity program at Westminster Seminary in Philadelphia. Some PCF members who had earlier made his acquaintance introduced him to the congregation and it was soon agreed that he should be the fellowship's pastor. Under his guidance, the congregation continued to grow steadily throughout the 1980s. Pastor

Chang set an emphasis on strong biblical teaching and discipleship as well as on stressing the need for fellowship members to engage in personal evangelism with family, friends, and co-workers. In 1984, PCF officially changed its name to Princeton Christian Church, though again there were voices of dissent on this from those who were uncomfortable with what they saw as a step toward "institutionalizing" the fellowship. Nevertheless, Pastor Chang made a concerted effort to strengthen the structure of the congregation, particularly by establishing the board of deacons to oversee the church's ministries and take responsibility for administration.

***Growing and Moving*:** As the congregation's membership continued to increase, finding adequate facilities became a recurring problem. In 1977, the fellowship had moved out of the Baptist church and into the United Methodist Church on Nassau Street, right in the heart of Princeton. It was not long, however, before a new meeting space had to be found, and the congregation soon began renting the Arts Council building on Witherspoon Street. Eventually, this too proved to be inadequate and a new search was begun for another facility. This endeavor was not an easy one and it was some time before a promising opportunity became available in the township of Kendall Park, several miles north of Princeton. However, the fact that moving to this new facility would take PCC out of Princeton became the subject of much intense debate. Several key members of the congregation insisted that PCC's calling was to be in Princeton and that moving away would signal a fundamental break with the long-standing mission and purpose of the fellowship. Other members argued that since no appropriate facilities seemed to be available in Princeton proper, there really was no other choice, given the inadequacy of the present meeting space, but to relocate. Arguments went back and forth for several months, but eventually the practical pressures of the situation convinced most of the members that moving to Kendall Park was the only option.

Yet just when it appeared certain that a final decision in favor of this move would be made, a new opportunity opened up. One of the members, a woman who had only recently obtained a staff position at Westminster Choir College, realized that her new employer had plenty of facilities available. In fact, Westminster, located just a few blocks from the Arts Council building, not only had ample space but also was in need of some additional income as its own financial situation at that time was shaky (Westminster has since become part of Rider University). So, in what many PCC members saw as a sign of God's providence, the congregation quickly came to an agreement with the choir college and moved to its present facilities on Westminster's campus. That move and the timely manner in which it came about continues to be perceived by many members today as confirmation of God's particular calling for this congregation in the Princeton area.

Although PCC continued to exhibit strong growth on many levels, with average attendance approaching two hundred adults, youth, and children by the end of the 1980s, internal conflicts had also arisen among key members of the church. It was not so much disagreement on particular issues as such but rather unfortunate clashes in personality and leadership style that led to increasing tension. The situation deteriorated to such an extent that in 1991 Paul Chang resigned as PCC's pastor. Still, he agreed to stay on until such time as the church could find a new minister, and it would be more than a year before Dr. Philip Liu would be called as the congregation's next pastor.

***New Opportunities for Ministry*:** The early '90s, therefore, represented a critical period of change for PCC. There was not only the departure of Pastor Chang and the arrival of Pastor Liu, but also the establishment of a second congregation within the church. Since the early days of its existence, the church had conducted its services, classes, and other programs only in Mandarin Chinese, with some limited English translation. However, when Joshua Suen, then a Master of Divinity student at Princeton Seminary, joined the church in 1992 and became available to serve, the leadership decided that it was time to begin a new, English language service. At the time, most of the English speakers in the church were the American born or American raised children of the members themselves, so the English congregation that was formed was essentially a youth congregation. Development and growth in this group was slow at first, but under the care of Pastor Suen, this group has grown rapidly since its inception. At present there are over one hundred members in all, with roughly equal numbers of adults and teens. It is a congregation that has also become quite multicultural, counting people of Korean, Malaysian, Filipino, Anglo, African, Indian, and Caribbean heritage among its members.

Meanwhile, in the last several years the Mandarin congregation has had to deal with the challenge of moving forward after the difficult ordeal of Pastor Chang's resignation and departure. A significant group of disenchanted members, including several deacons, also left the church. Yet the remaining leadership has shown a very high level of commitment to praying and working for the church's recovery and progress. In many ways, the old fellowship emphasis on active involvement by all members and on taking personal responsibility for the state of the community has provided PCC with the strength and resources needed for rebuilding.

A further challenge of a different sort has also presented itself to the Mandarin congregation in recent years. This is the influx into the Princeton area of new immigrants from the People's Republic of China. These mainlanders represent a very different population from the mostly Taiwan or Hong Kong born Chinese who have always formed the core of PCC's membership. Initially, congregation members expressed concern over how well the church would be able to reach out and effectively minister to these new arrivals. However, in keeping with its traditionally strong emphasis on personal evangelism, fellowship, and hospitality, PCC has been able to welcome and incorporate mainland Chinese into the life of the church with considerable success. Within the last ten years, students and professionals from the People's Republic have represented the fastest growing segment of PCC's membership. In fact, at present, fully forty percent of the Mandarin congregation's two hundred or so adult members are mainlanders.

PCC Today: 1998 marks the silver anniversary of PCC, yet despite its already long history the church continues to focus on new opportunities for expanding its ministry. Members in both the Mandarin and English congregations speak often of what they see as the still largely untapped potential of PCC's ministry. The leadership has emphasized that central to realizing this potential in the years to come will be the ability of the church to deepen its discipleship and teaching ministries while maintaining its traditionally strong vision for outreach in the Princeton area.

In the Mandarin congregation, Pastor Liu has made the Sunday School ministry a top priority. This was perhaps to be expected since prior to coming to PCC he was the elder in charge of Christian education at the Rutgers Community Church in Somerset, NJ, the largest Chinese

Christian congregation in the state. Until very recently, Sunday classes at PCC had been conducted without a set curriculum to guide overall progress. Certain members of the congregation would simply be invited to teach classes on a quarterly basis on various topics. With Pastor Liu's guidance, however, the Mandarin congregation has created a set education program that it hopes will catechize members more systematically. The English side is also considering such a program for its members. So while the Sunday School ministry in the past has not been seen as one of the primary strengths of PCC, significant steps are now being taken to bolster this key aspect of the church's life.

Nevertheless, evangelistic outreach continues to be the core of PCC's ministry. Imbued with a strong commitment to share the good news of Jesus Christ, church members generally perceive the Princeton area as a mission field ready for harvest. Sermon after sermon from both the English and Mandarin pulpits reinforce this vision. After all these years, the church remains focused on its purpose of reaching out to the ever-increasing number of ethnic Chinese, other Asians, and mixed couples in the community. Clearly, PCC's membership roll has benefitted from the continuing migration of these groups of people into central New Jersey. While incoming students at Princeton and other local campuses account for a portion of the annual increase in membership, most of the church's new members are professional people. Almost all of these moved to the area because of job offers received from one of the numerous large pharmaceutical, high-tech, telecommunications, or financial consulting companies in and around Princeton.

As in the early days, new arrivals learn about PCC through word of mouth, usually from a co-worker or classmate who happens to be a member. From these initial contacts, visitors are introduced to the church service and the Friday night fellowship meetings. It is in these latter gatherings that newcomers are especially treated to the hospitality of the church. There are at present twelve separate fellowship groups in the church, six in each congregation. With the exception of the seniors fellowship, the other groups are arranged according to region, with members generally attending the fellowship that is nearest their residence. Fellowship meetings, which are held at members' homes, usually center around Bible study or the sharing of personal testimonies, but there is also ample time before and after to chat, enjoy refreshments, and make new friends. Special activities and outings are periodically scheduled, and potluck dinners are a particular favorite among members and visitors alike. (As is the case with most Chinese churches, "food fellowship" plays a very large role in PCC's ministry). It is in this smaller, more comfortable Friday fellowship setting, then, that people are made to feel welcome, and PCC's growth throughout its history has depended to a greater extent on the hospitality of these home group meetings than on the Sunday services.

It is also within the fellowships that the church's ministry of care and support largely occurs. Among their fellowship brothers and sisters, church members give and receive guidance, encouragement, comfort, consolation, and prayer support. While both pastors do take on the responsibility of making special visitations and providing counseling, PCC's approach has always been that all members of the church ought to be ministers to each other. While this is still in some ways an ideal, it is nonetheless a perspective and a calling that many in the two congregations take very seriously. Pastoral care is not perceived to be solely the domain of the pastors, but rather the responsibility of each member.

Indeed, PCC's approach to its pastors has always been something of an anomalous one. Neither Pastor Liu nor Pastor Suen is ordained, and the church has not sought such a step for either of them, or earlier for Pastor Chang as a matter of fact. They do perform all the duties and functions of the pastorate, including preaching, baptizing, and presiding over the holy communion, but they do not receive the title of Reverend nor are they ever addressed as such. This is essentially a reflection of the continuing influence of Watchman Nee's local church perspective, in which ordination is seen as unnecessary. There are indications now, however, that PCC may be gradually moving away from such a position but any real changes in the near future are unlikely. In any case, the pastors do exercise all the spiritual authority that would be proper to an ordained minister within the life of the church.

As for decision-making, authority in the church rests with the two pastors and the board of deacons. There are ten deacons in all, nominated and elected by the congregations for one year terms. With the exception of the deacon chairperson, who oversees the board itself, each deacon has specific responsibility over one aspect of the church's life and ministry. These are worship, education, outreach, youth ministry, English adult ministry, fellowships, special events, facilities, and finance. Of the ten present deacons, eight are from the Mandarin side and two from the English. This disparity reflects not only the difference in size between the two congregations but also the fact that most of the fifty or so regular adult members on the English side are relatively new to the church. Because of this, they are as yet unable to assume leadership on a par with their Mandarin congregation counterparts.

This state of affairs, however, has led to a certain amount of discontent at times from the English side. Although all the leaders are very conscious of the need to work together, lack of communication in a few situations has caused some occasional tension. The English congregation does have a separate committee of co-workers who assist the pastor in carrying out some of the ministries on the English side, such as Sunday School, music ministry, discipleship, etc. Nevertheless, there is sometimes frustration over the fact that the ability of this committee to make decisions is still quite circumscribed. One expects that as the English congregation continues to grow and come into its own, it will have much more of a role to play in the decisions of the church as a whole. Still, certain, often subtle, differences between the two congregations in terms of culture, ways of communicating, and leadership style will probably continue to provide potential energy for future conflicts. Whether those inevitable conflicts can be handled in constructive ways still remains to be seen. In this, though, PCC is by no means unique among Chinese American churches.

Fresh Challenges: As the '90s draw to a close, the church as a whole is facing yet more challenges, and along with these more opportunities. Once again, space has become an issue. With total church membership now well beyond three hundred and steadily climbing, even the capacious facilities of Westminster Choir College are beginning to feel quite cramped. Fortunately, the church several years ago initiated plans for the eventual construction of its own building. Indeed, a sizable lot has been purchased along Route 206 on Princeton's northern border with the neighboring township of Montgomery. If all goes according to schedule, PCC will have its own, brand-new facilities ready for use by the start of the new millennium. Of course, the dilemma still remains about what to do before then. Many suggestions have been proffered but no satisfactory solution has yet been found.

Other significant problems are also presenting themselves. The youth group, now about fifty strong, is in desperate need of a full-time youth minister. The children's ministry is also growing too big for the current lay volunteers to handle. In addition, new worries are arising about how the financial commitment needed to support the building fund will affect other aspects of the church's ministry. No doubt, these issues are daunting ones, and PCC is struggling to find ways to deal with these pressing needs.

Despite the tremendous amount of growth that PCC has undergone in its twenty-five year history, its ministries have remained essentially quite basic. That has, of course, both positive and negative consequences. On the one hand, PCC has stayed true to its perceived calling in the Princeton area and has been very successful in its efforts to reach out and share the gospel. On the other hand, the church has accomplished relatively little in terms of other ministries to the community at large. One of the major weaknesses of the church, something that is in fact beginning to be recognized by the leadership, is its lack of participation in social welfare ministries. Although there is a growing desire on the part of many in the church to correct this imbalance, few as yet have the experience to take concrete steps in the right direction. It will be some time, therefore, before PCC is ready to be as active in other ministries as it is now in evangelistic outreach.

***The Significance and Uniqueness of PCC*:** Indeed, PCC is still learning in many ways how to be a "church" as such. Its own internal ministries, such as Sunday School, youth group, children's program, etc., are still coming into shape. The church has much yet to learn about how to structure and effectively carry out a broader range of ministries. As PCC's leadership, especially the younger deacons and co-workers, continues to develop in the next few years, the challenge will be upon them to take on this task with vigor and creativity.

In many ways, this is still a church in process. Although it clearly has the numerical size and the long history of a full-grown church, PCC remains at heart the fellowship that it has always been. Herein lies its strength. Hospitality and friendship, a family atmosphere, and a simple yet dynamic approach to ministry continue to be the hallmarks of this community. PCC's uniqueness rests with these very features. And its significance as a church, as a ministry, is to be found at the point where these fellowship qualities intersect with the firm conviction that God has called this community to be a witness in Princeton.

Thus despite the challenges that face the church today, PCC's members are confident about the future. Both congregations are still growing and more opportunities for ministry await. Throughout its history, the brothers and sisters of this church have remained convinced that as God has shown much mercy to the church over the years and blessed it with great increase, so God has provided and will provide the guidance and resources needed to nurture that increase and continue the work of ministry.

Chapter Fifteen

Korean Wives of American Servicemen in Shadow Land

Chester Kim

Introduction

The history of the United States is an immigration narrative. The last half of this century has been no different, recording its own immigration pattern.

> In 1940, only one-eighth of Californians were foreign-born. Today everyone in Los Angeles is a member of a minority group. This is not only an inner-city phenomenon. What is true of Southern California is becoming the case in every major urban area in the United States, indeed throughout the world. Our cities are increasingly becoming mirror images of the global village.[1]

In response to recent trends, pastoral theology has been taking a keen interest in cross cultural issues. This is evidenced not only by Paul Schurman's observations but also by David Augsburger[2] and several contributors to the collection of essays in *Pastoral Care and Social Conflict.*[3] My specific focus in this paper will be on the Korean wives of American military personnel as well as biblical, theological and psychological implications involved and the pastoral response of military town churches in America.

Rev. Yee-Seop Park reports that since the Korean War, which ended in 1953,[4] approximately 300,000 Korean women emigrated to other parts of the world, particularly to America. These women did not go overseas as regular emigrants, that is, with their Korean families:

instead, they left Korea as wives of foreign-born males whose language, race and culture were distinctively different from their own.

When these Korean brides went to America or other parts of the world, they did not just become assimilated into the cultures of their spouses. These women started their new married lives encountering cultures that were new and very different from their own. Just as countless immigrants' dreams of life in America have been shattered in their struggle, many of these Korean wives had to face a similar fate. Many of these women eagerly became the wives of American servicemen in hopes that they would be able to escape their low social and economic status in Korea. However, before long, they came to realize that they could not run away from the eyes of status-conscious Korean American communities. Soon they were forced to become marginal,[5] living in isolation from mainstream American society. These wives of American servicemen were "marginal, both to the dominant community and to the Korean community, and the high rates of social problems were attributed to their marginal positions."[6] Due to their despised and shamed social status from the past and adverse situations in present life, it is generally argued that these war brides may never be able to live as a part of the mainstream society.

Yet, my thesis is that they can become a part of the mainstream society and even contribute to the unity of the churches if the churches adopt the role of the kinsman-redeemer, which was the role of Boaz in relation to Ruth.[7] Out of concern for their struggle and lost identity, I will make an argument to shed light upon the lives of Korean military wives and the churches ministering to them in the following areas: reasons for their invisibility in Korean immigration history, their lost identity, their American spouses, their struggles for survival, a biblical analysis of their status and the church as their kinsman-redeemer, and theological and psychological implications. I will then propose pastoral guidelines for Korean churches in military towns to help these women become a part of the mainstream society. In the end a final remark will be made on the future of the military town churches, as well as on the unity of the Korean and American churches in the States.

1. Invisible Koreans

Considering Korea's nationalistic pride in a homogeneous race, Rev. Park's claim that 300,000 Korean women, married to foreigners, went overseas, mainly to the United States, is not an easily accepted statement for the traditional Korean mind-set. For many Koreans, 300,000 is too large and too shameful a number. Even among scholars and statisticians, there is disagreement over the exact number of Korean women who have married Americans, especially U.S. servicemen. Interviews with several people who are familiar with bicultural and bilingual churches in military towns produced little support for this number.

Therefore, out of a yearning to bring to light the identity of the many invisible interracially-married Korean women and a genuine desire to help them through the ministry of the churches, I questioned Park, who made the statement in his book *As a Hen Gathers Her Chicks under Her Wings*, on the validity of the number. In a telephone interview, Park admitted that probably no one could provide an exact number. He stated that he came up with the figure quoted through one of the books he had read long ago when he was working on the subject. Instead of 300,000, what Park found in one publication was that 200,000 Korean women married Americans, mainly U.S. servicemen, and came to America as wives of foreign males. He surmised that at least one out of three women went to places other than America. Using this rationale, if 200,000 Korean women went to the U. S. and 100,000 to other places of the world, then the figure of 300,000 women leaving their homeland as wives of foreign males is not so inconceivable. However, Park's explanation and method for arriving at his figure leaves much to be desired. As a result, it seemed necessary to conduct research on the topic of Korean immigration history.

In his 1985 publication, Daniel Lee states that "during the past three decades, nearly 80,000 Korean women emigrated to the U.S. as dependents of American servicemen."[8] Adding the approximation of 30,000[9] Korean women to Lee's figure, it is estimated that 110,000 Korean women had emigrated to the United States by 1994. This figure is 10,000 higher than the figure Paul Kim estimated in his article "Families of Love, Overcoming the Barrier of Biculturalism."[10] Accordingly, an educated guess on the total number of Korean military wives in the States can be estimated at somewhere between 91,000 and 110,000.

In addition to these Korean brides came their relatives by invitation of their daughters or sisters who came to America as military wives. As Lee reports, "more than half of Korean spouses. have brought out their relatives to the United States."[11] Therefore, the number of Korean relatives can easily double the number of Korean female immigrants. Accordingly, the figure of 200,000 which Rev. Park mentioned has some basis, strongly bolstering the assumption that 200,000-300,000 is not simply someone's unfounded guess. Based on these statistics, the place of the Korean wives of US servicemen should play an integral part in Korean immigration history because this figure is close to one third of all the Korean immigrants living in America. However, as previously stated, these women seem to have been omitted from immigration history.

Why have these Korean women been ignored and despised by the rest of Korean immigrant societies throughout America? Lee urges us to pursue the answer to this question with his statement, "there was a gross neglect and underestimation of the significance of the role that transcultural marriage has played in the course of Korean immigration, Korean-American relations, and transculturation of people across boundaries, creed, and ethnicity.[12]

2. Reasons for Their Invisibility

Several possible explanations can be offered for the questions above. However, to investigate beneath the surface of superficial assumptions, one has to understand the way the traditional Korean mind-set works. Even though it is nearly impossible to define the typical Korean mind-set within a few lines, a few aspects can shed some light on the rationale behind the Korean perspective.

First, one reason for ignoring the identity of these women is nationalistic pride in a homogeneous race. Koreans are proud of their long history, which can be traced back to the Neolithic period, 3,000 B.C., which gives the country an age of 5,000 years.[13] Throughout these years, Korea has maintained the purity of one race and is very proud of this fact. This pride is reflected in a "nationalistic spirit . . . [that] sees Korean history as a history of brilliance and glory."[14] Thus, it is regarded that marrying someone outside the Korean race is detrimental to the nationalistic pride of racial purity.

Second, there is a national propensity for Koreans to hide any shameful thing. This may help to explain why there is limited publication regarding Korean women's interracial marriages and related issues. Although many books have been published regarding Korean immigration history, hardly have any dealt directly with the issues of Korean women married to American servicemen in any detail and acknowledged the true weight of their presence in American societies. Most publications avoid the subject; if they do approach the subject, it is only briefly mentioned, as if these women were not an important part of Korean immigration history.

A third reason for their lost identity is found in the unwillingness of these women to reveal their identities because the Korean war brides are despised by other Koreans living in America. Therefore, there is a strong tendency for interracially married women to hide themselves away from the public eye. They are self-conscious of their identity as wives of American servicemen. This uneasy feeling is further reinforced by the reluctant attitudes of family members: "The relatives may even be reluctant to disclose their association with their Korean American kin because of bias against transcultural marriage.[15] This general feeling is also described by the authors of *Women in Shadows*: "It is common for an Asian woman to be ridiculed or disowned by her family and community once she begins to date an American serviceman.[16] Thus, hiding beneath the rubble of self-degrading thinking, these Korean women and even their relatives became invisible to the Korean communities in America. What then caused them to marry American servicemen? And who are these Korean women?

3. Korean Wives of American Servicemen

The majority of Korean people living in military towns in America are either Korean women married to American servicemen or their relatives. In comparison to other Korean women in America, it has been supposed that these women have substantially lower educational backgrounds. This notion is corroborated by Lee's article regarding the educational level of the wives of American military personnel: "The majority [of Korean wives] were comparatively disadvantaged by less than six years of education, unemployment, and the necessity of renting a home.[17] This is also what Brooke Brewer reports in her Ph. D. dissertation: "A study completed by the Chaplain's Service in the Second Infantry Division found that 66% had less than a sixth-grade education."[18]

Ill Kim reports the following educational data on Koreans living in New York: "High school (12%), Junior college (16%), College (67%), and other (5%)."[19] This contrast between the educational level of Korean wives living in military towns and their counterparts living in non-military towns further underscores why these Korean women and their relatives are despised by other Koreans in America. That is, Koreans tend to judge others by the level of education.

Another noticeable characteristic of Korean military wives is their high divorce rate.[20] Based on my experience working at the sampled church for eight years, it is conjectured that the divorce rate of Korean women living in the Ft. Hood area is about 50% or higher. Yet, more research has to be done for more objective data on their marital status. Statistics on this topic are not readily available.

Another negative stigma about these military wives might stem from their former occupation in Korea. Sil Dong Kim, a social worker, says that "very few women meet their husbands through legitimate work; most women meet them while working as prostitutes."[21] In general, this appears to be true of Korean wives who came prior to 1980. However, although it is hard to support an argument without further research in this area, based on my eight years of experience working as an interpreter for a bicultural church, the notion that most Korean wives were former prostitutes appears to have been formed from old research data, not from recent data. Lee appears to be of the same mind quoting a study done on the subject: "In his [McCullagh's] study of 264 randomly selected transcultural marriage applicants . . . McCullagh concluded that the facts do not support the common assumptions that . . . the majority of girls married by soldiers are prostitutes."[22] Thus, although it is hard to corroborate the above notion without further research in the area, it may be cautiously concluded that about half of all the Korean wives may have met their American spouses through channels other than prostitution. From the stories gathered from Korean wives who came to America recently, I was often told that many of these women met their husbands through their jobs on or around various military installations

4. American Husbands of Korean Women

In her Ph. D. dissertation, Brewer says that "many Korean women believe that all Americans have the wealth of those Americans portrayed in the movies and read about in the newspapers. Since it is extremely difficult for Koreans to leave Korea to travel, marriage to an American provides a passport and facilitated departure from Korea, if desired."[23] In this sense, for these women who want to leave or escape their present situation in Korea, American servicemen appear to them as tickets to America -- that is, as a kinsman redeemer who can deliver them from their desperate situations. The following data was collected concerning these men.

Compared to their wives' educational level, it appears that the American men surveyed had higher levels of education. From my experience working with American members of the congregation in the past, there is a general belief that Korean pastors, compared to American pastors, are much more conservative and more Scripture-oriented. This may imply that many American servicemen who are married to Korean women are generally more conservative and do not like the current liberal trend in American society. In comparison to American women, many Korean women tend to be more conservative due to the influence of Confucian philosophy on many Korean customs and lifestyle. Furthermore, they are brought up with the Korean tradition that it is a woman's virtue to listen to and obey her husband. In this respect, at least for those American soldiers who are divorced from their American wives[24] or who have not been accepted by American women, the idea of Korean women's submissiveness would have been less a threat to their maleness, as reported by Brewer.

> The American soldier who intermarries more likely had dated little prior to arrival in Korea and more likely comes from a lower socio-economic class family confronted by stress and strain. One can surmise that he perhaps has felt, due to stress while growing up, as an isolate within his own culture and from a psychological perspective compensates for this feeling of rejection and inadequacy by intermarrying one who is even more deprived and isolated. The result is some feeling of

> dominance, esteem, power and recognition needed by this . . . 'emotionally strained' male, this marginal man.[25]

This notion is further shared by the authors of *Women in Shadows*: "The majority of men marry API [Asian Pacific Island] women as a way of escaping from what they construe to be 'bossy, domineering, and castrating' American women."[26]

Furthermore, if the American husbands attending Korean churches in military towns are truly conservative and prefer a lifestyle from the past, this further explains why they chose less educated Korean women over American women. To a certain extent, Korean women's general submissiveness to their husbands may have influenced these American men's decision to take Korean women as their wives over American women. As military men, these husbands are already accustomed to a lifestyle of rank and order. For these reasons, it is easier to understand how these interracial unions are formed. These Korean brides follow their husbands back to America not quite prepared for the shocking realities that lie in wait for them.

5. Invisible Koreans' Struggles for Survival

As most immigrants come to America with the expectation of sharing a piece of the American dream, Korean wives also come to the States with much expectation and hope. Once in America, they expect that they will no longer be looked down upon by society because of their marriage to American servicemen or their degrading previous profession in Korea. They dream of having a happy life in a new land. Part of this happy life is expected to come from the supposed love, care, and help of their husbands.

From the stories gathered from some of the Korean wives, the attitudes of many husbands are not considerate but instead are very selfish and uncaring. Regarding the attitude of American husbands toward their wives, the authors of *Women in Shadows* state that "upon returning to the United States . . . many husbands fear and oppose 'Americanization' of their API wives. They set up barriers to prevent the wife's contact with the outside world. They openly or covertly oppose her learning English, driving a car, visiting Americans. Any activities which would make her self-sufficient are discouraged, usually with flimsy excuses.[27] Regarding the isolation of Korean military dependents, Brewer states that Korean wives of American servicemen are one group of people who are most isolated,[28] "both culturally and socially, in the US. This group has been noted for its severe culture shock, lack of education, impoverishment, isolation, malcommunication in the family, lack of occupational skills, high divorce rate and general alienation.[29] Thus, the wives' wishes to hide their former shameful identity by coming to America may result in being locked up within the walls of their own homes in the new land. Consequently, many of these women have little or no contact with the rest of American society,[30] and so become overly dependent upon their American husbands. As a result, many Korean military wives cannot function independently of their husbands.

It is true that some of these women have happy marriages in America, but as Harry Kitano and Roger Daniels state, there are also many who have failed marriages.[31] Subsequently, from these failed marriages many of these women are "left alone with two or three children with no means of support."[32] There are also many cases of "suicide, and attempted suicide."[33] Remembering clearly what they had to go through in Korea as wives of American soldiers, these women realize that they cannot go back to their native country, especially now being divorced and with racially mixed children. One woman who had become engaged to a serviceman while still in Korea said, "As soon as people around my office heard about my engagement to John, they looked down on me. I was made to feel dirty and unworthy."[34] That being the experience of a woman engaged to an American serviceman, a divorced Korean woman with racially mixed children would certainly have an even harsher life if she were to return to Korea. Not only would she be left abandoned by the society, but she would also be abandoned by her family. Many suicide attempts by military wives have been caused by this kind of tragic predicament.

But there are also many women who refuse to acquiesce to the present reality. Considering the lives of Korean wives of American servicemen, their courage and strong willpower have been the key to their survival in the midst of their harsh and hopeless situations. It is true that most of these military wives do not have much of an education. Their past is often not something of which they can be proud. Yet, they may have been the victims of poverty-stricken families. Whatever their situations may have been, Korean military wives often emerge from backgrounds in which they were rejected and ridiculed by society. Most of them have also been rejected and intentionally forgotten even by their own Korean families.

Whatever their present situation may be, most of these women have been the decision-makers for their own lives. Even for those women who had participated in prostitution, whether they had been influenced by impoverished circumstances or not, they had acted upon their own decisions. That is, they probably believed that their move to a military town to make a living was better than staying in their previous situations.[35] When the decision came to marry American servicemen, they thought that life in a new land[36] would be better than the life in Korea. In order to improve their situations, if they could be assured safe passage to America, they did not mind coming to America as wives of foreign-born males. Once in America, although most of these women have struggled in their new lives, they have shown strong determination in doing their best to survive here. As they struggle in America, they come to realize that they can never return to live in Korea again.

Analyzing the decisions of these women and their actions from this perspective, it may be concluded that they have exercised their survival instinct to the best of their ability. Furthermore, in their decisions and actions, they have discovered courage and willpower which are not normally found in most Korean women who have been taught to live within the confines of a traditional patriarchal society. However, at least for these military wives, it was their own struggle and their own choice to free themselves from the bondage put upon their lives by society. Their decisions may have led to immorality or extreme difficulty but one thing that should be remembered is that these women have responded to their situations in the best way they knew how.

6. Biblical Analysis: Korean Military Wives & Kinsman-Redeemer Model

1) *Korean Military Wives*: In the Gospel according to St. Matthew, five women appear within the genealogy of Jesus Christ: Tamar, Rahab, Ruth, Bathsheba and Mary. Like the Korean military wives, out of these five women save Mary, all the others were foreigners.[37] Like some Korean military wives, four of these women were

involved in some type of sexual scandal,[38] whether it was from their own choice or not. Most Korean military wives came to America out of choice, just as Ruth went to Bethlehem with Naomi out of her own choice, even though she did not have to go.[39] It was due to her decision to move to Bethlehem, a foreign land, that she became directly involved in the genealogy of Jesus Christ. Had she decided not to move to a foreign land, she would not have been a participant in the history of a nation and a Savior.

Ruth, a Moabitess, "married a Hebrew man living in her land."[40] She probably would not have been able to survive in a foreign land -- Bethlehem in Israel -- without the involvement of Boaz, the kinsman-redeemer. Boaz came into her life to bring her out of her dire situation. To a certain extent, these women are in a similar situation struggling to survive in America, a foreign land. As Ruth needed help from Boaz in order to survive her life's struggle, many of these military wives need help from someone. The help for these women can and should come from the churches in military towns. As Ruth had been helped, these women can be helped by the churches. With the church's involvement in their lives, they can be encouraged eventually to stand on their own and may even contribute to the future of the churches in these towns. Like the Samaritan woman who encountered Jesus at the well, with the gospel of love and care they receive from the churches, they can be guided to go out into society and become God's messengers of the gospel.

Like some Korean military wives, Rahab had been involved in prostitution for a living. But, out of all the people in Jericho, it was Rahab who had recognized through her faith the mighty saving act of God working with the Israelites at that time.[41] Not only did she gain a place in history through helping the Israelite spies, but she was also given the honor of giving birth to Boaz,[42] the kinsman-redeemer. And this Boaz was the one who came to the aid of Ruth when she arrived in Bethlehem, the land of promise. In a similar manner, Korean American women who are now despised and rejected might have an important role to play in their community in the future.

Still, despite their important potential role in the future of the Korean churches in America, their present situation is very harsh and bleak. Thus arises the following question: What can the churches do to help these women in the military towns? Can the churches provide them with any help to their present needs through their pastoral response?

2) *The Kinsman-Redeemer*: The churches can enter the lives of these women and adopt the kinsman-redeemer role. From those broken families, the church can take in these bruised women -- modern day Ruths -- as spiritual brides. For those who are still in marriage but abused, isolated, and oppressed, the church can unite them by building a safe community for them. Among themselves, these women can relate to one another with understanding. Being in the same boat, they do not have to disguise themselves from each other. Inn Sook Lee reports that Korean women's "isolation and emotional turmoil comes largely from the lack of compassion and understanding of the people around them."[43] Outside the church community, these wives of American servicemen will get easily hurt and isolated, but inside the faith community, they can be protected by their own bond, the "sisterhood" engendered "to serve, care for, and stand by . . . in spite of what lay ahead."[44]

For those who are divorced, they can encourage and uplift each other so that they can function as whole persons instead of being crippled by shame because of their failed marriages. Without conscious and constant encouragement and uplifting, these women will find themselves further isolated from society. One thinks for example of the divorced Samaritan woman who met Jesus when she came out to draw water at an odd hour and place. As one commentator has written: "The woman had a bad reputation. She chose the time and the place to avoid other women.[45] However, in their own community there is hope because there are older women who can serve as role models, because they themselves have survived the bitterness and hardship of divorce. As it was with Naomi and Ruth, what will eventually help them survive in the new land is "their mutual cooperation."[46] When a trusting relationship is established between the church and these women, signs of healing may come from these women's lives and in their involvement in the community. However, in order to lift them up from their given situation, the church first has to work with them. But what can the church do to lift them up from their isolated and oppressed situation? What kind of pastoral response can the churches give to these women in military towns?

7. Theological and Psychological Implications

In the incarnation of Jesus Christ, "God has come all the way to where we are, entering into the depths of our sin and misery, making . . . [God] to be the Subject who lives a human life, who suffers and dies,"[47] and then rises up again from death to restore broken humanity. During Jesus' earthly ministry, Scripture reveals that this Jesus went out to be with those in society who were oppressed and afflicted in order to be their healer and reconciler. Having fully experienced their pain and suffering, Jesus Christ -- fully divine and fully human -- could restore their broken and wounded selves to full humanity and reconcile them with God and with themselves.

Scripture acknowledges that everyone -- male and female -- is created equal and should be treated and respected accordingly. Nonetheless, due to the hierarchical nature of male dominant and tradition-conscious Korean society, women, especially the wives of foreign military spouses, have been stripped of their basic rights to work and live as equal members of the society, even in God's covenantal community. These women then have been forced to live and made to feel ashamed of their identity in their marriages to foreign-born males and their former occupations.

Scripture points out that "there is no longer slave or free, no longer Gentile or Jew, male or female; for all of you are one in Christ Jesus."[48] Namely, in Christ all are one and equal. From the perspective that Korean women's spouses failed to live out the role of the "kinsman-redeemer" for them, as agents of Christ, the church should come to these suffering women as their kinsman-redeemers. Therefore, by adopting them into the life of the covenantal community and nurturing them in the way Christ cared for those oppressed and afflicted in society, we can be instruments of healing.

In order effectively to help these suffering women who are emotionally and psychologically scarred from their abused past, the church should work with them, incorporating both disciplines of theology and psychology. It is acknowledged that Jesus Christ alone brings salvation to a suffering and broken humanity.[49] Since salvation is made possible through the incarnation and resurrection of Jesus Christ by God-initiated action, it is important to recognize theologically the work of God in restoring broken humanity. Thus, in the Korean churches, traditionally healing has been viewed from a primarily theological/spiritual perspective.

However, it is my conviction that in order adequately and functionally to work with abused women who suffer from psychological and spiritual complications, the church needs to recognize in its work the unique role of psychology for the needs of these women's treatment, especially if the church is not adequately equipped in offering help to these women's psychological dysfunction. In treating women who suffer from obvious psychological disorders, if the church insists on working with them only from the spiritual realm and thus refuses to acknowledge the function of the psychological discipline, much harm can easily be brought to these already suffering women. For this reason, the Korean church's traditional rigidity in overlooking the applicability of psychological work in the context of the church's ministry could exacerbate instead of improve these women's problems. Thus, in the church's working with psychologically and spiritually abused military wives, the spiritual community needs to work by actively using resources from both arenas of theology and psychology in order to bring true healing to them.

Furthermore, since broken humanity ultimately cannot be restored as a whole by the psychological treatment alone,[50] it is important for the psychological discipline to recognize the limitation of its function as well.[51] When the disciplines of both theology and psychology can work harmoniously in the spiritual community, acknowledging the unique function of each other's discipline, true healing can be brought to many of these military dependents who suffer from spiritual and psychological dysfunction. Then, the once shamed, wounded, and broken humanity of the Korean military wives can be made whole, finding peace from their restored selves in the church's ministry to their pain and suffering engendered by their abused past.

8. Pastoral Implications

In the military town church's ministry,[52] genuine love, understanding, and true desire to treat these women as whole human beings is an attitude that needs to be possessed by people working with Korean military wives in America. These women probably will experience subtle forms of discrimination, making them feel as if they are not fully human. From this perspective, the Korean churches in America can learn from African Americans in their civil rights struggles. As a further step, this should also be the attitude of Korean congregations of Korean immigrant families toward the military wives in their church. Since most of the Korean military wives have been despised, rejected, and treated inhumanely,[53] their self-esteem is almost non-existent. As a result, they have a natural tendency "to withdraw and remain alone in order not to be hurt again.[54]

As Paul Watzlawick explains, in order genuinely to help these women with their self-esteem, the help must come from the outside,[55] at least at the initial stage. This is true because they themselves can not help themselves in boosting up their own image due to their given circumstance. However, when other people begin to treat them with respect and dignity, and as these wives begin to feel that they are being accepted by other Koreans in the church, then they will begin to develop respect for themselves.

It is further acknowledged that it will not be easy for other Korean immigrants genuinely to change their views toward the military wives. Yet, in order to break down the invisible walls within the church, pastors and church officials have to work together intentionally with the goal of unity in mind. Either through Bible studies or sermons, slowly the unity of the church must be emphasized under the pastor's leadership. In order to break the bondage set upon the military wives by Korean congregations, Korean immigrants must also be reeducated so that they can open themselves to the Korean wives of American servicemen within the church. They have to come to appreciate the importance of these women's place in Korean immigrant history. Thus, in a way, the pastoral task should first begin with the Korean congregation. They need to be reeducated in their negative attitudes toward the military wives. In order to change their views of interracially married women, their perception of these women needs to be altered by changing the criteria of their value judgments.[56]

When these women begin to appear to the other Korean congregation members as people that need to be taken care of instead of targets for their criticism and ridicule, the invisible wall dividing the Korean immigrant families and the military wives can be torn down. Since much of the hurt has been caused by the people in the congregation, a change of heart and mind needs to take place among them. It will be important for the pastor and church leaders to give unity and the healing of the congregation priority through example, prayer and sermons.

In summary, in order to provide meaningful pastoral care for these women in military towns, the people working in these churches must have caring hearts and empathy for their situations. These women need to be shown genuine love and respect from the Korean congregation. As the trust level develops between the women and the church, the military wives may eventually open themselves up and become active in the church community.[57] The concluding question, then, is, "that will future Korean churches look like in these towns?"

9. Concluding Remarks

It is difficult to describe what will happen ten or more years in the future. However, a few topics can be discussed with some assurance. One issue is the number of military personnel. Currently there is a trend of troop reduction with ongoing peace talks around the world. With the reduction in the number of servicemen, the population of various military towns will gradually decrease and those people leaving the armed services will likely return to the places where they lived before they joined the service. From this perspective, the future of the church depends chiefly on the attitude of second generation youth in the church at the present time. It is not likely that other Koreans will move into military towns because, given the choice, they tend to avoid military towns.

Another influential factor will come from talks about closing all U.S. military bases in Korea. This appears to be a strong possibility. If this occurs, interracial marriages between Korean women and U.S. servicemen stationed in Korea will likely come to a halt. In any case, because of the improving Korean economic situation, fewer Korean women have been marrying American servicemen in recent years. Therefore, fewer Korean women and their relatives will move into military towns in coming years.

When the influx of military families to the church stops, the future of the church will depend on how the people within the church react through the coming years. In ten years, most of the current leading members of the church will have either retired or become less active. For these reasons, it is critical for the church to focus on the youth presently growing up in the church. If these youngsters are taught to think and believe that the church they are growing up in is truly their church and that they have a responsibility to care for the church's future, then the church will surely have a strong chance to grow into the future.

Most students will move to other places when they go to college, but if they have a strong sense of the importance of their role in the church, they may return to these towns and settle down with their future families. With these people, the churches in military towns can continue to grow. However, if the youths in the church are not nurtured to understand the importance of the church, then the church will gradually fade into extinction. The task of the church, then, lies in the hands of the current leadership to educate other church members to understand the urgency of educating the growing generation within the church. At the same time, the church leadership has to find and educate young people who can work together toward these common goals. Once this is accomplished, these churches will not only have a strong chance to survive the danger of extinction in future years, but they can also grow into bigger churches, able to provide for the needs of people who will continue to live in these areas.

As for the future of the Korean churches throughout America, at present, it is very uncertain. It should be acknowledged that Korean American churches cannot easily assimilate or acculturate into the mainstream of white American churches due to their ethnicity. As Korean American churches face an uncertain future in the States, like Ruth and Korean military wives, they will need assistance. What people will rise to help unite and harmonize the churches? The strongest candidate for this role appears to be from the children of the mixed families. As Daniel Lee states, "through parenting, their aspirations and dreams for transcultural harmony and success may well be fulfilled by their American offspring.[58] Like Esther -- "a Hebrew woman who married a gentile in a strategic time in the history of Israel to help preserve the nation from destruction"[59] -- if these children are raised to appreciate their mothers' Korean cultural heritage in harmony with their fathers' American heritage, they can participate in the leadership of the churches in America, and possibly connect both Korean and American churches. Accordingly, it is critical and urgent for the churches to devote much needed pastoral care to interracial families, especially to the suffering women.

To these suffering women who have been crying out for help, shedding the tears of agony, humiliation, shame, and suffering forced upon them by a class-conscious society in the margins of the society, the churches should adopt the role of the kinsman-redeemer. It was precisely for such as these that Jesus Christ came, who was himself born from the line of Ruth and Boaz, her kinsman-redeemer. By inviting these Korean war brides of American servicemen into the faith community, the body of Christ, the work of the churches' pastoral responses will have a positive impact on the future unity and harmony of the Korean churches in America. Ultimately, this team spirit of the churches working together in their efforts of helping these women[60] may encourage all churches to come together as "one body, being joined and knit together as are the limbs of a body in the same spirit of God."[61]

Chapter Sixteen

Korean Preaching:
The Evaluation of Its Present Situation[1]

Eun Joo Kim

When Protestant Christianity was introduced to Korea in the late-nineteenth century, it was welcomed by the enlightened Koreans as a new religious spirit. This century was the time when the energies of the Yi dynasty had run out politically, socially, and religiously. Politically, the Yi dynasty persistently refused to make any kind of treaty with foreign countries, whose imperialism caused a crisis of national identity and sovereignty. However, the dynasty could not protect the country from Japanese imperialism and Western expansionism.[2] Moreover, natural disasters, governmental corruption, peasant uprisings, and plagues recurred so frequently that Korean society became unstable morally and economically.[3] In this critical situation, Confucian and Buddhist philosophies that had sustained society for many centuries had become so hardened with formalities and the rigid literate mentality that they failed to provide spiritual leadership for the country at that time. Although nineteenth-century Korea was in chaos politically and socially, it could not generate a new spirit to confront its internal and external crises.[4]

These political, social, and religious conditions fostered a desire for a new leading spirit. Toward this end, Koreans did not wait for Christianity to be introduced by missionaries. Before the first Protestant missionaries arrived in Korea in 1884 and in 1885, many Koreans were already being converted by Korean believers who had encountered Christianity in Manchuria and in Japan. One of those who had accepted the faith in Manchuria established Korea's first church.[5]

Furthermore, when the first ordained American missionaries--Horace G. Underwood and Henry G. Appenzella--came to Korea through Japan, they carried with them the Gospels which had been translated into Korean by Soo-Jung Yi, who had studied in Japan and was called Rijutei by the Japanese. However, upon arrival the missionaries were surprised to find that the Bible, translated into Korean in Manchuria, had already been distributed nationwide by the Korean colporteurs.[6]

As such, in the Protestant mission in Korea, Koreans were "the primary agents of evangelism." Even after Western missionaries entered Korea in large numbers, Koreans actively participated in the missionaries' activities. As Martha Huntley describes,

> While the missionaries were catalysts and in some cases enablers, the Koreans were the primary agents of evangelism. Koreans participated in all aspects of the work, laboring beside the missionaries in writing the Bible, compiling hymnals, translating textbooks, teaching classes, caring for the ill, building church buildings, preaching the Word and making the rules. As in the case of women missionaries, Korean church leaders were underpaid and underacknowledged, but they were valued and very real partners in the mission enterprise.[7]

Since the time when Protestantism was introduced into Korea by pioneer Korean Christians and Western missionaries, it has grown rapidly throughout the nation's downtrodden history during Japanese annexation, the division of the nation, the Korean War, dictatorial governments, and now during the country's modernization. Such historical and sociological factors have influenced not only the external relations of the church to society but also its internal situation. Directly and indirectly, they have caused the rapid growth of the Korean Protestant churches, which today have become one of the predominant religions in Korea, with membership exceeding 10 million. Considering this quantitative growth, its impact on the individual and the society cannot be ignored, although it has a relatively short history in Korea compared with other indigenous religions.

At this juncture, it is important to reflect on the practice of preaching in the Korean Protestant churches. Preaching is deeply involved in contemporary conditions inside and outside the church. The practice of preaching reflects how the church understands the changing situation of society and responds to it theologically and homiletically. The preacher determines the content of a sermon by connecting the biblical text to the congregational context according to his or her own pre-understanding of Christian theology. Furthermore, what the preacher decides to preach as the gospel also determines the homiletical method, which is a medium for fulfilling the sermon's function. Thus, we can assume that contemporary Korean sermons reveal the present situation of Korean Protestantism to a great extent.

In this article, I will focus on the internal situation of contemporary Korean preaching. An evaluation of contemporary sermons according to a certain standard will show us not only the reality of Korean Protestantism but also the theological and methodological problems of Korean preaching and, furthermore, give us insights into the renewal of Korean preaching as Protestantism matures in Korea.

Regarding the evaluation of contemporary Korean preaching, it should be noted that contemporary Korean sermons are so diverse and complex that it is difficult to categorize them simply and clearly. In order, then, to know the current tendency of Korean preaching in general, we need to apply a certain method. Confronting this methodological demand, I visited Korea in the summer of 1994 and interviewed 40 pastors, randomly selected for the purpose of identifying preachers who represented contemporary Korean preaching. Through interviews, I obtained 15 preachers' names and chose 45 sermons from their recent sermon books.[8] On the basis of these sample sermons, I tried to extrapolate the general tendency of contemporary Korean preaching in its theology and method. While this research is based on only 45 sample sermons, it allows us to perceive with informed accuracy the probability of the reality of Korean preaching.

The review of the sample sermons reveals that contemporary Korean preaching can be divided into three categories according to their focus and function[9]: (1) Preaching of individual moral perfection, (2) preaching of personal success, and (3) preaching of social consciousness.[10] In the process of analysis, it should be made clear that not all Korean sermons fall into the three categories decisively and distinctively. In some cases, the first and second types are mixed together. Other sermons cannot be categorized easily into any of the three types. Further, sermons which share a particular category on the basis of their contents sometimes differ from one another in degree or detail. Nonetheless, the study of Korean sermons according to these three categories helps us access contemporary Korean preaching and understand the major homiletical forces in the contemporary Korean church. The following section will examine each type, focusing on the homiletical categories of biblical exegesis, the image of the preacher, and sermonic form and language. In addition, considering that contemporary Korean preaching cannot be understood apart from the homiletical traditions of the Korean church, each type will be investigated in relation to its historical roots.

1. Preaching of Individual Moral Perfection

The most popular type of contemporary sermon preaches about individual moral perfection. This type of preaching sees its primary function as moralistic exhortation. It understands Christianity as a religion of high morality and demands the listener the moral renewal of individual life. The function of preaching is to exhort the listeners to right behavior and obligation with moral guidelines drawn from the literal sense of the text. The main concern of this type of preaching is personal piety or legalistic moral behavior.

It is worth noting that this type of preaching is not a new development in the church. According to the analysis of 1,123 sermons recorded in the books *Great Preaching*, Volumes I-XII, which are the sermon collections of the Korean church over a 100-year period, most Korean sermons have focused on such moral issues as how Christians ought to behave or how they might live a converted life differently from the past.[11]

(1) *Biblical Exegesis*. In this type of preaching, the text is regarded as the source which contains the perennial and timeless value of moral discernment. The text is viewed as a timeless truth-claim on the basis of the belief that the Bible has unique authority as the Word of God. This type of preaching becomes a "scripture lesson" whose structure is deductive and propositional. That is, the preacher first of all reads the plain sense of the scriptures based upon a literal interpretation. If the text contains passages that seem to contradict one another or sound absurd by literal interpretation, they are read allegorically without consideration of the situation of the text. Second, the preacher abstracts the subject matter of the text and applies its enduring value to the standards for the listeners' behavior and attitudes. Finally, the preacher arranges three or four points

pulled from the text, combining them with a few illustrations for further elaboration of each point.

This hermeneutical method often tends to transfer the description of the historical people of the text into a prescription for people today. Biblical accounts are used as either positive or negative models for the individual believer's morality.

(2) *The Authority of the Preacher and Homiletical Language.* The preacher has authority as a moral teacher or a sage who knows the truth and has enough knowledge to move his or her followers to appropriate moral behavior. Likewise, the relationship between preacher and listener is comparable to that of teacher and pupil, which is vertically hierarchical rather than horizontally egalitarian.

In this hierarchical relationship, preachers often give orders to the listeners with authority as if they were issuing the commands of God. They speak in hortative tone rather than descriptive language, and in an imperative rather than affirmative mood. The speech pattern is that of a monologue. The listeners are regarded merely as passive recipients, invited neither to participate in the event of preaching nor to stimulate their imagination to reconsider their life before God.

(3) *The Sermonic Structure.* There are two kinds of sermonic form in this type of preaching: One is a topical point-making sermon, and the other is an expository point making sermon. The former is the traditional Korean style, rooted in early missionary preaching and still popular among Korean preachers.[12] According to the research of Sung-Ku Chung, a professor of homiletics at the Presbyterian General Assembly Theological Seminary, the nineteenth-century missionaries practiced topical point-making sermons, which were popular in the North American church of those times.[13]

While this method has been popular in Korean preaching until the mid-twentieth century, these days Korean preachers having reflected on this traditional method have come to believe that traditional topical preaching allows the preacher to read his or her own private opinions or philosophy of life into the Bible, preaching such ideas as the Word of God while ignoring what the text itself says.

As an alternative, the expository point-making sermon was introduced after 1970 by such Western preachers as Martyn Lloyd-Jones, Dennis Lane, and John Stott, and strongly attracted the conservative moral preachers. The basic ideas of the sermon come "from the text" rather than from the preacher's own thoughts or experience. The preacher usually focuses on a single verse or even on one word and explores the basic idea by means of three or four divisions.[14] This means the expository point-making sermon has a deductive propositional structure based upon movement "from the general truth to the particular application or experience."[15]

However, this deductive movement seems to be only concerned with how the preacher conveys his or her knowledge to the listener, rather than with how the listener receives the sermon. In addition, while the point-making style, whether topical or expository, takes advantage of introducing the speaker's idea clearly and logically, we cannot overlook the fact that the traditional three-point sermons are easily in danger of destroying the unity of the sermon and of ignoring the interest of the listener.

(4) *The Historical Background.* The popularity of moral preaching in the Korean church can be traced to the early missionaries' influence and to indigenous Korean cultural elements. The early missionaries who came to Korea in the late-nineteenth century were those "who had been most affected by the evangelical awakening and kindred revivals of the eighteenth and nineteenth centuries."[16] In North American religious history, a series of revivals took place in the early nineteenth century, culminating in the Second Great Awakening, which solidified the power of evangelicalism in the Church.[17] Evangelicals universally affirmed "the final authority of Scripture, the deity of Christ and the sufficiency of his atoning work on the cross, the necessity of a conversion experience, the importance of evangelism and mission, and the call to a sanctified life."[18] According to J. Christopher Soper, emphasis upon personal faith and moral practice led Evangelicals "to highlight issues such as drinking, gambling, and sexual practices while largely ignoring matters of economic justice or foreign policy where the connection between individual choice and social outcome [was] far less certain."[19]

The large majority of the missionaries in Korea, regardless of their denominations, were Evangelicals influenced by the strong Puritan heritage of New England.[20] Among the forty ordained missionaries serving in Korea in 1922, sixteen were from Princeton Theological Seminary, eleven from McCormick, four from San Anselmo, three from

Union, New York, and the rest from Moody and New York Bible Schools.[21] They came to Korea with a strong passion for Jesus and his mission in their hearts. Their preaching was a plain moral preaching urging restraint from such immoral behaviors as drinking and smoking.[22]

This preaching was easily accepted by Koreans who had lived with Confucian moralism. Among the first converted Christians in Korea, there were Confucian scholars who had been removed from office and sometimes exiled by the government.[23] They not only contributed to the translation of the Bible and other Christian documents but also might be attracted by the moral teaching of the Bible, and readily became "Bible-reading people." The missionaries' biblicism corresponded to the method of Confucian learning which was "thoroughly textual"; it included constant reading and studying until the student eventually memorized the entire text.[24] As such, Korean Christians understood that to memorize certain passages or even entire books of the Bible was a simple expression of one's faith. By extension, for a preacher to recite as many biblical passages as possible constituted proper biblical preaching. Converted Christians also found that the Bible's teachings and its moral wisdom, particularly in the Old Testament, corresponded to that found in Confucian texts, and applied these literal instructions to their contemporary life as the standard for living a Christian life. Likewise, the early evangelical missionaries' biblicism and moralism had a cross-cultural appeal for a people long grounded in their indigenous Korean culture.

The early missionaries' biblicism and moralism were further solidified later on by American fundamentalism.[25] For example, Hyung-Nong Park (1897-1978), one of the dominant figures in the Korean church, studied under J. G. Machen at Princeton Theological Seminary from 1923 to 1926 (Th. B., Th. M.) and gained a Ph.D. in Apologetics at Southern Baptist Theological Seminary in 1933.[26] After returning home, he helped establish the theological foundation of the conservative Korean Presbyterian church on the basis of his fundamentalist faith and theological knowledge.[27] Like American fundamentalists in the early twentieth century, the majority of Korean Christians assumed that Biblical accounts could be proved by an exact science, and accordingly they attempted to keep the literal sense of scripture, rejecting biblical criticism.[28] Until recently, this conservative biblicism has been a predominant theological standard for the majority of Korean preachers.[29] Their preaching creates a moralizing sermon on the basis of the unique authority of scripture or the doctrine of biblical inerrancy.

As we have seen, preaching individual morality has a long history in the tradition of Korean preaching. Considering that since Protestantism was first introduced into Korea, Korean society has been in a chaotic condition morally and psychologically, as well as politically and socially, we can evaluate this type of preaching positively in a sense. That is, throughout Church history, this type of preaching has helped provide Koreans with moral guidelines and with principles for their individual lives. The sage or teacher image of the preacher has appealed easily to Koreans, who had lived in the hierarchical structure of Confucian society. Moreover, the propositional "scripture lesson" style of preaching might also have taken advantage of introducing doctrines and knowledge of Christianity to the novices. The point-making structure of the sermon probably helped the preacher to deliver his or her knowledge clearly and logically.

However, it is important for contemporary preachers to notice that through rapid industrialization, modern Korea has changed not only externally and socially but also internally and individually. Modern Korea has changed not only externally and socially but also internally and individually. Modern contemporary Koreans are under the influence of corporate despair and nihilism, moralism and individualism, and materialism and hedonism and need the Christian gospel existentially and ontologically to liberate them as whole human beings. If preaching is limited to moralization or legalization of the gospel, it cannot liberate the listeners from their own existential predicaments. Rather, the traditional way of moral preaching, in its content and style, often leads them to misconstrue the Christian message as law first and grace second, and imposes on them the burden of legalization and moral perfection. Through this type of preaching, it is hard to proclaim the humanizing dimension of the Christian gospel. In this sense, contemporary Korean preaching demands a different way of interpreting the gospel. Literal interpretation, by failing to delve into deeper textual meanings in relation to the historical context and literary genre of the text, along with ignorance of the particular context of the listener, cannot create a liberating meaning of the text for the renewal of the world.

Moreover, the intellectual level of the Korean congregation has been enhanced in contemporary Korea, due to higher educational levels and by the development of secular educational methods, which have produced diverse approaches to communication and teaching, and a tendency to discard the conventional Confucian method. In addition, modernization and a swift assimilation with Western culture have been demolishing the hierarchical structure of society. In this changing situation, Korean preaching is challenged to develop a new method of communication which can appeal more effectively to contemporary listeners, and to reconsider the image of the preacher based on a new understanding of the preacher's authority.

Consequently, it is questionable whether this first type of preaching is an effective response to the changing situation in the Korean church. The contemporary Korean church demands a different understanding of preaching in its biblical hermeneutics, of the authority of the preacher, and of the homiletical structure and language.

2. Preaching of Personal Success

This second type of preaching is also popular in the Korean church. While the first type has a tendency to impose on the listeners a literal reading of the Bible as a timeless moral guideline ignoring the present context of the congregation, the second is more situational. It seems to challenge what it considers to be irrelevant and uninteresting moral preaching, and claims that preaching should first and foremost meet the realistic needs of the listeners. It contends that the place to begin a sermon is not with the biblical text but with the congregational context in which many realistic problems take place. That is, the preacher's main concern is how preaching can respond to the problems of human life. Such problems are generally understood to include economic poverty, physical or mental illness, failure in business, and psychological depression or despair.

The content of such preaching is an affirmative message in response to these problems. The main subjects of the sermons usually concern "a key to being blessed" or a key to being successful in this world. The key to success, according to Yong-Gee Cho, who is the senior pastor of Yoido Full Gospel Church in Seoul, which is the largest Protestant church in the world, is to have positive thinking and faith.[30]

Thus, the sermon's function is to transform the negative consciousness of the listeners into a positive one and to encourage the listeners to have a successful life in this world without suffering.[31]

(1) *Biblical Exegesis.* The hermeneutics of this type of preaching are the same as for the first type in that they stress the unique authority of the Bible on the basis of the inerrancy of the scriptures. How ever, unlike the first type, this kind of preaching does not seek any moral guideline or ethical norm from the text but instead looks for instruction for such spiritual experiences as the baptism of the Holy Spirit, speaking in tongues, miraculous healing, etc.

In order to testify about the personal experience of the Holy Spirit, the preacher often uses the miracle stories or personal success accounts in the Bible as the sermonic text and stresses that such stories can become "our stories" by faith. In other words, the Bible is used as a series of proof-texts regarding God's blessing to the individual. Biblical accounts are read neither as past historical events nor as pointing to a future-oriented hope, but as present answers of God to the life-burdens of the listeners in the present situation.

The hermeneutical movement in this type of preaching seems to be inductive in the sense that the sermons start with the human dilemma. However, it is difficult to regard this hermeneutic as inductive as Fred Craddock defines it,[32] since most sermons of this type fail to arrive at "the general truth" implied in the text. This is because, first, the text is selected by the preacher's prejudice, based on his or her ideology of personal success. Second, the text is often read superficially, merely to confirm the preacher's ideology. The preacher's personal thoughts derived exclusively from his or her own experience and learning neither fully engage nor deeply reflect on the biblical witness for the creation of a new meaning out of the text. Such interpretation easily results not from exegesis but from eisegesis, which uses the text as a supplemental resource but human experience as the primary source.[33]

(2) *The Sermonic Form and Illustrations.* The typical form of this type of preaching follows a topical point-making style. The preacher departs from the text to find his or her own points. Through this style, the content of the sermon easily syncretizes the preacher's thoughts with secular culture and ideology.

Stories and experiences play a major role in this type of preaching as illustrations. The sermon is given authority by many miraculous healing stories, personal testimonies based upon ecstatic experiences, and references to the numbers of people in and out of the Bible who attained successful lives through positive thinking and faith.

Illustrations are important in preaching. As Thomas Long says, "Stories, images, analogies, and experiences are not mere decorations in sermons; they are active ingredients of communication."[34] They help the preacher provide concrete reality for abstract concepts. Illustrations should be carefully selected and appropriately used in both a theological and rhetorical sense, considering the important role they play in preaching.

Long classifies illustrations as simile, synecdoche, and metaphor according to their functions. He defines simile as the speech figure which aims to give clear understanding to theological ideas through familiar examples, using the words "like" or "as" to make the connection between the examples and the ideas.[35] Synecdoche is the literary mechanism where "a part of something represents the whole." This figure of speech does not use comparison connectors such as "like" or "as" but names the essence of one thing by an example. That is, an illustration is used to say, "This is what it is; this is the heart of the thing itself in human life."[36] Metaphors employ one object or idea in place of another to suggest a likeness or analogy between the two. Metaphoric illustrations place "experience and concept side by side and invite the hearers to make imaginative connections." They aim "to create new meaning, to help us experience the reality of something in a new way."[37]

According to Long's analysis of speech figures, preaching of personal success is based on the illustrations of synecdoche. In this type of preaching, biblical and personal stories testifying to the success of an individual's life function as the essence of the Christian gospel. They provide the listeners with the conviction that such stories can be their stories. The fulfillment of the blessed life in this world illustrated by various positive experiences of healing and answered prayer is understood as the essence of the Christian life.

However, Long indicates the danger in this figure of speech in that the sermons centered on such illustrations sometimes ignore the reality of

> . . . the many faithful people who will not experience such a healing but who cling nevertheless to the gospel promise that the disease destroying their bodies does not have the power to speak the final word. We live in a Good Friday world, where Christians must pray for reconciliation as yet unrealized hope for liberation even as people lie captive, water the seeds of forgiveness where there is still enmity, apply the oil of healing while pain and death yet rage, and pray with all our might, "Come, Lord Jesus."[38]

In other words, "synecdoche-style" illustrations in this type of preaching run the risk of ignoring the future-oriented eschatological vision of the Christian faith because they illustrate the Kingdom of God as a fulfilled reality, at present existing among those who have experienced the miracles of healing or personal blessing. The illustrations are not used as eschatological signs which help the listeners understand the present situation in light of the promise of God.

In this sense, preaching of personal success, based on synecdochal illustrations of personal success and healing, is a theological problem. That is, such preaching gives the listener an impression that the gospel itself is success-oriented, and Christianity is the"religion for winners."

(3) *The Image of the Preacher.* In this type of preaching, the preacher has a great deal of authority as a charismatic figure. The image of the preacher is that of the traditional spiritual leader, the shaman, who prays for the blessing of the people in this world. The congregation expects the preacher to be a charismatic leader who works the miracles of healing, converts sinners, or prays worldly blessings upon believers.

This understanding of the preacher's authority creates a vertical relationship between preacher and listener, so that communication between them is characterized by the preacher's imperative mood. The listener often draws a one-to-one correlation between the power of the preacher and the power of the gospel, and entirely depends upon the charismatic power of the preacher.

(4) *The Historical Background.* To discover the origins of this experience-centered spiritual preaching, we can go back to early Korean preaching. Influenced by nineteenth century revivalism and

evangelicalism, particularly in the Wesleyan or Methodist tradition, the missionaries often stressed personal experience in their preaching and frequently regarded a dramatic personal conversion as a sign of Christian salvation.[39]

These missionaries desired to share their religious experience with Koreans and held Bible conferences and prayer meetings. Their efforts to heighten spiritual experiences among Korean Christians brought about the Great Revival of 1907, which became a movement sweeping all the churches in Korea.[40] The Great Revival strongly appealed to the emotions and aspirations of Koreans who, under the Japanese imperialistic invasion, longed for security, comfort, and inward peace.

The influence of this movement exists in contemporary Korean Christianity. That is, its emphases on a personal experience or being "born-again" with God, an ecstatic experience of the Holy Spirit, and an obligation to share one's faith with others all combine to characterize Korean Christianity as "evangelical." While this evangelical legacy has been shared by most Korean Christians, the emphasis on the personal experience of an immediate ecstatic encounter with the Holy Spirit, for example, speaking in tongues or miraculous healing, has been particularly stressed by such Korean revivalists as Ik-Doo Kim and Yong-Do Kim.[41]

From the middle of the twentieth century, the doctrine of the Holy Spirit was reinforced in Korea by the introduction of American Pentecostalism. The doctrine of the Holy Spirit was understood by Koreans who were living in the shamanistic spiritual world as something similar to a shamanistic spiritual experience. Such an understanding led the people to identify the Christian message with shamanistic ideology and the notion of worldly blessing, and has become popular in the Korean church since the 1960s when Korea was struggling to achieve economic success and prosperity. The Park government began to campaign for economic growth by infusing a positive spirit in the people, and keeping step with this national trend, the propagation of the Christian message as the key to success in this world corresponded with that national desire. In this historical context, the preaching of personal success appealed to the individual's basic human desire for prosperity and to the shamanistic ideology of wish-fulfillment.

Considering this second popular type of preaching in relation to the Korean historical context, we should admit that through Korea's tragic national history and during the country's strenuous period of industrialization, the preaching of positive thinking and faith-healing has provided the people with psychological stability by its message that God exists and watches over us. This type of preaching has prompted ecstatic, even frightening spiritual encounters; listeners often experience the presence of God, the revelation of Godself to them through the experience of a dramatic conversion experience, or "faith-healing" during the preaching. It also gives the listeners the religious confidence that if they have faith in God and live according to God's Word, they will be blessed in the world.

Although this type of preaching reinforces listeners' faith to a certain extent by spiritual proofs and offers them temporary psychological comfort, we cannot overlook its theological inadequacy. In this type of preaching, there is no message of struggling to find the existential meaning of suffering in relation to the cross. This type of preaching understands that the cross of Jesus Christ is a vicarious event for the believers, so that they do not have to suffer in this world. What is promised Christians is that they will enjoy God's blessing in this world through experiencing the miraculous works of the Holy Spirit in their individual lives as the reward of their faith.[42] Its message corresponds to the secular ideology and desire to be blessed in this world.[43] It does not distinguish human needs from human desires. Therefore, this type of preaching jeopardizes the essence of the Christian message. It risks syncretizing Christianity with secular culture and ideology, and producing non-biblical characteristics in Korean Christianity, such as selfish individualism and present-centered privatism while ignoring Christian responsibility for one's neighbors, society, and nature.

3. Preaching of Social Consciousness

While the previous two types of preaching represent the mainstream of contemporary Korean preaching, this third type is a lesser voice in the Korean church.[44] Whereas the main concern of the first two types revolves around the personal problems without any socio-political consciousness, this type of preaching sees the problems of the congregation not on a personal but on a socio-political level.[45] Preachers sharply analyze socio-political phenomena surrounding the community of faith and state their theological views in relation to biblical texts for the purpose of transforming the fundamental structure of an unjust and oppressive society. They see social problems from the perspective of such victims of national industrialization as poor industrial workers, urban squatters, and impoverished farmers. They also criticize traditional social values like sexism and classism for being an outgrowth of patriarchal Confucian ideology, and the undemocratic political situation as the result of the "colonial ideology" of the superpower nations. They understand that their listeners are oppressed politically, socially, economically, and culturally by internal and external social factors.

At this juncture, preaching is important because it is a means for liberating people from their oppression. That is, through preaching, the preacher provides the congregation with critical insights about society and conscientizes them to face up to the real problems of society. The preacher also imposes on the listeners a sense of social and political responsibility for transforming the socio-political structure.

(1) *Biblical Exegesis.* In this type of preaching, the Bible has its authority not as a timeless sacred book but as a historical heritage of the community of faith. The biblical text is an "enabling resource" which helps the reader become liberated from oppression and injustice, rather than "a normative immutable archetype" which represents unconditional truth or guidelines for life.[46] So, the preacher's main concern is to discern "how historically and culturally determined writings can have any theological significance and authority for contemporary persons without losing their historical character and being transformed into historical universal principles and timeless norms."[47]

For this purpose, the preacher on the one hand uses the historical-critical method in order to understand the particular context of scripture. A socio-political analysis of the text helps the preacher discover what the text meant at its time and place, and suggests relevance to the contemporary congregational context. On the other hand, the preacher approaches the contemporary experience of the listeners socio-politically in order to create contemporary meaning for the listeners. The preacher's political and socio-economic analysis of the situation analogically relates the text to each congregational context. Thus, in this hermeneutical process, the preacher requires enough knowledge and accurate information about society.

(2) *The Sermonic Form.* While the preacher inductively approaches biblical interpretation by beginning with the socio-political experiences of the congregation and arriving at the general truth of the text, the typical sermonic style of this type is the traditional deductive proposition. That is, most sermons present the thesis that the preacher derives from the text by the deductive point-making style.[48] The content, which is discovered by the inductive approach, is arranged logically for the best presentation like a lecture, by means of three or four divisions. The preacher here seems to understand that interpretation and application are separate processes in the formation of a sermon. Thus, the sermonic structure of this type of preaching is exactly the same as that of the first type of preaching.[49] This style of preaching might appeal to the listener's intellectual level and make it possible to conscientize the listeners rationally.

(3) *The Authority of the Preacher and Sermonic Language.* The preacher is understood as a leading spirit or a prophet who penetrates the present situation of society and realizes the will of God in advance. With the authority of a prophet, the preacher often criticizes the present political and social structure and sends a judgmental message to the listeners as the Word of God. The preacher, as a prophet, usually uses the hortatory and imperative mood for encouraging the listeners to do act in response to his or her prophetic message. In contrast to the second type of preaching which always encourages the listeners to think positively by telling the bright side of the world, this type of preaching employs illustrations related to the negative aspects of reality.

(4) *The Historical Background.* This type of preaching is not something new to the Korean church. It has a long history in Korean Christianity, although its theological perspective has been held by the minority leaders of the church.

When Protestantism was introduced to Korea during its turbulent era, some enlightened Koreans realized the urgent need to modernize the country for the defense of the nation, and identified Christianity with the power of modernization. They wanted the nation to remain independent from any direction or invasion by foreign countries and to be reformed by means of the new religious message of Christianity understanding that the Christian message had revolutionary power for the country.

During the national ruin caused by Japanese annexation (1910-1945), Korean Christians interpreted the events of political liberation in the Old Testament in the context of their own political crisis. They resisted Japanese imperialism on the basis of their Christian faith. As a result, in the later part of the occupation, the Japanese government forbade the Korean Church to preach from the Old Testament.[50] The conscientized Christians played a major role in the country's independence, organizing political clubs, such as those leading to the March First Independent Movement in 1919, and inspiring in the people a national consciousness on the basis of the liberating message of the scriptures.[51]

However, missionaries whose faith was of an evangelical-conservative stripe did not want to bring political matters into the church from the early period of their mission in Korea. When the Japanese government severely persecuted the churches and individuals that were involved in the Korean independent movements, missionaries reinforced their efforts to separate politics from the church in order to avoid ecclesial persecution by the Japanese government.[52]

Since the tight surveillance of the Japanese government after the March First Independent Movement, Christian activists could no longer remain in the church.[53] Since that time, the prophetic voice has hardly been heard from the Korean pulpit. Those Christians who were quiet about national issues could survive in the church and became the mainline church leaders.[54]

On the other hand, Jae-Joon Kim and other Korean theologians, the pioneers of liberal theology in Korean Christianity, established Chosun Theological Seminary in 1940 as independent and free from the control of conservative Korean churches. This seminary retained liberal theological study and enhanced socio-political consciousness as an alternative way to do theology.[55]

The contemporary prophetic preaching which is identified with the preaching of social consciousness is best represented by the theologians and pastors who have shared the theological trend of this school. These preachers are open to the perspective of liberation theology. While political dictatorships have persecuted the intellectuals and the students who demonstrated for freedom of speech and the press since the 1970's, a few church leaders have also played their prophetic role in the pulpit and suffered for the sake of justice.

A noticeable fact in the contemporary Korean church is conspicuous presence of "minjung churches,"[56] which began with the particular theological concern of "Minjung Theology."[57] They proclaim the gospel in relation to the subjects of political and social issues, such as social justice, human rights, democratization, peace-making, and egalitarianism, on the basis of liberation theological perspectives. and of a "Women-Church" which is modeled after feminist theology.[58] The study of preaching of social consciousness reveals that although most Korean preaching has focused on personal faith isolated from social-political concerns, there has been a small prophetic voice in the Korean church. Although this voice has been represented by a few preachers, it has contributed to the prophetic role of the church throughout the darkness of Korean society. This type of preaching has used such advanced methods of biblical exegesis as historical-critical methods and socio-cultural analysis. The Bible is understood as a resource which enables the church through models of emancipatory praxis to struggle for liberation from oppression and dehumanization.

On the other hand, it is important to take into account a critical theological challenge to this type of preaching. Kwang-Shik Kim, a systematic theologian at Yonsei University, says,

> If we speak of salvation in the framework of Korean Theology, there are urgent problems such as reunification and the liberation of the oppressed. But in my view, the theological problems happening in the individual's ordinary life and struggles are as much important as socio-political problems. There is a tendency that we emphasize only the socio-political issues objectively and treat the personal issues lightly. I think this is the weak point of minjung theology. Because of this, minjung theology is neither welcomed by the majority churches nor by other Christians.[59]

Kim's criticism is supported by a survey taken regarding the situation in the minjung churches. According to the survey's findings, the main problems that the preachers of minjung churches experienced in their ministry were: a one-sided over-emphasis upon the evil structure of society (38.2%); an absence of ecclesiology (30.9%); the ignoring of individual problems (8.8%); and a separation between the liberational perspective of minjung theology and such practices as preaching(8.8%).[60]

As this survey reveals, if the people only hear about the big issues such as social justice and political democratization without any intimate relation to their daily lives, they will feel a distance between the subjects of the sermons and their personal lives. Furthermore, such preaching will make the listeners feel too heavy a responsibility on their shoulders. Its intellectual approach of deductive point-making style will be in danger of making the listeners only realize the limits of their power to take responsibility for social and political issues. It sometimes brings forth a sense of helplessness in the listeners rather than encouraging them with the revolutionary power of the gospel for the sake of the transformation of the society.

This is reflected in the consequence that the preaching of social conscientization is not fulfilling its theological goal realistically. Rather, this type of preaching risks becoming an information-providing sermon or impossible burden-giving sermon instead of helping the listeners make sense of their lives in light of the eschatological vision of the Christian gospel.

Notes

Chapter One

1. Joan Laird, "Women and Stories: Restorying Women's Self-Constructions," in *The Women in Families: A Framework for Family Therapy*, ed. Monica McGoldrick, Carol M. Anderson and Froma Walsh (New York: Norton, 1980), 435-436.

2. Ibid., 431. Emphasis mine.

3. Ibid., 437.

4. Ibid., 440.

5. James K. Morishima, "The Evacuation: Impact on the Family," in *Asian Americans: Psychological Perspectives*, ed. Stanley Sue and Nathaniel N. Wagner (Palo Alto, CA: Science and Behavior Books, 1973).

6. John Tateishi, *And Justice for All: An Oral History of The Japanese American Detention Camps* (New York: Random House, 1984).

7. Steven P. Shon and David Y. Ja, "Asian Families," in *Ethnicity and Family Therapy*, ed. Monica McGoldrick et al. (New York: The Guilford Press, 1982), 221.

8. Jeanne Wakatsuki Houston, *Beyond Manzanar: Views of Asian-American Womanhood* (California: Capra Press, 1985), 12. *Hakujin* means white people.

9. Ibid., 13.

10. Morishima, 15.

11. S. Frank Miyamoto, "The Forced Evacuation of the Japanese Minority during World War II," *Journal of Social Issues* 29 (1973): 21.

12. *Enryo* means self-imposed confinement.

13. Joe R. Feagin, *Racial and Ethnic Relations* (New Jersey: Prentice-Hall, 1984), 346. Also see Harry H. L. Kitano & Akemi Kikumura, "The Japanese American Family," in *Asian-Americans: Social and Psychological Perspectives,* vol. 2, ed. Russell Endo et al. (Palo Alto, CA: Science and Behavior Books, 1980), 8.

14. *Koko* means filial piety.

15. Daisuke Kitagawa, *Issei and Nisei: The Internment Years* (New York: The Seabury Press, 1967), 96.

16. Ibid., 87.

17. Morishima, 17.

18. Kitagawa, 87.

19. Morishima, 16.

20. Ibid., 17.

21. Kitagawa, 94.

22. Ann Umemoto, "Crisis in the Japanese American Family," in *Asian Women* (Berkeley: n.p., 1971), 107.

23. Kitagawa, 89-90.

24. Harry H. L. Kitano, "Does Culture Make a Difference?" in *Changing Perspectives in Mental Illness*, ed. Stanley C. Plog and Robert B. Edgerton (New York: Holt, Rinehart and Winston, 1969), 275.

25. Ibid., 275-276.

26. Kitagawa, 72.

27. Harry H. L. Kitano and Roger Daniels, *Asian Americans: Emerging Minorities* (New Jersey: Prentice-Hall, 1988), 69.

28. *Kibei* are American born *nisei* children who had been sent to Japan for education and were returned to America at the break of the Pacific War. See Kitagawa, 97-99, for further explanation of the situations of *kibei*.

29. Kitagawa, 107.

30. Ibid.

31. Ibid., 108.

32. For the ruling outcome of Misue Endo (a *nisei* woman) case by the Supreme Court, see Jacobus ten Broek et al., *Prejudice, War and the Constitution: Japanese American Evacuation and Resettlement* (Berkeley: University of California Press, 1958), 252-254.

33. Kitano and Daniels, 64-65.

34. Jeffrey Jay, "Terrible Knowledge," *The Family Therapy Networker* 15, no. 6 (1991): 25.

35. For further information, see Stanley Sue and James Morishima, *The Mental Health of Asian Americans*, especially chapter 2.

36. Kitano, "Does Culture Make a Difference?," 270.

37. See Shon and Ja, 219-222.

38. Laura M. Markowitz, "After the Trauma," *The Family Therapy Networker* 15, no. 6 (1991): 37.

39. Ibid.

40. Helen Murano, "Minidoka," in Tateishi, 42.

41. Ibid., 46.

42. Ibid., 44.

43. Ibid., 45.

44. Ibid., 42.

45. Ibid., 46.

46. Ibid.

47. Ibid., 47.

48. Ibid., 48.

49. Ibid.

50. Ibid., 50.

51. Violet De Cristoforo, "Tule Lake," Tateishi, 125.

52. Ibid., 126.

53. Ibid.

54. Question 27 and 28: Kitagawa paraphrases these in (116): 27) Do you pledge your loyalty to the government of the United States and promise to abide by the laws of this country? Answer Yes or No. 28) Do you forswear allegiance to the Emperor of Japan? Answer Yes or No. These questions placed *issei* in a no-win situation. The US government did not grant citizenship to *issei.* As permanent residents hoping to become US citizens, they were forced to maintain Japanese citizenship. To answer "No" to question 28 meant immediate deportation from the US. If answered "Yes" they would be considered traitors of the Emperor in Japan and there would not be a chance for them to return to their native land in case their US citizenship was to be revoked.

55. De Cristoforo, 128.

56. Ibid., 129.

57. Ibid., 131.

58. Ibid., 130.

59. Ibid., 132.

60. Ibid., 133.

61. Ibid.

62. Ibid., 136.

63. Ibid.

64. Ibid., 139.

65. Ibid., 128.

66. Ibid., 139.

67. Ibid., 140.

68. Ibid., 127

69. Ibid., 130, 132.

70. Ibid., 131. *Hotokesama* means Buddha, including the ancestral spirits in Japanese folk Buddhism.

71. Ibid., 134.

72. Ibid., 127.

73. Ibid., 134.

74. Ibid., 140.

75. Kitagawa, 57.

76. Christ United Presbyterian Church, *The Church's One Hundred Years in the Japanese American Community* (San Francisco: n.p., 1988), 61.

77. Ibid.

78. Ibid., 67.

79. Tateishi, 24.

80. Ibid., 147.

81. Ibid., 226.

82. Christ United Presbyterian Church, 62.

83. Tateishi, 15.

84. Christ United Presbyterian Church, 62.

85. Kitagawa, 57.

86. Tateishi, 15.

87. Ibid.

88. Shon and Ja, 222.

89. Laird, 440.

90. Ibid., 441.

91. Shon and Ja, 225.

92. Inn Sook Lee, "Children of Pilgrims: Asian American Identity," *APCE Advocate* (May 1989).

Chapter Two

1. Tom Mathew, "The Siege of L.A.," *Newsweek*, 11 May 1992, 30.

2. Angela Oh, "Two Facets of Los Angeles Riots," interview by ABC News in *An MPI Home Video Presentation,* 5 May 1992.

3. Ibid., 3.

4. "Eastern Pacific Troubles," *Far Eastern Economic Review* (May 1992): 7. Italics mine.

5. Nevertheless, it is not necessary to deny that African Americans want freedom from economic and political oppression as well.

6. Richard Schickel, "How TV Failed to Get The Real Picture," *Time*, 11 May 1992, 29.

7. Susumu Awanohara and Jae Hoon Shim. "Melting Pot Boils Over," *Far Eastern Economic Review* (May 1992): 10.

8. Elaine H. Kim, "They Armed in Self-Defense," *Newsweek*, 18 May 1992, 10.

9. David Ellis, "L.A. Lawless." *Time*, 11 May 1992, 28.

10. Oh.

11. James H. Cone, *For My People: Black Theology and the Black Church* (New York: Orbis Books, 1992), 142.

12. According to a poll, "78% of 200 blacks questioned, and 79% of 798 whites, said they thought before the verdict that the policemen would be found guilty." George J. Church, *Time*, 11 May 1992, 21.

13. Mathew, 30.

14. James H. Cone, *A Black Theology of Liberation* (New York: Orbis Books, 1992), xviii.

15. According to one report, in L.A., black unemployment was between 40 and 50%; the poverty rate was 32.9%; about 20% of black teenagers (ages 16 to 19) were both out of school and unemployed; an estimated 40,000 additional jobs were simply lost as a result of the civil unrest in May. Maxine Walters, "The L.A. Disturbances

Should Have Surprised No One," *Public Welfare* (Fall 1992): 11.

16. "Eastern Pacific Troubles," *Far Eastern Economic Review* (May 1992): 7. In a political sense, it is pointed out that the failure of President Lyndon B. Johnson's Great Society anti-poverty programs of the 1960s were responsible for "many of the root problems that have resulted in inner-city difficulties." Julie Rovner, "Rhetoric, Not Radical Change Likely Result of L.A. Riots," *Congressional Quarterly Weekly Report*, 9 May 1992, 247.

17. Tom Morganthau, "The Price of Neglect," *Newsweek*, 11 May 1992, 54.

18. Richard Lacayo, "This is Your Land, This is My Land." *Time*, 18 May 1992, 31. The report continues, "[a]bout half of America's 250 million people live in the suburbs, and only one quarter in central cities."

19. Morganthau, 55.

20. In this regard, the Korean merchants' behavior that most of them were living in a relatively wealthier region, not in the ghetto where their stores were located, should be blamed. Furthermore, it is important that this behavior has been regarded as a kind of exploitation by blacks. Nevertheless, we should not articulate this as typical behavior of the Korean American community or their racial discrimination of blacks. Rather, it should be regarded as one of the typical evil by-products of capitalism mingled with economic egoism. We shall discuss this later.

21. Lacayo, 29.

22. Morganthau, 54.

23. It is noteworthy that the significance of the violence committed in the L.A. riots was accepted in this meaning. Jim Wallis wrote, "In America, violence is about the only thing that makes us see the poor or even remember that they exist. The Los Angeles rebellion broke the long, frightening silence in both the media and the highest levels of national political leadership about the disintegration of life and society that now is the norm of existence in vast inner-city territories." Jim Wallis, "Violence, Poverty, and Separation," *Public Welfare* (Fall 1992): 15.

24. "Eastern Pacific Troubles," 7.

25. Cone, *For My People*, 142. In this regard, the attitude of Korean Americans in their personal relationships with other minorities, particularly with African Americans, should be reconsidered. It is noteworthy that for African Americans, Korean American merchants' treatment of them has been regarded as another racial prejudice. In other words, Korean Americans may not be exonerated from the same charge by which African Americans were condemned.

26. Jack E. White, "The Limits of Black Power," *Time*, 11 May 1992, 38.

27. Ibid., 39.

28. Ibid., 40.

29. Cone, *A Black Theology of Liberation*, xviii.

30. Later Cone acknowledges his weakness and the importance of the economic aspects of human oppression. "Anyone who claims to be fighting against the problem of oppression and does not analyze the exploitive role of capitalism is either naive or an agent of the enemies of freedom. I was naive and did not have at my disposal sufficient

tools for analyzing the complexity of human oppression." Ibid.

31. Kim, 10.

32. T. Clinton, "Hatred for Korean Americans; A Part of Black Culture?" *Korean Diaspora: Voices of the People & Gospel* 86 (June 1992): 11-12.

33. Daniel Hyukjoon Choi, "Can We Think of Ourselves As Successful Minority?" Ibid., 13-14.

34. James H. Cone, *Black Theology and Black Power* (New York: Harper San Francisco, 1989), 17.

35. The word "cultural flunkyism" is used for indicating a kind of mental character which is prone to feeling culturally inferior and being servile to any dominant culture. This cultural flunkyism is usually observed in the Korean American community. Those who acquire economic wealth or who work with relatively stable professions assimilated sooner than their competitors from other minorities as well as their own people.

36. Cone, *For My People*, 158.

37. Ibid.

38. Ibid., 159.

39. Ibid., 172.

40. Cone, *Black Theology and Black Power*, 63.

41. Tong Hwan (Stephen) Moon, "Korean Minjung Theology," in *Korean-American Relations at Crossroads*, ed. Wonmo Dong (San Francisco: Liberty Press, 1982), 27.

42. Cone, *For My People*, 167.

43. Regarding this, Cone writes: "The universal dimension of the gospel was revealed in the particularities of poor people throughout the world. It was this universalism in the gospel that prevented me from elevating the black experience or the African reality to an absolute norm in black theology. While there is no knowledge of Jesus' gospel apart from the particular struggle of the poor for liberation, we must never absolutize a particular struggle (whether black, African, Asian, or Latin) to the exclusion of others." James H. Cone, *My Soul Looks Black*, (New York: Orbis Books, 1992), 99.

44. Jonathan Burton, "Razed Hopes," *Far Eastern Economic Review* (Oct 1992): 26.

45. Kim, 10.

46. Ibid., 158.

Chapter Three

1. *Haole* is Hawaiian for "foreigner," and is popularly used in Hawai'i for people of European descent. *Hapa* is Hawaiian for "half." A person who is *hapa-haole* is "half-haole."

2. People of Japanese ancestry in Hawai'i usually identify themselves as simply "Japanese," rather than use a term such as Americans of Japanese Ancestry as is more common on the mainland United States. Japanese is not being used here to identify people born and raised in Japan.

Appendix

1. Information for this paragraph and the next is drawn from Mary Ishii Kuramoto, *Dendo: One Hundred Years of Japanese Christians in Hawaii and the Nuuanu Congregational Church* (Honolulu, 1986).

2. Takie Okumura, *Seventy Years of Divine Blessing*, (Japan, 1939), 2-3; quoted in Kuramoto, 45.

3. This paragraph is indebted to Masuo Ogoshi, *Makiki Christian Church: 75th Anniversary 1904-1979.*

4. Ogoshi, 7.

5. Ibid.

6. This chart is adapted from Hawai'i State Government: Department of Business, Economic Development and Tourism, "Table 1. 32-Ancestry: 1990," in *1997 State of Hawaii Data Book* [Database online]; Available from http: www. hawaii. gov/dbedt/db97/index. html; Internet. It is derived from U. S. Bureau of the Census, *1990 Census of Population, Supplementary Reports, Detailed Ancestry Groups for States*, 1990 CP-S-1-2 (October 1992), tables 1 and 3. The table includes persons who reported at least one specific ancestry group. No more than two groups per person were coded.

7. Shown separately for all groups over 50,000, plus several smaller groups of special interest in Hawai'i. The table has been modified by the addition of groupings according to European, Asian, and Pacific Islander Ancestry. People of Portuguese Ancestry are popularly distinguished in Hawai'i from other people of European Ancestry and are thus presented separately here. The ancestries grouped under European are popularly undifferentiated in Hawai'i, while those grouped under Asian as well as those grouped under Pacific Islander are strictly differentiated in the popular culture of Hawai'i.

8. Out of the 1,335,722 responses, 1,052,735 reported a first ancestry and 282,987 reported a second ancestry as well.

9. The U.S. total was 256,081.

Chapter Four

1. Phrase and concept introduced by Mark Taylor.

2. Lin, *Grounds For Remembering: Monuments' Memorial Texts* (Berkeley: Doreen B. Townsend Center for the Humanities, 1995), 22-23.

3. Dean MacCannell, *Empty Meeting Grounds: The Tourist Papers* (New York: Routledge, 1992), 282.

4. Hess, "Tale of Two Memorials," from Franklin Ng, "Maya Lin and the Vietnam Veterans Memorial"in *Chinese Historical Society of America 1994*, 214.

5. Ng, 212.

6. He is the veteran who developed the idea of the memorial.

7. Tiger Woods made that quote when he turned 18 and was allowed to play in the professional circuit. Youth and race were also discriminative factors against Woods.

8. Scruggs and Swerdlow, "To Heal" in Ng, 203.

9. Abramson, "Maya Lin and the 1960s," *Critical Inquiry*, 687.

10. Ng, 204.

11. Lin, 11-12.

12. Lin, quoted in Abramson, 704.

13. Lin, 11-12.

14. Ibid.

15. Ibid.

16. Ibid.

17. This does not include the non-American casualties, which would amount to a much higher human loss.

18. Lin, 11-12.

19. Ng, 210.

20. Abramson, 705.

21. Michael Vietnam; Internet.

22. Ng, 210.

23. Lin, 11-12.

24. Lin, quoted in Abramson, 697.

25. Ng, 217.

26. Ibid.

27. Mark Taylor, *Theology as Cultural Critique in America*, 129.

28. Abramson, 707.

29. Ibid.

30. Taylor, 129.

31. Ibid., 132.

32. Ibid., 138.

33. Greenblatt, 24.

34. Abramson, 707.

Chapter Five

1. Quoted in Amy Tachiki, Eddie Wong, and Franklin Odo, eds., *Roots: An Asian American Reader* (Los Angeles, CA: The UCLA Asian American Studies Center, 1971), 98-99.

2. *Hankuk Ilbo* (*Korea Times*), 28 February, 1979.

3. The term "Asian American" is used as a shorthand term for convenience. People such as the Pacific Islanders should not be excluded from the meaning of that term.

4. Everett V. Stonequist, *The Marginal Man: A Study in Personality and Culture Conflict* (New York: Russell & Russell, 1937), 8; and Charles Marden and Gladys Meyer, *Minorities in American Society* (New York: Van Nostrand Reinhold, Co., 1968), 44-45.

5. See H. F. Dickie-Clark, *The Marginal Situation: A Sociological Study of a Colored Group* (London: Routledge & Kegan Paul, 1966), 24; and E.C. Hughes and H.M. Hughes, *Where People Meet: Racial and Ethnic Frontiers* (Glencoe, IL: Free Press, 1952), 190.

6. See Victor Turner, *The Ritual Process: Structure and Anti-Structure* (Ithaca: Cornell University Press, 1969), 94-203.

7. The Asian immigrants' in-between liminality and their strangerhood caused by the American society's non-acceptance are two of the major themes that run throughout Ronald Takaki's masterful narrative of Asian Americans' history. See his *Strangers from a Different Shore: A History of Asian Americans* (New York: Penguin Books, 1989). For an interesting attempt to reinterpret the meaning of the Asian American experience of marginality from the perspective of the Asian world view, see Jung young Lee, "Marginality: A Multi-Ethnic Approach to Theology from an Asian-American Perspective," *The Asian Journal of Theology* 7, no. 2 (1993): 244-253.

8. See Harry H. L. Kitano and Roger Daniels, The Asian Americans: Emerging Minorities (Englewood Cliffs: Prentice Hall, 1988), 1-9.

9. Won Moo Hurh, "Comparative Study of Korean Immigrants in the United States: A Typology," *Koreans in America,* ed. Byong-suh Kim et al. (Memphis, TN: The Association of Korean Christian Scholars in North America, 1977), 95.

10. See n. 7.

11. See Alan C. Kerckhoff and Thomas C. McCormick, "Marginal Status and Marginal Personality," *Social Forces* 34 (October 1977): 50; and Won Moo Hurh and Kwang Chung Kim, *Korean Immigrants in America: A Structural Analysis of Ethnic Confinement and Adhesive Adaptation* (Rutherford, NJ: Fairleigh Dickinson University Press, 1984), 138-155.

12. For a discussion of the change process, see, for example, William Bridges, *Transitions: Making Sense of Life's Changes* (Reading, MA: Addison-Wesley Publishing Co., 1980).

13. I owe this reference to *Tao Te Ching* to Bishop Roy I Sano, "A Theology of Struggle from an Asian American Perspective," *Branches: Journal of the Pacific and Asian Center for Theologies and Strategies* (Fall/Winter, 1990): 8.

14. The meaning of the pilgrimage symbol I am adopting follows closely that of J.B. Soucek, "Pilgrims and Sojourners: An Essay in Biblical Theology," *Communio Viatorum* I (1958): 3-17. I have also found helpful Richard R. Niebuhr's observation: "Pilgrims are persons in motion -- passing through territories not their own -- seeking something we might call completion, or perhaps the clarity will do as well, a goal to which only the spirit's compass points the way." Richard R. Niebuhr,"Pilgrims and Pioneers," *Parabola* 9 no. 3, 7. Definitions of the term "pilgrimage" range from strict and narrow to comprehensive and broad. H. B. Partin, for example, finds four essential elements in pilgrimages: separation, journey to a sacred place, a fixed purpose, and a

hardship. E. B. Partin, "The Muslim Pilgrimage: Journey to the Center" (Ph.D. diss., 1967); quoted in William G. Johnson, "The Pilgrimage Motif in the Book of Hebrews," *Journal of Biblical Literature* 97/2 (1978): 244. Another anthropologist, Alan Morinis, however, offers a much broader definition. The term "pilgrimage", according to Morinis, "can be put to use wherever journeying and some embodiment of an ideal intersect."Alan Morinis, "Introduction: The Territory of the Anthropology of Pilgrimage,"in *Sacred Journeys: The Anthropology of Pilgrimage,* ed. Alan Morinis (Westport, CN: Greenwood Press, 1992), 3. For a recent discussion of the metaphor of pilgrimage with a different application from mine, see Margaret Miles, "Pilgrimage as Metaphor in a Nuclear Age," *Theology Today* 45 (July 1988): 166-179.

15. See Hurh and Kim, 84-86, 146-149.

16. Byung-sup Bahn, *Jil-Geu-Reut-Gat-Un-Na-Eh-Ge-Do (Even for Me an Earthen Vessel)* (Seoul: Yang-Suh-Kak, 1988), 97.

17. For one of my earliest attempts to relate the pilgrimage symbol to marginality, see "Called to Be Pilgrims: Toward a Theology Within the Korean American Context," in *The Korean Immigrant in America,* ed. Byong-suh Kim and Sang Hyun Lee (Montclair, NJ: The Association of Korean Christian Scholars in North America, 1980), 37-74. I have benefitted from numerous other theological reflections by Asian American scholars. In addition to those already mentioned, see also, for example: Roy I. Sano, *From Every Nation without Number: Racial and Ethnic Diversity in United Methodism* (Nashville, TN: Abingdon Press, 1982); Wesley S. Woo, "Theological Themes," in *Asian Pacific American Youth Ministry* (Valley Forge: Judson Press, 1988), 11-22; and Ha Tai Kim, *Tai-Pyong-Yang-Geun-Neu- Kanaan-Tang (The Land of Canaan Across the Pacific)* (S. Pasadena, CA: Korean Church of the Pacific, 1979).

18. H. Richard Niebuhr, *The Meaning of Revelation* (New York: The Macmillan Co., 1962), 116.

19. Darryl M. Trimiew, working out of his African American context, also critiques and learns from H. Richard Niebuhr's thought. See his *Voices of the Silenced: The Responsible Self in an Marginalized Community* (Cleveland, OH: The Pilgrim Press, 1993).

20. A series of insightful analyses of the tragic events of 1992 in Los Angeles appeared in a Korean American journal, *The Christian Herald*, in the spring of 1994. See, e.g., Chan-Hie Kim, "The April 29 Event from the Biblical Perspective and Koreans in America,"part 1-2, *The Christian Herald,* no. 635 (April 8, 1994): 20-22; no. 636 (April 15, 1994):14-17; and Sung-Do Park, "The April 29 Event and the Emergence of New Life," part 2, *The Christian Herald* no. 639 (May 6, 1994): 21-25.

21. See Helmut Koester, "Outside the Camp: Hebrews 13:9-14," *Harvard Theological Review* 55 (1962): 299-315; and William G. Johnson, "The Pilgrimage Motif in the Book of Hebrews," *The Journal of Biblical Literature* 97 no. 2 (1978): 239-251. For an important study of the letter to the Hebrews by an Asian American theologian, see Roy I. Sano, *Outside the Gate: A Study of the Letter to the Hebrews* (Cincinnati, OH: The United Methodist Church, 1982). For an instructive essay on the themes of home and the Christ "outside the camp," see Charles C. West, "Where is Our Home and Who is Welcome in It?", *The Presbyterian Outlook* 10 (June 1985): 14-15.

22. In the case of Korean immigrants, for example, almost 70 percent are affiliated with Korean immigrant churches, and about 85 percent of them attend church regularly. See Hurh and Kim, 129-169.

23. John H. Elliott, *A Home for the Homeless: A Sociological Exegesis of I Peter-Its Situation and Strategy* (Philadelphia: Fortress Press, 1981), 127, 130-131, 199. Elliott draws a sharp distinction between the "heavenly home," "beyond time and history," of the letter to the Hebrews and the "household of God," "a place of belonging" here and now, of I Peter. Ibid., 129-132, 224-227. Even if we suppose that this distinction is correct, it would seem that we would need both the transcendent dimension of the ultimate realization of God's kingdom in "The Letter to the Hebrews" as well as this-worldly embodiment of the kingdom in "I Peter."

24. Roy O. Samp,"Ministry for a Liberating Ethnicity: The Biblical and Theological Foundations for Ethnic Ministries," in *The Theologies of Asian American and Pacific Peoples: A Reader*, comp. Roy I. Sano (Berkeley, CA: Asian Center for Theology and Strategies, pacific School of Religion, 1976), 291.

25. See Won Moo Hurh, "Toward a New Community and Identity: The Korean-American Ethnicity," in Kim and Lee, 1-25.

26. Soomee Kim Hwang, "In-Between Colors Have Names, Too," *PAACE: Pacific and Asian American Christian Education Newsletter* 7 (March 1992): 10, quoted from Fumitaka Matsuoka, "Out of silence: Emerging Themes of Asian-American Churches," unpublished manuscript, 108.

27. Gaston Bachelard, *The Poetics of Space* (Boston: Beacon Press, 1969), 6, quoted from Sharon Daloz Parks, "Home and Pilgrimage: Companion Metaphors for Personal and Social Transform," *Soundings* 72 (Summer/Fall, 1989): 304.

28. Kwang Chung Kim and Won Moo Hurh, "The Wives of Korean Small Businessmen in the U.S.: Business Involvement and Family Roles," in *Korean American Women: Toward Self-Realization,* ed. Inn Sook Lee (Mansfield, OH: The Association of Korean Christian Scholars in North America, 1 985), 1-41. A good anthology of articles on Asian American women's experiences is: Asian Women United of California, eds., *Making Waves: An Anthology of Writings By and About Asian American Women* (Boston: Beacon Press, 1989).

29. See Inn Sook Lee, "Korean American Women and Ethnic Identity," in *Korean American Ministry*, exp. ed., ed. Sang Hyun Lee and John V. Moore, (Louisville: Presbyterian Church(USA), 1993), 192-214; Soon Man Rhim, "The Status of Women in Traditional Korean Society," in *Korean Women in a Struggle for Humanization,* ed. Harold H. Sunoo and Dong Soo Kim (Memphis, TN: The Association of Korean Christian Scholars in North America, 1978), 11-37; and Minza Kim Boo, "The Social Reality of the Korean American Women: Toward Crashing with the Confucian Ideology," in Lee, *Korean American Women,* 65-93.

30. For a discussion of women's "experience of nothingness" and its creativity, see, for example, Carol Christ, *Diving Deep and Surfacing: Women Writers on Spiritual Quest* (Boston: Beacon Press, 1980), 9-14.

31. The idea of the creation as God's "repetition" of God's inner being comes from Jonathan Edwards. See his "Concerning the End for Which God Created the World," *Works of Jonathan Edwards,* vol. 8, *Ethical Writings,* ed. Paul Ramsey (New Haven:

Yale University Press, 1989), 433.

Chapter Six

1. For more in depth discussion of distinctions between race and ethnicity see Miicael Omi and Howard Winant, *Racial Formation in the United States: From the 1960s to the 1990s* (New York: Routledge, 1994).

2. Many feminists who are women of color find themselves in this same situation. Powerful articulations of this tension are emerging from various communities. See, Alma M. Garcia, "The Development of Chicana Feminist Discourse"in *From Different Shores: Perspectives on Race, and Ethnicity in America,* ed. Ronald Takaki (New York: Oxford University Press, 1994); Maria Hong, ed., (New York: Avon Books, 1993); Sneja Gunew, ed., *Feminist Knowledge: Critique and Construct* (New York: Routledge, 1990); Idem, *A Reader in Feminist Knowledge* (New York: Routledge, 1991); Bell Hooks, *Feminist Theory: From Margin to Center* (Boston: South End Press, 1984); Patricia Hill Collins, *Black Feminist Thought: Knowledge, Consciousness, and the Politics of Empowerment* (Boston: Unwin Hyman, 1990); and Ada Maria Isasi-Diaz and Fernando F. Segovia, eds., *Hispanic/Latino Theology: Challenge and Promise* (Minneapolis: Fortress Press, 1996).

3. Franz Fanon, *The Wretched of the Earth* (New York: Grove press, 1963).

4. Lisa Lowe, *Immigrant Acts: On Asian American Cultural Politics* (Durham: Duke University press, 1996), 62-63.

5. Ronald Takaki, *Strangers From A Different Shore: A History of Asian Americans* (New York: Penguin Books, 1989).

6. Homi K. Bhabha, "Cultural Diversity and Cultural Differences," in *The Post-Colonial Studies Reader*, ed. Bill Ashcroft, Gareth Griffiths and Helen Tiffin (New York: Routledge, 1995), 206-210. See also Sang Hyun Lee, "How Shall We Sing the Lord's Song In a Strange Land?," *Journal of Asian and Asian American Theology* (1996): 77-81. He envisions the Asian Americans as the emerging "new ethnicity" and "creative minority."

7. Iris Marion Young, *Justice and the Politics of Difference* (Princeton: Princeton University Press, 1990), 156-171.

8. For more, see, Judith Roof and Robyn Wiegman, eds., *Who can Speak? Authority and Critical Identity* (Urbana: University of Illinois Press, 1995).

9. Sneja Gunew, "Feminism and the Politics of Irreducible Differences: Multiculturalism/Ethnicity/Race," in *Feminism and The Politics of Difference*, ed. Sneja Gunew and Anna Yeatman (San Francisco: Westview Press, 1993).

10. Judith Butler, "Contingent foundations: Feminism and the Question of 'postmodernism,'" in *The Postmodern Turn: New Perspectives on Social Theory* (Cambridge: University of Cambridge, 1994), 153-170.

11. Trinh T. Minh-ha, *Woman, Native, Other.*

12. Gary Okihiro, *Margins and Mainstreams: Asians in American History and Culture* (Seattle: University of Washington Press, 1994), 175.

13. Jane Gallop, *The Daughter's Seduction: Feminism and Psychoanalysis* (Ithaca: Cornell University Press, 1982).

14. For more in depth discussion see Albert Menni's *The Colonizer and the Colonized* (Boston: Beacon Press, 1965).

15. Seidman, 150.

16. Also see Judith Butler and Joan W. Scott, eds., *Feminist Theorize the Political* (New York: Routledge, 1992); and Helen Eisenstein and Alice Jardine, eds. *The Future of Difference* (New Brunswick: Rutgers University Press, 1990).

17. Minh-ha.

18. Diana Fuss, *Essentially Speaking: Feminism, Nature, and Difference* (New York: Routledge, 1989), 97-112.

19. Jung Young Lee, *Marginality: The Key to Multicultural Theology* (Minneapolis: Fortress Press, 1995), 62-63.

20. See Jung Ha Kim, *Bridge-Makers and Cross Bearers: Korean American Women and the Church* (Atlanta: Scholars Press, 1997).

21. Bell Hooks, *Yearning: Race, Gender, and Cultural Politics* (Boston: South End Press, 1990). Also see articles in Russel Ferguson et al., *Out There: Marginalization and Contemporary Cultures* (Cambridge: The MIT Press, 1990).

22. Lee, *Marginality*, 31.

23. Ibid., 46-47.

24. Also see Iris Marion Young, "The Ideal of Community and the Politics of Difference," in *Feminism/Postmodernism*, ed. Linda J. Nicholson (New York: Routledge, 1990).

25. See Andrew Sung Park, *The Wounded Heart of God: The Asian Concept of Han and the Christian Doctrine of Sin* (Nashville: Abingdon Press, 1993).

26. See Rita Nakashima Brock, "On Mirrors, Mists, and Murmurs; Toward an Asian American Thealogy," in *Weaving the Visions: New Patterns in Feminist Spirituality*, ed. Judith Plaskow and Carol P. Christ (San Francisco: Harper Collins, 1989), 235-243.

27. See Fernando F. Segovia, "In The World but Not of It: Exile as Locus for a Theology of the Diaspora," in Isasi-Dias and Segovia, 195-217.

28. Ibid., 203.

29. Ibid., 213.

Chapter Seven

1. Robert Kegan, *The Evolving Self: Problem and Process in Human Development* (Harvard University Press, 1982), 86-87.

2. Peter Berger, "Secular Theology and the Rejection of the Supernatural: Reflections on Recent Trends," *Theological Studies* 38 (March 1977): 41.

3. Ibid., 43.

4. Langdon Gilkey, *Catholicism Confronts Modernity: A Protestant View* (New York: Seabury, 1975), 59.

5. Kegan, 45-ff.

6. Erik H. Erikson, *Identity and the Life Cycle* (New York, London: W.W. Norton and Company, 1980), 94.

7. Idem, *Young Man Luther: A Study in Psycho Analysis and History* (New York, London: W. W. Norton & Company, 1962), 118.

8. Idem, *Identity Youth and Crisis* (New York, London: W. W. Norton & Company, 1968), 93.

9. Ibid., 96.

10. Idem, *Childhood and Society* (New York, London: W. W. Norton & Company, 1960), 262-263.

11. James E. Loder, *Transforming Moment*, 2nd ed. (Colorado Springs: Helmers & Howard, 1989), 99-ff.

12. See Lee A. Kirkpatrick and Phillip R. Shaver, "Attachment Theory and Religion: Childhood Attachments, Religious Beliefs, and Conversion," *Journal for the Scientific Study of Religion* 29 (Sep 1990): 315-334; and Gordon D. Kaufman, *The Theological Imagination: Constructing the Concept of God* (Philadelphia: Westminster, 1981), 67.

13. Paul Ricoeur, *Freud and Philosophy: An Essay on Interpretation,* trans. Denis Savage (New Haven and London: Yale University Press, 1970), 10.

14. S. G. F. Brandon, *Time and Mankind: A Historical and Philosophical Study of Mankind's Attitude to the Phenomena of Change* (London, New York: Hutchinson and Col, Ltd., 1951), 23.

15. Young Pai, "Toward a Reconceptualization of Community," (paper presented at the Conference for the Second Generation Ministry for Korean-Americans, Princeton, New Jersey, June 1990).

16. Hans-Georg Gadamer, *Truth and Method* (New York: Seabury Press, 1975), 141-142.

17. Ibid., 142.

18. Michael Rosenak, *Commandments and Concerns: Jewish Religious Education in Secular Society* (The Jewish Publication Society: 1987), 76-77.

19. Ricoeur, 7.

20. Refer to Chapter 8: "Culture as Mentor" in Sharon Park *The Critical Years: Young Adults & the Search for Meaning. Faith & Commitment* (San Francisco: Harper San Francisco, 1986), 176-205; and also I found it helpful to read C. Ellis Nelson's argument on "the formative power of culture" in his *Where Faith Begins* (Atlanta: John Knox Press, 1967), especially 35-66.

Chapter Eight

1. Many women immigrated because their husbands wished to gain further education or job training. Therefore, women themselves did not have a chance to choose the move on their own for their own purpose.

2. Rollo May, *Man's Search for Himself* (New York: Norton, 1953), 119.

3. Erik H. Erikson, *Identity, Youth and Crisis* (New York: Norton, 1980), 156.

4. Ibid.

5. Erik H. Erikson, *Identity and the Life Cycle* (New York: Norton, 1959), 132.

6. Ibid.

7. Ibid., 25.

8. Hesung C. Koh, "Women's Roles and Achievement in the Yi Dynasty," in *Korean Women in Transition*, ed. Eui-Young Yu and Earl H. Phillips (Los Angeles: California State University Press, 1987), 29.

9. Ibid.

10. Yung-Chun Kim, *Women of Korea* (Seoul: Ewha Woman's University Press, 1976), 98.

11. Laurel Kendall and Mark Peterson, eds., *Korean Women: View from the Inner Room* (New Haven: East Rock Press, 1983), 65.

12. Kim, 195.

13. Ibid., 198.

14. Ibid., 219.

15. Ibid., 241.

16. Alex R. Ramsey, "Koreans in America," in *Kore-Am Journal* (December 1987): 100.

17. Koh, 19.

18. Sucheng Chan, *Asian Americans: An Interpretive History* (Boston: Twayne, 1991), 140.

19. U.S. Census 1980.

20. Daniel B. Lee, "Transcultural Marriage and Its Impact on Korean Immigration," in *Korean American Women: Toward Self-Realization*, ed. Inn Sook Lee (Mansfield, OH: Association of Korean Christian Scholars in North America, 1985), 56; and personal conversation with the Rev. Nam Soo Kim at New York Theological Seminary in New York City on February 15, 1989.

21. Inn Sook Lee, "Korean American Women and Ethnic Identity," in *Korean American Ministry*, ed. Sang Hyun Lee and John V. Moore (Louisville: Presbyterian Church (USA), 1993), 198-199.

22. Ibid., 199.

23. Ibid., 198.

24. David Kim and Charles Choy Wong, "Business Development in Koreatown, Los Angeles," in *Asian Americans: Social and Psychological Perspectives*, ed. Russell Endo, Stanley Sue, and Nathaniel N. Wagner (Ben Lomond, CA: Science and Behavior

Books, 1980), 109.

25. Koh, 56.

26. Illsoo Kim, "Organizational Patterns of Korean American Methodist Churches: Denominationalism and Personal Communities," in *Rethinking Methodist History*, ed. R.E. Richey and K.E. Rowe (Nashville: Kingswood Books), 147.

27. Eun-Sik Yang, "Korean Women of America," *Amerasia* 11 (1984): 25.

28. Lee, "Korean American Women and Ethnic Identity," 199.

29. Ibid., 200.

30. Young Pai, "A Sociocultural Understanding of Korean American Youth Caught in the Web," in Lee and Moore, 277.

31. Sonia Shinn Sunoo, *Korea Kaleidoscope: Oral Histories* (New York: United Presbyterian Church, 1982), 6.

32. Won Moo Hurh, *The Korean Americans* (Westport, CT: Greenwood Press, 1998), 102.

33. Minza Kim Boo, "The Social Reality of the Korean-American Women: Toward Crashing with the Confucian Ideology," in Lee, *Korean American Women*, 83.

34. Hwain C. Lee, *Confucius, Christ and Co-Partnership* (Lanham, MD: University Press of America, 1994), 12.

35. Inn Sook Lee, "Women's Emancipation Movement within the Christian Context," in Lee, *Korean American Women*, 111.

36. Ai Ra Kim, *Women Struggling for a New Life* (Albany, NY: State University of New York Press, 1996), 72.

37. Jung Ha Kim, *Bridge-Makers and Cross-Bearers* (Atlanta, GA: Scholars Press, 1997), 138.

38. Lee, "Korean American Women and Ethnic Identity," 201.

39. Lee, "Women's Emancipation Movement within the Christian Context," 119.

40. Won Moo Hurh, "Korean American Pluralism the 1.5 Generation," in Lee and Moore, 217.

41. Bok Lim Kim, "Asian Wives of U.S. Servicemen: Women in Shadows," *Amerasia* 4 (1977): 91.

42. Inn Sook Lee, "Asian American Identity," *APCE (The Association of Presbyterian Christian Educators) Advocate* (May 1989): 6.

43. Harry H. Kitano and Roger Daniels, eds. *Asian Americans: Emerging Minorities*, 2nd ed. (Englewood Cliffs, NJ: Prentice Hall, 1995), 119.

44. Ibid., 120.

45. Inn Sook Lee, Class Discussion, Princeton Theological Seminary, November 1997.

46. Kitano and Daniels, 121.

47. Inn Sook Lee, Interview with Korean American Women in Los Angeles, March 1998.

48. Rosemary R. Ruether, *To Change the World: Christology and Cultural Criticism* (New York: Crossroad, 1981), 31.

49. Cherri Moraga and G. Anzaldua, eds., *This Bridge Called My Back* (Watertown, MA: Persephone Press, 1981), 71.

50. Sunoo, 7.

51. Kitano and Daniels, 119.

52. Deborah Woo, "The Socioeconomic Status of Asian American Women in the Labor Force," *Sociological Perspectives* 28 (July 1985): 321.

53. Hurh, *The Korean Americans*, 54.

54. Won Moo Hurh and Kwang Chun Kim, "The Wives of Korean Small Businessmen in the U.S.: Business Involvement and Family Roles," in Lee, *Korean American Women*, 27.

55. Ibid.

56. Barney G. Glaser and Anselm L. Strauss, *The Discovery of Grounded Theory: Strategies for Qualitative Research* (Chicago: Aldine Publishing, 1968).

57. Those who immigrated with parents or as foreign students at age eighteen and older are considered to be 1st generation immigrants. See Won Moo Hurh, *The Korean Americans*, and also Won Moo Hurh in *Korean American Ministry*.

58. Donald Capps, *The Depleted Self* (Minneapolis: Fortress Press, 1993), 117.

59. Kyeyoung Park, *The Korean American Dream: Immigrants and Small Business in New York City* (Ithaca, NY: Cornell University Press, 1997), 138.

60. Woo, 310.

61. Won Moo Hurh, "Toward A New Community and Identity: The Korean American Ethnicity," in *The Korean Immigrant in America*, ed. Byoung-suh Kim and Sang Hyun Lee (Montclair, NJ: Association of Korean Christian Scholars in North America, 1980), 22.

62. The labeling of stages in this article has been influenced by William S. Hall and William E. Cross, "Stages in the Development of Black Awareness: Exploratory Investigation," in *Black Psychology*, ed. Reginald Jones (New York: Harper & Row, 1972), 156-165; and by Donald R. Atkinson, George Morten, and Deral Wing Sue, eds., *Counseling American Minorities: A Cross Cultural Perspective* (Dubuque, IA: William C. Brown, 1979), 39; and quoted in Paul Pedersen, *A Handbook for Developing Multicultural Awareness* (Alexandria, VA: American Association for Counseling and Development, 1988), 62.

63. William Bridges, *Transitions* (Reading, MA: Addison-Wesley, 1980), 138.

64. C. Kay Allen, *The Ways and Power of Love* (American Fork, UT: Covenant Communications, 1993).

65. Kitano and Daniels, 119.

66. Karen Horney, *Self-Analysis* (New York: Norton, 1942).

67. Monica McGoldrick and Randy Gerson, *Genograms in Family Assessment* (New York: Norton, 1985).

68. Charles L. Whitfield, *Healing the Child Within* (Deerfield Beach, FL: Health Communications, 1989).

69. Melody Beattie, *Codependent No More: How to Stop Controlling Others and Start Caring for Yourself* (Center City, MN: Hazelden, 1992).

70. Anne Katherine, *Boundaries: Where You End and I Begin* (New York: Parkside, 1991).

71. Bridges, 138.

72. May, 119.

Chapter Nine

1. Andrew P. Morrison, "Shame, Ideal Self, and Narcissism," in *Essential Papers on Narcissism*, ed. Andrew P. Morrison (New York: New York University Press, 1986), 352.

2. Ibid., 349-352.

3. Helen Merrell Lynd, *On Shame and the Search for Identity* (New York: Harcourt, Brace and Company, 1958), 27.

4. Ibid., 27-32.

5. Erik H. Erikson, *Childhood and Society* (New York: W. W. Norton & Company, 1963), 252.

6. Nathaniel Hawthorne, *The Scarlet Letter* (New York: The New American Library of World Literature, Inc., 1959), 183.

7. Gershen Kaufman, *Shame: The Power of Caring* (Cambridge, Mass: Schenkman Books, 1980), 12.

8. Ibid., 13.

9. Ibid., 43-49.

10. Erikson, 253.

11. Lynd, 49-56.

12. Ibid., 50-51.

13. David W. Augsburger, *Pastoral Counseling Across Cultures* (Philadelphia: The Westminster Press, 1986), 115-116.

14. Erikson, 251-254.

15. Karl Barth, *Church Dogmatics*, vol. IV, part 1, *The Doctrine of Reconciliation*, ed. G. W. Bromiley and T. F. Torrance (Edinburgh: T & T Clark, 1965), 231, 234.

16. Lynd, 121.

17. Ibid., 71.

18. Lowell Noble in his book *Naked and Not Ashamed* (Jackson, MI: Jackson Printing, 1975), 4-6, notes different types of experiences of shame. This typology is adapted by Augsburger, 117. Augsburger writes:

> **Innocent shame**: shame felt when one's character is slandered without

justification
Guilty shame: Shame felt before others when one violates an ethical norm
Social shame: Embarrassment felt when one makes a social blunder or error
Familial shame: Disgrace from the behavior of another family member
Handicap shame: Embarrassment over some bodily defect or physical imperfection
Discrimination shame: Downgrading of persons treated as socially, racially, ethically, religiously, or vocationally inferior
Modesty shame: Shame related to sexual, social, or dress norms and proscribed behavior
Inadequacy shame: Feelings of inadequacy and inferiority from passivity, repeated failure, or abuse
Public shame: Open ridicule in the community as punishment or group pathology
Anticipated shame: The fear of exposure for any planned or desired behavior

19. Because of the stressed inferiority of women to men, a high rate of abortion of female fetuses exists in Asian American societies. This results in a higher percentage of males and a lower percentage of females among the population. As a result, marriage becomes more difficult for men since there are approximately two times the number of men to the number of women in society.

20. Jean Baker Miller, *Toward a New Psychology of Women*, 2nd ed. (Boston: Beacon Press, 1986), 27-48.

21. Racism includes more than the inferiority associated with physical attributes noted above. It pertains to the totality of the person, including various abilities.

22. John Bradshaw, *Healing the Shame that Binds You* (Deerfield Beach: Health Communications, Inc., 1988), 66-67.

23. Kaufman, 71-87.

24. Donald Capps, *Deadly Sins and Saving Virtues* (Philadelphia: Fortress Press, 1987), 28-32.

25. John Patton, *Is Human Forgiveness Possible* (Nashville: Abingdon Press, 1985), 73.

26. Kaufman, 11.

27. Lynd, 70.

28. Herbert Lockyer, Sr., ed., *Nelson's Illustrated Bible Dictionary* (Nashville: Thomas Nelson Publishers, 1986), 971.

29. Lynd, 66.

30. Ibid., 239.

Chapter Ten

1. Edward W. Gondolf, *Men Who Batter; An Integrated Approach for Stopping Wife Abuse* (Florida: Learning Publication, Inc., 1984), 27.

2. David Adams, "Treatment Models of Men Who Batter," in *Feminist Perspectives on Wife Abuse*, ed. Kersti Yllo and Michele Bograd (Newbury Park: SAGE Publications, 1988), 178.

3. Gondolf, 29.

4. Anthony Steven Kill,"Kohut's Psychology of the Self as a Model for Theological Dynamic," *Union Seminary Quarterly Review* 41, no. 1 (1986): 21.

5. Andrew P. Morrison, "Shame, Ideal Self, and Narcissism," *Essential Papers On Narcissism,* ed. Andrew P. Morrison (New York and London: New York University Press, 1986), 357.

6. Heinz Kohut and Ernest S. Wolf, "The Disorders of the Self and Their Treatment: An Outline," in Morrison, *Essential Papers on Narcissism*, 189.

7. James F. Masterson with Jacinta Lu Costello, *From Borderline Functioning Adult: Adolescent to the Test of Time* (New York: Brunner/Mazel. Publishers, 1980), 6.

8. Ibid., 8.

9. Ibid., 30.

10. Salvador Minuchin, *Families & Family Therapy* (Cambridge, MA: Harvard University Press, 1974), 55.

11. Y. S. E. Kim, *Korean Families and Family Therapy* (New York: Verlag Peter Lang, 1987), 219.

12. Masterson, 31.

13. Kohut and Wolf, 176.

14. Althea J. Horner, *Object Relations and the Developing Ego in Therapy* (Northvale: Jason Aronson Inc., 1989), 264.

15. Heinz Kohut, *The Restoration of the Self* (New York: International University Press, Inc., 1977), 121.

16. Ben Burnstein, "Some Narcissistic Personality Types," in Morrison, *Essential Papers On Narcissism*, 382.

17. Ibid., 384.

18. Adams, 190.

19. Bograd, in Yllo and Bograd, 4.

20. R. Emerson Dobash and Russell Dobash, *Violence against Wives* (New York: Free Press, 1979), 33.

21. Rita-Lou Clarke, *Pastoral Care of Battered Women* (Philadelphia: Westminster Press, 1979), 20.

22. Ibid.

23. Jong Sung Lee, *Korean Psychiatric Research* 1, no. 3 (Fall 1983): 64.

24. Kim, 216.

25. Bograd, 17.

26. Spender, 1980, quoted in Adams, 190.

27. Adams, 199.

28. Del Martin, *Battered Wives* (San Francisco: Glide Publishers, 1976), 64.

29. James B. Nelson, *The Intimate Connection* (Philadelphia: Westminster Press, 1982), 19.

30. Ibid., 68.

31. Quoted in Bussert, 79.

32. Nelson, 71.

33. Walter Brueggemann, *Genesis*, Interpretation (Atlanta: John Knox Press, 1982), 31.

34. Ibid., 34.

35. Ibid.

36. Bernard Loomer, "Two Conceptions of Power," *Criterion* 15 (1976): 13.

37. Ibid., 13.

38. Ibid., 14.

39. Nelson, 101.

40. Ibid., 20.

41. Ibid., 21.

42. Loomer, 27.

43. Gondolf, 98, from Domestic Abuse Project (Minneapolis, MN).

44. Adams, 192.

45. Jennifer Baker Fleming, *Stopping Wife Abuse* (Garden City, NY: Anchor Books, 1979), 45.

46. Gondolf, 135.

47. Ibid., 195.

48. Bussert, 44.

49. Samuel Osherson, *Finding Our Fathers,* 40.

50. Ibid., 207.

51. Ibid., 187.

52. Gondolf, 158.

53. Ibid., 71.

54. Ibid., 154.

55. Andrew Kimbrel, "A Time for Men to Pull Together," *Utne Reader*, no. 45 (1991): 70.

56. Adams, 195.

57. Mark Gerzon, *A Choice of Heroes: The Changing Faces of American Manhood* (New York: Houghton Mifflin, 1982), 238.

58. Alice Jardine and Paul Smith, *Men in Feminism* (New York: Methuen Inc., 1987), 34.

Chapter Twelve

1. Refer to Sharan B. Merriam and Rosemary S. Caffarella, *Learning in Adulthood* (San Francisco: Jossey-Bass Publishers, 1991).

2. Refer to U. S. Department of Education, Office of Educational Research and Improvement, Center for Statistics, (Washington, D. C.: Department of Education, 1986).

3. Ibid, 67.

4. J. W. E. Johnstone and R. J. Rivera, *Volunteers for Learning: A Study of the Educational Pursuits of Adults* (NY: Hawthorne, 1965), 143.

5. Ibid., 144.

6. Merriam and Caffarella, 81-82.

7. Ibid., 84.

8. B. R. Morstain and J. C. Smart, "Reasons for Participating in Adult Education Courses: A Multivariate Analysis of Group Difference," *Adult Education* 24, no. 2: 83-98. For further reference, see also Robert W. Gardner, Robey Bryant, and S. Smith Peter, *Asian Americans: Growth, Change, and Diversity* (Washington D. C.: Population Reference Bureau, 1985).

9. Won Moo Hurh and Kwang Chung Kim, "Religious Participation of Korean Immigrants in the United States," *Journal for the Scientific Study of Religion* 29, no. 29 (1990): 19-34.

10. Ibid.

11. Refer to Illsoo Kim, *New Urban Immigrants: The Korean Community in New York* (Princeton: Princeton University Press, 1981).

12. Hurh and Kim, 20.

13. Idem, *Korean Immigrants in America: A Structural Analysis of Ethnic Confinement and Adhesive Adaptation* (Cranbury, New Jersey: Fairleigh Dickinson University, 1984), 131.

14. Idem, "Religious Participation of Korean Immigrants in the United States," 20.

15. Ibid.

16. Bong-youn Choy, *Koreans in America* (Chicago: Nelson Hall, 1979), 258.

17. Hurh and Kim, "Religious Participation of Korean Immigrants in the United States," 135.

18. For more detailed discussion, refer to Peter Berger, *The Noise of Solemn Assemblies* (New York: Doubleday, 1961), 22.

19. Robert N. Bellah, "Civil Religion in America," *Daedalus* (1996): 22.

20. For more discussion, refer to Henry C. Simmons, "Critical Psychology and Ministry," *The Ecumenist* 23: 76-80; and Edmund V. Sullivan, *A Critical Psychology* (New York and London: Plenum Press, 1984).

21. For Coe, the adjective "social" is crucial to understand all human phenomena, as if "social" is the opposite of "individual" or "individualistic." Coe emphasized the importance of the community (i.e., being together) of all human beings. Refer to George Albert Coe, *A Social Theory of Religious Education* (New York: Charles Scribner's Son, 1917). This concept of "social" has been prevalent in the history of Oriental culture. In pictorial Chinese Language, "*IN*" means a person, which depicts two persons leaning on each other. In Korean culture, the concept of "mine" is less frequently used in depicting one's family members. For example, when we introduce children, we do not say, "they are my children." Rather, we say that they are "our" children, because it is assumed that our children belong to a community and in return the community as a whole is responsible to raise and nurture children together.

22. Hurh and Kim, "Religious Participation of Korean Immigrants in the United States," 22.

23. See the table in Ibid., 24.

Chapter Thirteen

1. This essay is revised from a paper that was originally written for Mark Taylor's Cultural Anthropology and Theology course at Princeton Theological Seminary. The names of the youth mentioned have been changed in order to protect their anonymity.

2. The National Convocation of Asian American United Methodist Churches, "An Affirmation of Our Community," *Engage/Social Action* 7 (March 1979): 32-33.

3. James L. Peacock, *The Anthropological Lens: Harsh Light, Soft Focus* (Cambridge: Cambridge University Press, 1986), 55.

4. See Won Moo Hurh and Kwang Chung Kim, *Korean Immigrants in America: A Structural Analysis of Ethnic Confinement and Adhesive Adaptation* (Rutherford: Fairleigh Dickinson University Press, 1984), 44-49; and Bong Youn Choy, *Koreans in America* (Chicago: Nelson Hall, 1979), 253-260.

5. Sang Hyun Lee, "Korean American Presbyterians: A Need for Ethnic Particularity and the Challenge of Christian Pilgrimage," in *The Diversity of Discipleship: Presbyterians and Twentieth-Century Christian Witness,* ed. Milton J. Coalter, John M. Mulder, and Louis B. Weeks (Louisville: Westminster/ John Knox, 1991), 314.

6. Won Moo Hurh, "Comparative Study of Korean Immigrants in the U. S.: A Typological Study," in *Koreans in America*, ed. Byong-suh Kim et al. (Montclair: The Association of Korean Christian Scholars, 1977), 95; quoted in Lee, 315.

7. Won Moo Hurh and Kwang Chung Kim, "Religious Participation of Korean Immigrants in the United States," (paper presented at the annual meeting of the Association of Asian Studies, Washington D.C., March 17-19, 1989), 7; quoted in Lee, 318.

8. President's Commission on Mental Health, Report of the Special Populations Subpanel on the Mental Health of Asian/Pacific Americans, *Task Force Panel Reports* 3, 1978, 785; quoted in The United States Commission on Civil Rights, *Civil Rights Issues Facing Asian Americans in the 1990's* (Washington D. C., 1992), 19-20.

9. Ibid., 19.

10. Ibid. For a historical perspective on the "model minority" stereotype, see Glenn Omatsu, "The 'Four Prisons' and the Movements of Liberation: Asian American Activism from the 1960's to the 1990's," in *The State of Asian America: Activism and Resistance in the 1990's*, ed. Karin Aguilar-San Juan (Boston: South End Press, 1994), 63.

11. Ibid., 64.

12. Lee, 317.

13. Elaine H. Kim, "Between Black and White: An Interview with Bong Hwan Kim," in Aguilar-San Juan, 75.

14. Florence Yoshiwara, "Success Through Education: The Asian American Myth," *Church and Society* 64, no. 2 (1973): 24-25.

15. Kim, 90.

16. Frank Y. Ichishita, "Asian American Racial Justice Perspectives," *Church and Society* 72, no. 4 (1982): 30.

17. Ibid.

18. Ibid.

19. Sonia Shah, "Presenting the Blue Goddess: Toward a National Pan-Asian Feminist Agenda," in Aguilar-San Juan, 154.

20. Margaretta Wan Ling Lin and Cheng Imm Tan, "Holding up More Than Half the Heavens: Domestic Violence in Our Communities, A Call for Justice," in Aguilar-San Juan, 324.

21. Recently, Jane and her family have decided to take legal action against her perpetrator. This is a big step, especially in an Asian American context, in that it means that both she and her family will likely be ostracized from the larger clan. Jane's family are currently seeking emotional and spiritual support from their local church. As well, Jane has taken the first steps toward healing. Through some encouragement she has decided to undergo therapy. This is also a big step for her in view of the issues discussed above. Her case characterizes the struggles that many Asian American women face as they seek wholeness apart from a family system that has betrayed them.

22. The National Convocation of Asian American United Methodist Churches, "An Affirmation of Our Community," *Engage/Social Action* 7, no. 3 (1979): 34-35.

Chapter Fourteen

1. Harry L. Kitano and Roger Daniels, *Asian Americans: Emerging Minorities* (Englewood Cliffs, NJ: Prentice Hall, 1988), 19. This number would double to 60,000 by the beginning of the following decade.

2. Ibid., 48. The Chinese American population is projected to rise above 1.6 million by the year 2000. See Ibid., 161.

3. Gail Law, *Chinese Churches Handbook* (Hong Kong: Chinese Coordination Centre of World Evangelism, 1982), 243.

4. This is according to the Directory of Chinese Churches, Bible Study Groups, and Organizations in North America, compiled and published by Ambassadors for Christ, Inc.

5. The Ambassadors for Christ directory lists over two dozen denominational affiliations among the Chinese churches.

6. See Law, 243.

7. The reader should not take PCC as being representative of all Chinese American churches, as if in knowing about this one church one thereby knows all Chinese churches. While PCC shares many qualities and has had some experiences in common with other Chinese congregations, as will be pointed out in subsequent pages, it is ultimately PCC's uniqueness that makes its story so interesting.

8. Three other pastors had ministered at PCC for short periods prior to this, but Pastor Chang was the church's first full-time, long-term minister.

Chapter Fifteen

1. Paul G. Schurman, "Pastoral Care Across Cultures," in *Handbook for Basic Types of Pastoral Care & Counseling*, ed. H.W. Stone and W.M. Clements (Nashville: Abingdon Press, 1991), 89.

2. David W. Augsburger, *Pastoral Counseling Across Cultures* (Philadelphia: The Westminster Press, 1986). Cross-cultural issues are extensively discussed in the following works as well: Paul Pedersen et al. eds., *Counseling Across Cultures*; and Paul Pedersen, *Culture-Centered Counseling Interventions.*

3. Pamela Couture and Rodney Hunter, eds., *Pastoral Care and Social Conflict* (Nashville: Abingdon Press, 1995). Couture's work focuses on the needs of pastoral counseling and the church's work with minorities.

4. Yee Seop Park, *As a Hen Gathers Her Chicks under Her Wings* (Homewook: Korean United Methodist Church of South Suburban Chicago, 1991), 136. More than 40,000 U. S. military personnel have been continuously stationed in Korea since 1953: "Since the withdrawal of most U. S. military personnel from Indochina, South Korea is made tangible by an infantry division, four squadrons of fighter-bombers and tactical nuclear weapons." Daniel B. Lee, "Transcultural Marriage and Its Impact on Korean Immigration," in *Korean American Women*, ed. I. S. Lee (Mansfield: Association of Korean Christian Scholars in North America, 1985), 47.

5. Sang Lee defines a marginal person as "one who is 'in between' two cultures or societies without wholly belonging to either one." Sang Hyun Lee, "Called To Be Pilgrims," in *Korean American Ministry*, ed. Sang H. Lee and John V. Moore (Louisville: Office of Korean Resource Development of the Division of Congregational Ministries PC(USA), 1993), 41.

6. Harry H. L. Kitano and Roger Daniels, *Asian Americans* (Englewood Cliffs: Prentice Hall, 1988), 110.

7. Boaz, it will be remembered, is the one who is "a descendent of Judah who married Ruth the Moabites and fathered Obed, the grandfather of David . . . Both agree at Ruth's request to act as the family's kinsman-redeemer by purchasing the land offered

for sale by Naomi and by marrying Ruth to 'perpetuate the name' of her deceased husband Mahlon. *The Anchor Bible Dictionary*, s.v. "Boaz," by Kenneth A. Matthews. See Ruth in the Old Testament.

8. By looking at the date of the article's publication, I found this was the figure he came up with either in 1984 or 1985. Lee, "Transcultural Marriage," 42.

9. In *Korean Immigrants in America*, the authors state that approximately 30,000 Koreans have been admitted annually since 1970. They further state that each year 3,000 Korean women -- 10 percent of the immigrants -- came to the United States with American husbands. This implies that 30,000 women came to the United States from 1985 to 1994. Hyung Chan Kim and Patterson Wayne, eds., *Korean Immigrants in America* (New York: Oceana Publications, 1974), 314.

10. The Rev. Paul Kim writes in his article that "about 100,000 Korean women came to America since the Korean War," as wives of American soldiers. The Rev. Kim has ministered to St. Luke United Methodist Church in Texas as senior minister. The American congregation membership of St. Luke UMC is about 100 out of the 350 members of the church. This is where the author served as the official worship interpreter for eight years, interpreting the service from Korean into English. Paul Kim, "Families of Love, Overcoming the Barrier of Biculturalism," *United Methodist Family* (Spring/Summer 1990): 7.

11. Lee, "Transcultural Marriage," 53.

12. Ibid., 43.

13. *Encyclopaedia Britannica*, 1986 ed., s.v. "Korea."

14. Mahn Yol Yi, "A Christian Understanding of Korean History," in *Essays on Korean Heritage and Christianity*, ed. Sang Hyun Lee (Princeton Junction: Association of Korean Christian Scholars in North America, 1984), 3.

15. Daniel B. Lee, "Transcultural Marriage," 54.

16. Bok-Lim C. Kim et al. eds., *Women in Shadows* (La Jolla: National Committee Concerned with Asian Wives of US Servicemen, 1981), 13.

17. Lee, "Transcultural Marriage," 51.

18. Bascom W. Ratliff, "Intercultural Marriage: The Korean-American Experience," *Social Casework* 59 (April): 222; quoted in Brooke Lilla Brewer, "Interracial Marriage: American Men Who Marry Korean Women," (Ph. D. diss., Syracuse University, 1982), 21.

19. See Table 1.7 in Il Soo Kim, *New Urban Immigrants: The Korean Community in New York* (Princeton: Princeton University Press, 1981).

20. Jai P. Rhu, "Korean in America," in *The Korean Diaspora*, ed. Hyung Kim (Santa Barbara: ABC Clio, 1977), 212; quoted in Brewer, 22. Harry H. L. Kitano and Roger Daniels, *Asian Americans* (Englewood Cliffs: Prentice Hall, 1988), 110.

21. Bok-Lim Kim, "Casework with Japanese and Korean Wives of Americans," *Social Casework* 53 (1972): 277.

22. Chaplain McCullagh's report is in the minutes of the Human Self Development and Planning Unit, the Office of Eights US Army Chaplains (25 Sep 1973) under the title "A Study of the International Marriage between American Servicemen and

Koreans"; quoted in Lee, "Transcultural Marriage," 49.

23. Brewer, 48.

24. Brewer reports the following from Barnett: "Among those who undertake an interracial marriage a greater than average number have been previously married." Larry D. Barnett, "Research on International and Interracial marriages," *Marriage and Family Living* 25 (February 1963): 107; quoted in Brewer, 54.

25. Brewer, 91.

26. Kim et al., 53.

27. Ibid., 49.

28. Unlike the experience of the Korean war brides, the experience of post World War II European G. I. brides is comparatively positive, as evidenced by the words of an European G.I. war bride: "Speaking for myself and from my association [European] with my G. I. brides friends," says Rose . . . "we feel that America has been very kind to us all. They opened their arms to us and made us as welcome as anyone could." Pamela Winfield, *Sentimental Journey* (Constable: Constable and Co., 1984), 207.

29. Jai P. Ryu, "Koreans in America: A Demographic Analysis," in Kim, *The Korean Diaspora,* 212; quoted in Brewer, 22.

30. Unlike the Korean wives, the European G.I. brides are very much in touch with the main stream of the society, as evidenced by the words of Ronald Reagan, the former U.S. president: "The approximately one million European women who married American servicemen . . . America has indeed been fortunate to have had the benefit of the strength and ability of these citizens and I proudly join with so many others in saluting their impact and their continuing gift to this great land." Elfrieda Shukert and Barbara Scibetta, *War Brides of World War II* (Nobato: Presidio Press, 1988), 260.

31. Kitano and Daniels, 110.

32. Inn Sook Lee, "Korean American Women and Ethnic Identity," in Lee and Moore, 198.

33. Bok-Lim Kim, *The Korean American Child at School and at Home* (Washington, D. C.: Government Printing Office, 1980); quoted in Kitano and Daniels, 110.

34. Idem, "Asian Wives of US Servicemen: Women in Shadows," *American Journal* 4, no. 1 (1977): 97; quoted in Kim, *The Korean American Child,* 14.

35. "their paradoxical dilemma . . . maid-service provided by a woman from a low-income family can be tantamount to slavery, whereas a bar girl position has better financial incentive although it is degrading. Her alternatives are to be a good girl with no hope or a bad girl with some hope," Lee, "Transcultural Marriage,"48.

36. Their decision to marry a foreign male comes from their understanding that the solution to their present situation is a reflection of the second order change, that is, changing the place of their social context from Korea to America. Since nothing would have changed their situation if they continued to live in Korea, as an effort to change their social status socially and economically, they have decided to come to America by marrying American military personnel. Thus, the result was to bring out the change in their context of life. Paul Watzlawick, John Weakland, and Richard Fisch, *Change:*

Principles of Problem Formation and Problem Resolution (New York and London: W. W. Norton & Co., 1974), 82-83.

37. See the genealogy of Jesus Christ in Matthew 1:1-16.

38. "Rehab in the History of Judah," *Koo-Mal-Ssum* 29 (December 1994): 75.

39. "Where you go, I will go; where you lodge, I will lodge; your people shall be my people, and your God my God. Where you die, I will die -- there will I be buried." Ruth 1:16-17, NRSV.

40. John F. Walvoord and Roy B. Zuck, *The Bible Knowledge Commentary* (USA: Victor Books, 1985), 415.

41. See Joshua 2:8-14, NRSV.

42. "Boaz, who was the son of Rahab, a former prostitute in pagan Jericho (Hos. 2:1; Mt. 1:5), did marry Ruth." *The Hebrew-Greek Key Study Bible: New American Standard* (Chattanooga: AMG Publishers, 1977), 362; "Rahab was a Canaanite harlot in Jericho who became an ancestress of Boaz." Walvoord and Zuck, 417.

43. Lee, "Korean American Women and Ethnic Identity," 193.

44. Renita J. Weems, *Just a Sister Away* (San Diego: LuraMedia, 1988), 29.

45. Leon Morris, *The New International Commentary on the New Testament: The Gospel According to John* (Grand Rapids: WM. B. Eerdmans Publishing Co., 1992), 258.

46. Weems, 31.

47. Bruce McCormack, "Lecture Note: Systematic Theology II," (Princeton: Princeton Theological Seminary, 1994), 42.

48. See Galatians 3:28, NRSV.

49. For it is only when "God is present in life, [can] persons become empowered to full humanity and to relationships of wholeness with one another," Cynthia Campbell, *Theologies Written From Feminist Perspectives* (Louisville: Office of the General Assembly, 1988), 30.

50. "Psychological health is not understood only as an end in itself but also as a relative good within a larger context of faith," Deborah van Deusen Hunsinger, *Theology & Pastoral Counseling* (Grand Rapids: W. B. Eerdmans Publishing Co., 1995), 149.

51. Rebecca Propst states that through psychotherapy, "it is possible to have an impact on the emotional ills." Although psychotherapy has the psychotherapeutic approach alone to true healing, thus nowhere does Propst put forth an exclusively psychotherapeutic approach alone to true healing, thus implying its limitation. L. Rebecca Propst, *Psychotherapy in a Religious Framework* (New York: Human Sciences Press, 1988), 9.

52. Kwon Lee reports that there are about 2,500 Korean churches in America as of October, 1991. Out of 2,500 Korean churches, about 15 percent, that is, about 375 Korean churches are present in military towns throughout America. Kwon Lee, "Stress and Burnout among Korean-American Pastors in American Culture: Implications for Pastoral Care," *Ministry and Theology* 65 (November 1994): 118, 120 and 126; according to a Korean church address-book of the *Christian Herald*, as of October 1991,

the number of Korean churches listed throughout America is 2,489.

53. Russell reports that "many of the G. I. brides have great difficulty, often rejected by Korean congregations because the women were formerly bar women and entertainers." Letty M. Russell, *Church in the Round: Feminist Interpretation of the Church* (Louisville: Westminster/ John Knox Press, 1993), 63.

54. Marguerite Shuster, *Power, Pathology, Paradox* (Grand Rapids: Zondervan Publishing House, 1987), 220.

55. In their book, Weakland and Fisch defines "first and second order change" as follows: "There are two different types of change: one that occurs within a given system which itself remains unchanged [first order change], and one whose occurrence changes the system itself," that is, "a change to an altogether different state [second order change]." In relation to the second order change, Watzlawick further says, "It cannot generate from within itself the conditions for its own change; it cannot produce the rules for the change of its own rules." Watzlawick, Weakland, and Fisch, 10, 22.

56. See also Donald Capps, *Reframing: A New Method in Pastoral Care* (Minneapolis: Fortress Press, 1990), 169

57. "When the meaning changes, the person's response and behaviors also change," Bandler and Grinder; quoted in Capps, 10.

58. Lee, "Transcultural Marriage," 43.

59. Walvoord and Zuck, 415.

60. I strongly agree with Sang Lee that "we cannot overemphasize our responsibility to cooperate with all Christians of all races in a common struggle for humanization and justice." Sang Hyun Lee, "Asian American Theology in Immigrant Perspective: Called To Be Pilgrims," in Lee and Moore, 61.

61. John Calvin, *Institutes of the Christian Religion,* 2nd ed., ed. John T. McNeill, trans. Ford L. Battles (Philadelphia: The Westminster Press).

Chapter Sixteen

1. This article is reprinted from Eun Joo Kim, "The Preaching of Transfiguration: Theology and Method of Eschatological Preaching from Paul Lehmann's Theological perspective as an Alternative to Contemporary Korean Preaching" (Ph.D. diss., Princeton, NJ, 1996), 45-80.

2. In its first involvement with a Western nation, Korea opened diplomatic relations with the United States in 1882. Japan's victories in the Sino-Japanese War of 1894-1895 and Russo-Japanese War of 1904 conducted on Korean soil accelerated the colonization of Korea. The United States and the United Kingdom provided Japan with financial support during the Russo-Japanese War, and the United States came to support Japan in its efforts to colonize Korea based on Japan's willingness to remain indifferent to American colonialism in the Philippines. MacDonald, *The Koreans*, 237; Soon-Kyung Park, *The National Reunification and Christianity* (Seoul: Hangilsa 1986), 35.

3. According to Martha Huntley, in 1812-13 drought and famine produced a record death toll in Korea; it was said that about 4.5 million persons died. In addition, a million or more perished in cholera epidemics in the summers of 1821 and 1822. There

were also large scale revolts in 1804, 1811, 1813, 1817, 1833, 1862, and 1885. The biggest was the Tonghak Peasant Movement in 1894. Martha Huntley, *Caring, Growing, Changing: A History of the Protestant Mission in Korea* (New York: Friendship Press, 1894), 1-2, 7.

4. Sok-Hon Ham, *Queen of Suffering,* trans. E. S. Yu (London: Friends World Committee For Consultation, 1985), 132.

5. The first church in Korea was "Sorae Church," established in Sorae in Hwanghae Province in 1884 by Sang-Yun Suh, who had become a Christian in Manchuria. Man-Yeul Lee, *Korean Christianity and National Consciousness* (Seoul: Gishik, 1992), 82.

6. John Ross and John MacIntyre, Scottish Presbyterian missionaries residing at New Chwang, Manchuria, translated the Bible into Korean by the help of Korean merchants and scholars who were proficient in Chinese: Ung-Chan Yi, Sang-Yun Suh, Hong-Joon Paik, Sung-Kyun Choi, et al. In 1883, the Gospels and the Acts were completely translated, and the Epistles were finished in 1886. In 1882, Luke and John were printed for the first time and distributed to those Koreans who had lived in the eastern Manchurian valleys. Later, in 1884, Sang-Yun Suh distributed them in Seoul and in his hometown of Sorae. See Lak-Joon G. Paik, *The History of Protestant Mission in Korea: 1832-1910* (Seoul: Yonsei University Press, 1987), 51-53; Lee, 41-47, 76.

7. Huntley, i.

8. I randomly selected and interviewed a total of 40 pastors, 30 on three different seminary campuses at my own convenience and 10 who were my acquaintances. The group included 35 men and five women. To my question, "Who is your preaching model?" they reported 15 preachers. Of those, six were from the moderate Korean Presbyterian denomination (Yeachang Tonghap: Sun Hee Kwak, Young-Soo Rim, Sam-Whan Kim, Yong-Jo Ha, Jong-Soon Park, Jong-Yoon Lee), two from the conservative Korean Presbyterian (Yeachang Haptong: Sung-Jong Shin, Han-Heum Oak), three from the liberal Korean Presbyterian (Kichang: Keun-Soo Hong, Joong-Pio Lee, Sook-Ja Chung), one from Methodist (Sun-Do Kim), one from Pentecostal (Yong-Gee Cho), one from Baptist (Choong-Gee Kim), and one from the Holiness Church (Young-Jae Rim).

I purchased their recently published sermon books and selected three sample sermons from each of them, the first, middle, and last ones. The titles of the books are as follows: Sun-Hee Kwak, *The Ultimate Concern*; Young-Soo Rim, *What Shall We Believe and How Shall We Live*; Sam-Whan Kim, *Look Uprightly*; Yong-Jo Ha, *Ask, Seek, and Knock*; Jong-Soon Park, *The People Who Live Righteously*; Jong-Yoon Lee, *The Exposition of James*; Sung-Jong Shin, *There Are No Day and Night for the Disciples Who Have a Dream*; Han-Heum Oak, *Those Who Are Saved Live Like This*; Keun-Soo Hong, *If Jesus Came to Seoul*; Joong-Pio Lee, *The Leader of the Other World*; Sook-Ja Chung, *Collection of Sermons*; Sun-Do Kim, *We Want to Win*; Yong-Gee Cho, *The Portrait Painted with the Blood*; Choong-Gee Kim, *The God Who Reigns*; and Young-Jae Rim, *Before Death Comes*.

9. Thomas G. Long defines focus as "what the sermon aims to say," and function as "what the sermon aims to do." Thomas G. Long, *The Witness of Preaching* (Louisville: Westminster/John Knox Press, 1989), 86.

10. The first type includes the sermons of Sun-Hee Kwak, Han-Heum Oak, Yong-Jo Ha, Chung-Gee Kim, Sung-Jong Shin, Jong-Yoon Lee, and Jong-Soon Park; the second type: Young-jae Rim, Sam-Whan Kim, Yong-Gee Cho, and Sun-Do Kim; and the third type: Keun-Soo Hong, and Sook-Ja Chung.

11. Boo-Woong Yoo, "Biblical Preaching and Its Application to the Pulpit of the Korean Church," (D.Min. diss., Fuller Theological Seminary, 1984), 88. Yoo analyzed 1,123 sermons preached from 1884-1970 in the church on the basis of 10 categories such as doctrinal, christological, ecclesiastical, etc. and found that the preaching of individual morality was the most frequent theme (306 sermons).

12. According to Boo-Woong Yoo's sermon analysis of the Korean church for 100 years on the basis of the books *Great Preaching*, vol. 1-12, topical preaching was 71.7% during 1884-1919, 73% during 1920-1930, 80% during 1931-1940, 87.2% during 1941-1950, 84.8% during 1951-1960, and 66.3% during 1961-1970. Ibid., 22-23.

13. Sung-Kuh Chung, *A History of Preaching in Korean Church* (Seoul: The Presbyterian General Assembly Theological Seminary Press, 1986), 18.

14. For example, Jong-Yoon Lee preaches the text, James 5:19-20, focusing on the word "wandering." By the exploration of the word, he moralizes the text and exhorts the listeners not to deviate from right behavior. *The Exposition of James, A Sermon Collection* (Seoul: Pilgrim, 1994), 343-48. Also see Sung-Jong Shin, *There Are No Day and Night for the Disciples Who Have a Dream, A Sermon Collection* (Seoul: Hana, 1994); and Han-Heum Oak, *Those Who Are Saved Live Like This, A Sermon Collection* (Seoul: Duranno, 1994).

15. Fred Craddock, *As One without Authority* (Nashville: Abingdon Press, 1971), 54.

16. Kenneth S. Latourette, *A History of the Expansion of Christianity: The Great Century in Northern Africa and Asia, A.D. 1800-A.D. 1914,* vol. 6 (New York & London: Harper & Brothers Publishers, 1944), 336.

17. George M. Marsden, *Understanding Fundamentalism and Evangelicalism* (Grand Rapids: William B. Eerdmans Publishing Company, 1991), 2.

18. Richard Lints, *The Fabric of Theology* (Grand Rapid: William B. Eerdmans Publishing Company, 1993), 30.

19. Christopher C. Soper, *Evangelical Christianity in the United States and Great Britain* (Houndmills, Basingstoke, Hampshire, & London: Macmillan, 1994), 56.

20. A. J. Brown, *The Memory of the Far East* (New York: Scribners, 1919), 540.

21. Korea Mission, Presbyterian Church, U.S.A., Annual Report, 1922, 17; quoted in Sung-Bihn Yim, "The Relevance of H. R. Niebuhr's 'Ethics of Response' to Korean Christian Context: A Critical Inquiry into Niebuhr's Ethics from a Non-Western Context," (Ph.D. diss., Princeton Theological Seminary, 1994), 67.

22. Chung, *A History of Preaching in Korean Church*, 53.

23. Lee, *Korean Christianity and National Consciousness*, 44.

24. Chi-Young Kay, "A Study of Contemporary Protestant Preaching in Korea: Its Exegesis, Hermeneutics, and Theology," 19, 21.

25. According to Marsden, the American Evangelical coalition was split in two by means of the vast cultural changes of the era from the 1870s to the 1920s. "On the one hand were theological liberals who, in order to maintain better credibility in the modern age, were willing to modify some central evangelical doctrines, such as the reliability of the Bible or necessity of salvation only through the atoning sacrifice of Christ. On the other hand, there were conservatives who continued to believe the traditionally essential evangelical doctrines. By the 1920s a militant wing of conservatives emerged and took the name fundamentalist . . . fundamentalism was at first almost as broad and complicated a coalition as Evangelicalism itself. It included militant conservatives among Baptists, Presbyterians, Methodists, Disciples, Episcopalians, Holiness groups, Pentecostal, and many other denominations. After fundamentalism lost its initial national prominence by the 1930s, the term 'fundamentalism' began to take on a more limited meaning. Many fundamentalists were leaving the mainline Protestant denominations . . . by the 1960s 'fundamentalists' usually meant separatists and no longer included the many conservatives in mainline denominations." Marsden, 3. In this historical context, when I mention here "fundamentalism," it means the "militant wing of conservatives" represented by J. G. Machen.

26. Yim, 56.

27. Ibid., 57.

28. Marsden, *Fundamentalism and American Culture* (Oxford, New York, Toronto, Melbourne: Oxford University Press, 1980), 61.

29. For example, Yong-Jo Ha, who is one of the famous expository preachers today, blames liberal theology as the words of false prophets in his sermon, "Protect Yourself from the False Prophets." Yong-Jo Ha, *Ask, Seek, and Knock, A Sermon Collection* (Seoul: Dooranno, 1994), 102.

30. Yong-Gee Cho, *I Preach This Way* (Seoul: Seoul Bookstore, 1984), 154.

31. See Sam-Whan Kim, "The Way of the Cross," in *Look Uprightly, A Sermon Collection* (Seoul: The Word of Life, 1993), 13-26; and Sun-Do Kim, "Christians are to Possess Only the Best," in *We Want to Win, A Sermon Collection* (Seoul: The Kwanglim Publishing Co., 1993), 183-94.

32. Craddock, 45.

33. For example, Yong-Gee Cho, "Three Beat Blessing," *Famous Sermons in Korean Church, Volume 2*, ed. Shin-Myung Kang (Seoul: Korean Document Mission, 1983), 773-90; and Kim, *Look Uprightly.*

34. Long, 157.

35. Ibid., 162-63.

36. Ibid., 165-66.

37. Ibid., 172-73.

38. Ibid., 171.

39. Kyung-Bae Min, *A History of the Korean Christian Church* (Seoul: The Christian Literature Society of Korea, 1982), 252-53.

40. Paik, 367-70.

41. Min, 353-56.

42. For example, see Yong-Gee Cho, "Things That are Inside Us," *A Self-Portrait Painted by the Blood of Jesus Christ*, A Sermon Collection (Seoul: Seoul Book Store, 1993), 195-202.

43. For example, Kim, *We Want to Win*; and Young-Jae Rim, *Before Death Comes* (Seoul: Korean Holiness Church Publisher, 1990).

44. According to Sung-Kun Kim, a sociologist at Suhwon University, 95% of Korean Protestant churches are conservative. He identifies the characteristics of these churches with the "emotional, conservative, spiritual (Pentecostal advent of the Holy Spirit), individualistic, and other-worldly (in its eschatology). "Korean Protestantism and the Problem of Fundamentalism." Sung-Kun Kim, *The Christian Thought Monthly* (May 1988): 155-156.

45. See Sook-Ja Chung, *Collection of Sermons* (Seoul: Women-Church, 1993); and Keun-Soo Hong, *If Jesus Comes to Seoul* (Seoul: Hanwool, 1992).

46. Elisabeth S. Fiorenza, *Bread Not Stone* (Boston: Beacon press, 1984), xvii.

47. Ibid., 23.

48. While most male preachers in this type of preaching follow the traditional propositional point-making style, women preachers who have a feminist perspective make an effort to attempt different styles of sermons. See Chung, *Collection of Sermons*.

49. For example, see Keun-Soo Hong, "That the Church Become the Body of Christ," in *If Jesus Comes to Seoul*, 13-21. He draws a subject matter from the text (Ephesians 1:15-23) that Christ is the head of the church and the church is the body of Christ, and explains what it means by means of three points.

50. Cyris Hee-Suk Moon, *A History of the Interpretation of the Old Testament in the Korean Church: 1900-1977* (Seoul: The Christian Literature Society of Korea, 1984), 77.

51. Lee, *Korean Christianity and National Consciousness*, 358-65.

52. Min, 322-23; and Allen D. Clark, *A History of the Church in Korea* (Seoul: The Christian Literature Society of Korea, 1971), 158.

53. Clark, 312-14.

54. Ibid., 187, 202.

55. Min, 448.

56. According to Tae-Su Rim's research, there are ninety-nine Minjung churches near metropolitan areas. Tae-Su Rim, "The Survey of the Situation of Minjung Church and Its Consciousness," *The Christian Thought Monthly* (September 1994): 252-53.

57. David Kwang-Sun Suh briefly explains about Minjung Theology as follows: " . 'Minjung theology' is a Korean theology of liberation. Minjung theology is deeply rooted in the people's struggles for liberation, and in the Korean Christians' political hermeneutics of the Gospel. 'Minjung' is a new term even to Korean Christians, but it is a Korean word. It is a combination of two Chinese characters 'min' and 'jung.' 'Min' may be translated as 'people' and 'jung' as 'the mass'. . . 'the people' is close to what 'minjung' seeks to convey, sociologically and theologically as well. . . minjung theology is an accumulation and articulation of theological reflections of the political experiences

of Christian students, laborers, journalists, professors, farmers, writers and intellectuals, as well as theologians in Korea in the 1970's. . . The theology of Minjung is a socio-political biography of myself and my father and my mother under the Japanese occupation. At the same time it is a theological story about Korean Christians in the political struggle for freedom in the 1970's of Korea. It is theologically and historically rooted in the theological awareness of the oppressed in the Korean political situation, a theological response to the oppressors, and it is the response of the oppressed to the Korean Church and its mission. . . It is the way in which we have lived and acted under the Japanese occupation, under the Communist government of the North and dictatorial regimes in South Korea." David Kwang-Sun Suh, *The Korean Minjung in Christ* (Hong Kong: The Christian Conference of Asia, 1991), 23-24.

58. See Fiorenza, 1-23. There is a "Women-Church" in Korea, established in the 1980s by Korean clergy woman Young Kim. The goal of the church is to develop "the discipleship community of equals," that is, to liberate Korean women from traditional patriarchal structures of society and church through the interpretation of the Bible from a feminist perspective, the creation of new models of liturgy, etc.

59. Hyung-Mook Choi, "Symposium: The Situation and Task of Korean Theology," *The Theological Thought Quarterly* 21 (Fall 1993): 30. (Translation mine.)

60. Soo-Kyung Ahn, "A Survey of the Situation and Consciousness of Minjung Church (II)," *The Christian Thought Monthly* (August 1994): 272. This research surveyed 68 minjung church pastors.

Contributors

Peter Thiam Chai Chang—Ph.D. candidate, Harvard University; M.Div., Princeton Theological Seminary

Kurien George—Priest, Diocese of North American of the Mar Thoma Syrian Church of Malabar, India; M.Div., Serampore University; special student, Princeton Theological Seminary

Young Hoon Hwang—Assistant Professor of Pastoral Care, Seoul Women's Universiy; Ph.D., Th.M., Princeton Theological Seminary; M.Div., Fuller Seminary

Wonhee Anne Joh—Associate Professor of Theology, Garrett Theological Seminary; Ph.D., Drew Universiy; M.Div., Princeton Theological Seminary

Chester Kim—Pastor, Benardsville Presbytarian Church; Ph.D. candidate, Drew University; Th.M., M.Div., Princeton Theological Seminary.

Douil Kim—Associate Professor of Christian Education, Presbytarian Theological Seminary and College; Ed.D., Presbytarian School of Christian Education; M.Div., Princeton Theological Seminary

Eun Joo Kim—Associate Professor of Homiletics, Ilif Theological Seminary; Ph.D., Th.M., M.Div., Princeton Theological Seminary

Inn Sook Lee—Professor-Adjunct, Practical Theology, Princeton Theological Seminary; former Professor of Pastoral Theology, New York Theological Semiary; Ed.D., M.A., Columbia University

Jae Myung Lee—Pastor, River Edge Presbytarian Church; Ph.D., Th.M., Princeton Theological Seminary; M.Div., Chong Shin Theological Seminary

Sang Hyun Lee—Professor of Systematic Theology, Princeton Theological Seminary; Ph.D., S.T.B., Harvard University

Noel Yuen Lin—Youth Pastor, Princeton Christian Church; M.Div., Princeton Theological Seminary

Angella M. Pak—Associate Professor of Religion, Drew University; Ph.D., Th.M., M.Div., Princeton Theological Seminary

Hanry Wolfgang Rietz—Associate Professor of Religious Studies, Grinnell College; Ph.D., M.Div., Princeton Theological Seminary

Timothy D. Son—Assistant Professor of Christian Education and Youth Ministry, Pittsburgh Theological Seminary; Ed.D. candidate, Columbia University; Th.M., M.Div., Princeton Theological Seminary

Haruko Nawata Ward—Associate Professor, Columbia Theological Seminary; Ph.D., Th.M., Princeton Theological Seminary; M.Div., Southeastern Baptist Theological Seminary

Frank M. Yamada—Associate Professor, McCormick Theological Seminary; Ph.D., M.Div., Princeton Theological Seminary

www.ingramcontent.com/pod-product-compliance
Lightning Source LLC
LaVergne TN
LVHW020529100826
845148LV00010B/1399

* 9 7 8 1 6 0 6 0 8 5 4 6 2 *